Debbie
Miske
11/82

SOMEONE CRY FOR THE CHILDREN

SOMEONE CRY FOR THE CHILDREN

The Unsolved Girl Scout Murders of Oklahoma and the Case of Gene Leroy Hart

MICHAEL WILKERSON
AND
DICK WILKERSON

THE DIAL PRESS   NEW YORK

Published by
The Dial Press
1 Dag Hammarskjold Plaza
New York, New York 10017

Joan, Barbara, and Crying Wolf are real people, but their names and certain identifying details have been changed to insure their privacy and personal safety.

Copyright © 1981 by Michael Wilkerson and Dick Wilkerson

All rights reserved. No part of this book may be reproduced or transmitted in any form or by any means, electronic or mechanical, including photocopying, recording or by any information storage and retrieval system, without the written permission of the Publisher, except where permitted by law.

Manufactured in the United States of America

FOR MOM AND DAD

A most gentle union

The authors wish to thank the men and women of the Oklahoma State Bureau of Investigation for their cooperation and support while writing this book.

Special recognition is also given to Dr. Robert L. Phillips, of the Oklahoma Psychiatric Clinic and Barkouras Foundation, whose narrative is included in this book.

Special gratitude is owed to Kathie Blackmon for her hard work and unwavering faith and enthusiasm.

Finally, we gratefully acknowledge the cooperation of the Great Cherokee Nation; our kinsmen.

Michael Wilkerson
Dick Wilkerson

CHAPTER I

LOCUST GROVE, OKLAHOMA, IS SIMILAR TO OTHER SMALL TOWNS IN northeastern Oklahoma. It lies sleepily at the junction of State Highways 82 and 33 in the heart of what the Department of Tourism calls Oklahoma's Green Country: thirty-four miles east of Tulsa, forty-one miles west of the Arkansas border, and twenty-five miles north of Tahlequah, the capital of the Cherokee Nation. Many of Locust Grove's citizens, in their sharp-toed boots and western hats, are second and third generation residents. They are a distinct, independent breed that strangers might categorize as hillbillies or cowboys. Like all of surrounding Mayes County, Locust Grove boasts a large Cherokee population among its thousand or so residents.

Cherokee. The name conjures images of great warriors, classic battles, and stoic dignity. According to legend, the Great Spirit gave the Cherokee fire and told them that as long as the fire burned the Cherokee would survive and prosper. But an evil sorcerer stole the sacred fire. A young brave pursued the sorcerer to a mountain and, with great cunning, he caused the sorcerer to be consumed by the very fire he had stolen. The brave then returned the gift of fire to the Cherokee people, whose medicine men guard it to this day.

The Cherokee are one of the original Five Civilized Tribes that were forcibly moved to Oklahoma to make way for the expansion of the land-hungry settlers. This removal is the great tragedy of the Cherokee Nation. In the eighteenth century they were the largest tribe in America. They were a trusting, intelligent people and they were lied to time after time. By the end of the nineteenth century all that remained to them was their dignity, their industry, their religion, and a binding hatred and mistrust of the white man.

Paradoxically, it's difficult to find a person in northeastern Oklahoma who does not have Indian blood. Unlike the citizens of many other states with large Native American populations, the people of Oklahoma are fiercely proud of their Indian blood. With the largest Indian population of any state, evidence of Indian culture is everywhere. Even the name Oklahoma itself means "the Home of the Red Man." There are towns with names like Seminole, Wewoka, Tahlequah, Wetumka, and Weleetka, and counties named Pushmataha, Pottawatomie, Cherokee, and Sequoyah. The University of Oklahoma calls itself the *Big Red,* Oklahoma City University is designated the *Chiefs,* and the Cimarron and the Indian Nation turnpikes traverse the state. The capitals of the Cherokee, Choctaw, Chickasaw, Seminole, Creek, and Osage are all located in Oklahoma.

To the outsider, it may sometimes seem that the transition from warrior to businessman has taken place quickly and completely, but a closer study reveals that the Indians cling tenaciously to their old ways. Their belief in "medicine," spiritualism, ancient power, and magic are kept alive, especially in the hills of northeastern Oklahoma. It is impossible to separate Cherokee law and religion, they are so intertwined. Many Indians still solve critical problems by smoking the sacred pipe or by consulting medicine men whose powers are legendary. This mysticism rarely surfaces, however, and to the white man it is all but nonexistent. The Cherokee are a proud, private people who do not share their "medicine" with whites.

In Locust Grove, pickup trucks, the predominant mode of transportation, abound. The three-block-long business district seems to be the only part of town meant for strangers to see. Irregular streets, some dirt, some paved, with their ancient frame houses, wind up and down the small wooded hills, nature appearing to be the chief landscaper.

Surrounded as it is by the thick blackjack, locust, and oak woods, Locust Grove could have remained lost to the world and even to most of Oklahoma were it not for the white-tailed deer which each year draw hundreds of hunters to the area who plunge into the thickets and do battle with the ticks, chiggers, and dense brush in hope of bagging one of the elusive creatures.

There were other reasons a stranger might know of Locust Grove's existence. Maybe he drove through on his way to Arkansas and had to stop at the town's one stop light. Maybe he passed through coming from or going to the Trail of Tears reenactment in Tahlequah of the Cherokee's long march to their present home, or even had an accident at the four-way stop at the junction of State Highways 82 and 33. Maybe he visited his son at Camp Garland Boy Scout Camp south of town or his daughter at Camp Scott Girl Scout Camp a mile or so closer to town just off State Highway 82. Still, were it not for a night in mid-June 1977, Locust Grove, Oklahoma, could have remained one of those wide spots in the road that people pass through and whose name, if they ever knew it, they quickly forget—one of those dozens of small towns in eastern Oklahoma whose only identity is its proximity to Tulsa.

But in June of 1977 that changed.

Camp Scott had been operated by the Magic Empire Council of Girl Scouts since 1928. The Magic Empire Council covered a six-county area—Tulsa, Mayes, Rogers, Payne, Creek, and Osage counties—with most of the girls coming from the Tulsa metropolitan area. The camp, which housed both Girl Scouts and Brownies, also accepted non-scouts. The girls were anywhere from second grade levels through high school. Perfect for boating, hiking, camping, and fishing, the camp covered 410 acres that had been chopped out of the wilderness and was a checkerboard of permanent wooden tent floors set well off the ground. With facilities for one hundred and forty children and a staff of thirty counselors, the camp was divided into ten units named after Indian tribes. The counselors were older girls, sixteen to twenty-five, usually from Oklahoma; some, however, were from elsewhere, from the deep South to the Pacific Northwest.

As the bus pulled through the gate of Camp Scott, all the children crowded the left side of the bus to look out of the window. Some of them chanted in unison the names of the signs that designated the camp units:

"Osage! Chickasaw. Creek. Seminole. Choctaw."

The chanting grew louder as the excitement built. A shout of "this side, this side" brought children scrambling to the opposite side of the bus. Everyone had seen their sign except the Kiowa Unit. One of the older girls who had been there before explained that the Kiowa area was on the outer edge of the camp, on the other side of Quapaw Unit.

Before the three buses were even in sight, coming up Cookie Trail, the counselors could hear the children laughing and squealing above the roar of the engines. When the buses arrived, the children were assembled by camp areas, with counselors carefully checking each name. Their bags were loaded onto a pickup truck and transferred to the appropriate units by the counselors and the camp ranger, Ben Woodward. Twenty-seven girls had been assigned to the Kiowa Unit. A last-minute change in assignments left Tent Number 8 one girl short.

The counselors assigned to Kiowa were Carla Sue Wilhite, age twenty-three; Dee Elder, twenty; and Susan Emery, eighteen. They had been hired by Camp Director Barbara Day and had attended a week-long pre-camp conference earlier in the month. During the conference, activities were planned, camp areas assigned, and the camping units were inspected. During the inspection the counselors noticed that Tent Number 2 had a rip in the fabric. They reported it to Ben Woodward, who later repaired it.

The counselors had arrived a couple of hours before the buses. They had unloaded their luggage into their tent and had made another inspection of the area. They noticed that someone had cut off the flap on Tent Number 6. Carla reported the damage to Mrs. Day and the tent was repaired with a linen material thinner than the tent canvas. Carla wondered why anyone would tear a flap from a tent when there was canvas in the storage area in the middle of the site.

The counselors marched the children to Kiowa Unit, which was more isolated than the rest of the units. It had been cut out of the dense woods at the westernmost boundary of the camp and was accessible only by a service road that came to a dead end at the campsite.

The afternoon was spent getting the girls settled. They were shown where the outdoor bathrooms and the counselors' tent were located, and generally given the do's and don'ts that they had to live by for two weeks. The children were more or less allowed to select their tentmates. After the selection, three girls were left. They were left because they did not know anyone in the unit and they had been too shy to make friends on the bus ride to the camp. Lori Farmer, Denise Milner, and Michelle Guse were introduced to each other and seemed to get along well. Although Denise was very homesick, she tried hard to be brave and not show it to the other girls. They unrolled their sleeping bags and put them on three of the four cots. Lori and Michelle took the cots on the south end of the tent and Denise took the first cot on the north side. They used the remaining cot to store their belongings.

By 4:30 P.M. the girls had completed moving in and appeared to be settled. The sky was beginning to cloud as Carla took a group of *hoppers* to the great hall cafeteria located less than a quarter of a mile southeast of the unit. Hoppers were girls assigned to set and clear the tables for the evening meal. Carla helped the girls set the tables and a few minutes later the scouts arrived and the evening meal was served. As the girls ate, it began to rain—only a few drops at first, but during the course of the meal it built into a heavy thunderstorm. Food was usually served between 6:00 and 7:00 P.M. but, because of the thunderstorm and the first-night jitters, mealtime was extended until 7:30 P.M. After dinner all of the girls met under the porch of the Great Hall and Dee led the whole camp in song. The clouds were still hanging ominously and it was still raining moderately when the Kiowa counselors decided to make the trek back to their unit. With counselors in the lead, the children went half-running into the dusky darkness.

By the time they got back to their campsite, everyone was soaking wet. The counselors told the girls to go to their tents, change into dry clothes, and get ready for bed. At about 8:00 P.M. the counselors decided they would have a campers' meeting in the kitchen area located in the middle of the unit. The kitchen was nothing more than a roof supported by cornerposts with a storeroom and shower located at the north end.

When all of the girls were under the structure, a head count was made and all the campers accounted for. A counselor from Comanche Unit told Carla that she had a girl who was supposed to be in Kiowa Unit. Carla told her to let the girl stay in Comanche for the night and they would move her the next day. Unit representatives were elected and the girls were told what their activities would be at the encampment. It was explained that each of them would have duties on different days. Their duties would be rotated on a regular basis and all the girls would have each job at least once. Because of the thunderstorm, activities had been cancelled and the girls were told to return to their tents and write letters to their parents.

Each counselor had two hours of free time daily. These off-duty periods had to be scheduled so that at no time were all of the counselors away from the unit. Carla's free time was scheduled between 9:00 and 11:00 P.M. Shortly after the meeting, she left Kiowa Unit and walked to the Arapaho site to visit some friends.

A very homesick Denise Milner approached counselor Dee Elder at her tent and asked if she could make a phone call to her mother.

Dee Elder knew from past experience that Denise didn't like Camp Scott and wanted to go home. She also knew that the homesickness would probably pass when the youngster got to know her tentmates better and joined in the camp activities. She comforted Denise and told her to stick it out and that she could call her mother in the morning, if she still wanted to. The child returned to Tent Number 8.

As a counselor in Comanche Unit walked from the latrine, she noticed a dim light in the woods. It appeared just beyond the tree line surrounding the camp. She knew that no one should be in the area and shone her flashlight in that direction. As her beam of light hit the tree line, the dim light went off. She turned hers off and waited. In a few minutes the wan light returned and began moving northwest, in the direction of Kiowa Unit. She shone her flashlight toward the woods once again, and again the mystery light went off. She turned her flashlight off again and the light returned. By this time uneasiness, bordering on fear, began to creep into her consciousness. After several minutes she switched her flashlight back on and ran back to the safety of her companions.

Somewhere around ten o'clock Dee Elder decided to make a tent check of the Kiowa Unit. She went to every tent and talked with each girl. The last tent she visited was Number 8. All three of the girls were finishing their letters home by flashlight.

Dee told them that it was time for bed and made small talk to make their first night in camp a little easier. After a few minutes she closed the flap on the tent and returned to her own. The girls carefully folded their letters, put them in envelopes, and packed them away to be mailed the next day. They changed into their nightclothes, said their prayers, and crawled into their sleeping bags.

Susan Emery was returning to the counselors' tent at about eleven o'clock. She had been with several counselors-in-training chatting about the encampment. There were no outside lights or fires in Kiowa Unit and without a flashlight it was impossible to navigate. The trees blocked any light from the surrounding area and she literally could not see her hand in front of her face.

Susan and Dee decided to retire for the night and took the two cots closest to the front of the tent. A short time later Carla returned from her visit with her friends in Arapaho Unit. As she arrived she heard several scouts laughing and talking loudly in their tents. She decided that she had better remind the scouts of the big day that they would have tomorrow. She went to each tent where she had heard the noise and told the children to be quiet and to go to sleep. After checking Tent Number 6, she stood near Number 7 and listened. No noise came from either Tent 7 or 8 so she turned and walked back to the counselors' tent. She changed into her nightclothes and took off her glasses and put them beside her flashlight on the floor. She set the alarm clock for six and retired for the evening.

Carla had been asleep for about an hour when she was awakened by some scouts from Tent Number 2 banging on the door of the latrine and chattering. She got out of her bed, flashlight in hand, went to the latrine and escorted the girls back to their tent. Again she walked back to her tent and went to sleep.

In Quapaw Unit, which abutted Kiowa in the east, screams of young scouts rang through the darkness. Counselors ran to see what had happened. One frightened child explained that she was walking from her tent to the latrine when someone grabbed her by her raincoat. Other girls told of something stalking around their tents. Another youngster said that on her way back to her tent, she had dropped her towel. As she bent down to pick it up, the beam of her flashlight had struck a man's legs clad in khaki pants.

The counselors walked to the tents and to the latrine but found nothing. Finally they attributed the excitement to first night jitters and practical jokes by other campers.

Carla was awakened again at 1:30 A.M. by the girls giggling in Tent Number 5. She yelled at the girls, telling them to go to sleep, and at the same time shone her light on the tent. Dee had also awoken. As they lay awake on their cots they heard a noise that caused each to give the other a questioning look. It seemed to be a low guttural moan. The two counselors got up and stepped outside. Together they went toward Tent Number 5, listening to the sound. Carla suggested that Dee walk toward the moaning to see if it was an animal, while she checked Tent 5 itself. Carla, however, changed her mind and decided to investigate the noise herself before she looked in on the scouts. The eerie sound continued as she walked toward the road that led to the camp. When she reached the road, she pointed her flashlight in the direction of the sound. When the light beam hit the trees the moaning stopped.

Carla turned and began walking back toward the tents. The moaning started again. She stopped, turned around, and went back toward the road, but once more the sound stopped.

The night seemed to get a little darker as she turned her back on the sound and, with a quickened step, walked back to the tent area. It must be an animal, she thought to herself. It must be an animal.

She walked back to the tent area and with Dee checked out Tent Number 5, then returned to the counselors' quarters. As Carla lay down on the cot, the moaning began again and continued, until it was a part of her dreams.

The odd light appeared in Kiowa Camp somewhere around two in the morning. It was not a flashlight; it was much dimmer. It appeared to be a very dull glow rather than a beam of light. As it moved silently through the unit, the light would disappear for minutes, then reappear suddenly on the other side of the unit.

As the counselors slept, the flaps of their tent were taken off the hook screws and a dark figure slid silently underneath the canvas. Dee's and Susan's purses and Carla's glasses were taken. The light again appeared and moved toward Tent Number 7. A ten-year-old occupant watched the light approach through a mended panel. The other three girls had their heads covered when the panel was jerked open and light flooded the tent. The child watched in mute terror as a large dark figure glared into the tent for a moment, then dropped the panel back down and moved on to Tent Number 8. The light disappeared as the male figure moved to the back. Slowly and quietly the hook screws holding down the back of the tent were removed.

In Arapaho, Kiowa, Quapaw, and Cherokee low-pitched moaning was heard throughout the night. In Quapaw Unit a girl heard someone screaming, "Momma, Momma." She remembered how Lori Farmer had been frightened before at Fort Gibson Scout Camp and wondered if Lori was unable to sleep.

CHAPTER 2

THE RINGING OF THE ALARM CLOCK JERKED COUNSELOR CARLA SUE Wilhite from the comfortable distances of sleep. She shut off the clock, sat up on the side of the cot, yawned, and rubbed her eyes. She had awakened thirty minutes before the rest of the camp so she could take a hot shower at the staff house a few hundred yards up the service road. She felt around in the darkness for her flashlight. Being careful not to awaken her bunkmates, she found a fresh change of clothes and a clean towel. After putting on her sneakers, she tiptoed out of the tent and down the steps. A beautiful day greeted her. The rain had brought a fresh smell to the woods, and for a moment she drank in the serenity. The only sounds were the chirping of birds and her footfalls on the gravel surface trail leading from her tent to the road. She approached the intersection of the trail and the road when a flash of bright yellow caught her eye, and she walked over to invesitgate. Her eyes began feeding her sleepy brain bits of information. Sleeping bag—child lying down—wonder what she's doing sleeping away from the tent? Looks like more than one bag. When she walked up to the pile of debris all the information rushed together.

"No! No! No!" she screamed. "My God, no." With tear-clouded eyes she turned, almost falling, and ran back to the counselors' tent. Collecting her thoughts, she threw the flap open and screamed, "Dee, get up!" Dee and Susan both looked up from their beds. "Get up. We have to count the girls."

"Why?" asked Dee sluggishly.

"Because there's a body out in the road."

"Oh, my God. You've got to be kidding," gasped Dee.

"No. We've got to count the girls."

The counselors grabbed their clothes and ran toward the line of tents in which the scouts slept. Carla and Susan started at Tent Number 2 and Dee at Tent Number 8. The counselors were racing into every tent and touching each one of the girls as they counted them. Dee came running back from Tent 8.

"God. Tent Eight is empty," she cried.

"Maybe they're asleep in somebody else's tent," Carla said hopefully, and the counselors continued the count.

They tallied all the scouts in the unit and came up with twenty-four girls. Carla went back to Tent 8. There was blood on the floor and mattresses.

"Maybe one of the girls started her period and became frightened." She was clinging to any hope that the girls in the pile at the intersection were not from her unit. Turning to Dee, she told her to keep the scouts in their tents while she ran for help, and dashed off.

When she got to the staff house, she cut across the field toward the nurse's quarters, approximately 300 yards to the south. As she ran she heard a bloodcurdling scream coming from the area where the bodies were located. The counselors had not done as she had asked. Susan had gone to where the bodies were and had screamed uncontrollably at what she saw. Carla yelled out at the top of her lungs for Susan to be quiet and not to panic the others, not realizing that her shouts, too, would wake the camp.

As Carla continued toward the nurse's quarters, a sobbing, shaken Susan bent down and felt a lump in one of the sleeping bags. There was no movement. She felt the other lump. No movement there either. Dee ran to Susan and told her to get back to the unit and keep the girls inside their tents. Then she ran toward her car, parked at the staff house.

Carla sprang up the front stairs of the nurse's quarters and began beating on the screen door. "Maryanne, Maryanne. Get up!" she screamed.

Maryanne Alabeck, the camp nurse, came to the door in her nightclothes. "What's the matter?" the nurse asked.

"Something terrible has happened. There's a body down in our unit," Carla panted.

The nurse grabbed her clothes and hurried to her car. Carla raced next door to the director's office and banged on the door. She woke Director Barbara Day and her husband, Richard, and told them what had happened.

As the camp nurse drove to Kiowa Unit, she was met by Dee in her car. The nurse asked Dee what had happened and the counselor told her, "There are those little girls down there and I think they're all dead."

The nurse drove on to Kiowa Unit and was met by Susan. "Where?" the nurse asked. Susan pointed in the direction of the bodies. Nurse Alabeck could see the brightly colored sleeping bags from where she was standing. She walked over and saw a young black girl lying on her back, her legs spread wide apart. She bent down, put her hand on the girl's throat, and applied pressure to the carotid artery to determine if there was a pulse. When she squeezed the artery, blood gushed from the child's mouth and nose. The nurse instinctively tried to pull the girl's hands from behind her to find her wrist but couldn't. The girl's hands were tied. Richard and Barbara Day had arrived and she screamed, "Over here! Over here!"

Barbara Day stayed at the car while Richard ran over to the nurse. He couldn't believe what he saw as he reached down, picked up a loose sleeping bag, and covered the girl's nakedness. He was certain she was dead. Richard was a surgical technician at a large Tulsa hospital. He had seen death, but nothing to compare with this. Not until after he had covered the little girl did he notice the other two sleeping bags. He felt each one and knew that they, too, contained bodies. He told the nurse to stay there and walked back to where his wife was standing and told her that they should call the police. They got in their car and drove to the house of Camp Ranger Ben Woodward. They met Dee coming from the director's house. Her eyes seemed to plead for them to tell her that the whole thing was a bad dream.

Barbara looked at the counselor and said, "It's the worst that we could expect."

They first tried to knock on the front door of Ben Woodward's residence but could not awaken him, so they beat on the bedroom window until he awoke and let them in. They told the ex-marine what had taken place in the Kiowa Unit. As he hurriedly dressed, Barbara called the Highway Patrol.

Richard and Ben drove to the camp gate, where Richard stayed to guide the police to the scene while Ben drove on to the Kiowa Unit. Reaching the camp, Ben got out of his car and went over to where the little sleeping bags lay on the ground. As he stared in disbelief and on the verge of tears, he said, "This is the reason why we moved to the country. To get away from crazy people." As he looked at the scene, his eyes fell upon a red and white 9-volt flashlight and roll of dark duct tape lying near the bodies. "There's got to be fingerprints on those," he said hopefully. "What kind of animal would do this? I don't understand."

The counselors from the other units were informed about the murders. The other children, however, were not to be told. Buses were brought in to take the scouts back to Tulsa. The girls from Kiowa Unit were lined up and marched through the woods, out of sight of the bodies, to rendezvous with the other children. All of the girls talked and giggled, unaware of what had happened.

Ted Limke slid behind the wheel onto the rock-hard seat of the 1977 Pontiac police car. As he backed from the driveway of his rural home near Tahlequah, he noticed that the pipe fence needed to be straightened up at first opportunity. The large brick house and five acres was the first home he and his wife, Barbara, had owned in their nine-year marriage. Limke smiled. She deserved it and a lot more.

All agents of the Oklahoma State Bureau of Investigation, or OSBI, knew about Limke's perfect marriage. He had met Barbara when he was a detective sergeant with the Norman, Oklahoma, Police Department. Both had been married and divorced and both had two sons. Shortly before their marriage in 1968, he had accepted an appointment as an OSBI agent. After the initial indoctrination, Ted, with his new wife and her sons, moved to Muskogee where he had been assigned as resident agent. Five years later he was promoted and moved to Tulsa as Agent in Charge of the Northeastern Regional Office. Shortly after his promotion he led an investigation into the activities of a politically powerful judge who had set himself up as the Godfather of Northeastern Oklahoma. Subsequently the judge was removed from the bench and suspended from practicing law. But Limke had been a clog in the political system. The Regional Office in Tulsa, home of Gene Howard, President Pro Tempore of the state Senate, was closed. Howard had been a political ally of the ex-judge. It was rumored that Howard, whom Limke had allegedly called a crook, wanted Limke out of Tulsa. Otherwise no money would be appropriated for the OSBI. So the office was transferred to the small town of Tahlequah. It consisted of three agents, two secretaries, two forensic chemists, a sophisticated crime laboratory, and a regional office in this town of 18,000. Meanwhile Tulsa, a city of 330,000 people, had one agent who worked out of his home. Limke and his men had performed their duties as prescribed by law and as a reward they had been exiled to the boonies.

Still, he was proud to be part of the state bureau. A statewide organization, it offered forensic and investigative assistance to the smaller police departments and sheriffs' offices. Regional offices and laboratories were maintained in each quadrant of the state as well as at its headquarters in Oklahoma City. Agents were stationed at the regional offices, headquarters, and in smaller towns as resident agents.

Limke felt both pride and frustration in the fact that his region boasted the highest caseload of major investigations. Limke was known as a good supervisor, fiercely loyal to his agents and the Bureau. Quick to laugh, his easygoing manner was sometimes mistaken for weakness, but coupled with a volatile temper, this misconception rarely lasted long. At thirty-eight, Limke was an imposing figure at five feet eleven inches, two hundred and ten pounds. He had long since lost most of his curly brown hair but his baldness made him appear even more formidable.

It was nearly 8:00 A.M. when Limke urged the Pontiac onto State Highway 81 and began the eleven-mile drive to Tahlequah.

The OSBI Regional Office at Tahlequah was housed on the second floor of an ancient office building directly across the main street from the County Courthouse. Limke climbed the steep stairs, cursing all the way and wishing the new office building was ready for occupancy. Connie Heston, the receptionist-secretary, glanced up as Limke entered the reception room and headed toward his office.

"Ted, you're supposed to call Pete Weaver at Pryor. They think they have a homicide," she said.

Limke smiled and continued on to his office. Must be bad if Weaver is asking for help, Limke thought to himself. Glen "Pete" Weaver was the Sheriff of Mayes County. The two men had not spoken since Weaver had been the subject of an ouster action Limke had been assigned to investigate. That had been five years ago. Sheriff Weaver had been cleared of the charges but animosity between the agent and the sheriff had left a wound that had never healed.

Mike Wilkerson could hear fellow agent Cary Thurman asking directions on the radio. Wilkerson chuckled to himself as he followed Thurman's progress through several wrong turns that had ended up on a dead-end road. The two agents were probably no more than three miles from one another as the crow flies, but were several miles apart on the twisting roads. As Wilkerson drove through Locust Grove, he heard Thurman report his arrival at the crime scene. The usual things were running through Wilkerson's mind: will the crime scene be secured? what shape are the bodies going to be in? who discovered the bodies? All the things that a criminal investigator thinks of on his way to the place of a crime.

He had been with the Oklahoma State Bureau of Investigation for four years but still had not become accustomed to the aftermath of violent crime, even though he had been involved in over one hundred and fifty homicide investigations and boasted a 100 percent clearance rate in his cases. He had never quite gotten used to the bodies, the blood, the hair, the flesh, that was part of a death scene, but he managed to put on a professional face and do his job.

He was one of three brothers employed at the OSBI. At thirty-two, he was two years junior to Dick and seven years senior to his youngest brother, Pat. The Wilkersons were reared in rural east-central Oklahoma and, like so many Oklahomans, they too shared Indian blood. All three still proudly boasted that they were from Atwood, Oklahoma, population 80.

It was his brother, Dick, Chief of Investigative Operations in Oklahoma City, who had called Mike Wilkerson at his home in Tulsa two hours earlier and told him about an apparent triple homicide at Camp Scott, just south of Locust Grove. Agent Cary Thurman, out of Bartlesville, would meet him there and Ted Limke would be along later.

Wilkerson turned west off the highway onto a narrow blacktop road that twisted and wound through fields of dense green woods. He knew from personal experience that these woods were filled with ticks, chiggers, and rattlesnakes. After driving half a mile in, he approached the large aluminum gate that led into the camp. Wilkerson identified himself to the guards and passed through. The road continued to twist and turn until a large group of cars was visible over to his right. He pulled the 1976 Pontiac over to the side of the road, deciding to walk the last 300 feet to where a crowd was gathered.

As he approached the group, he recognized Agent Cary Thurman. Thurman looked around, clipboard in hand, and with a relieved smile walked up and shook Wilkerson's hand. Thurman, a new agent, had less than a year with the agency. Being the first OSBI agent on the scene, he had automatically been recognized as the expert and was being deluged with questions. Wilkerson recognized the look in Thurman's eyes, the realization of the awesome responsibility of a major homicide and the knowledge that the decisions made and actions taken could determine whether the perpetrator was apprehended or forever went free. He looked at Thurman and grinned. "It's lonely out here, isn't it, Cary?"

Thurman grinned sheepishly. "You bet it is."

Mike Wilkerson liked Thurman; his enthusiasm was contagious. His schoolboy appearance belied his years in law enforcement. At thirty-five, he could still pass for twenty-five. While new to the OSBI, Thurman was not new to the profession. He had risen through the ranks to become the Chief of Police of the small central Oklahoma town of Mustang.

A tall gray-haired man introduced himself: Sid Wise. He was the District Attorney. Wilkerson also met Mayes County Sheriff Pete Weaver, a county medical examiner, and Highway Patrolman Harold Berry.

"What have we got?" Wilkerson asked his fellow agent.

Thurman almost whispered, "Mike, we've got three little dead girls over there under that tree. One is lying over there naked; the other two appear to be in two different sleeping bags."

"Hasn't anyone looked in the bags?" Wilkerson asked. Thurman shook his head. Wilkerson turned to the medical examiner. "Have the two in the sleeping bags been declared dead?"

"No," the doctor replied. "I felt the bag and I didn't feel any movement."

Wilkerson's face reddened. It was 10:00 A.M., approximately four hours after discovery of the bodies, and no one had opened the bags.

"Doctor," he said, suppressing his anger, "I suggest that you check those bodies right now."

The doctor nodded and Wilkerson, Thurman, and the doctor walked over to the bodies. The first thing that was noticeable were the small lumps in one end of each sleeping bag. For some reason Wilkerson had not thought of the children as being that small, that young. It was only now that he realized they were under eleven. Either that or the bodies had been dismembered and were scattered around inside the sleeping bags.

The doctor opened the first bag. Cary Thurman had his camera ready. Thurman gasped as the bag opened. The tiny blond-haired girl was approximately seven years of age and wrapped in what appeared to be bloody bedclothes. "My God," Thurman said. "My God." The medical examiner declared her dead.

The next bag was opened and revealed the body of another little girl, brown haired, eight or nine years old. She too was covered with blood and was bound in a fetal position, cord around one hand which was looped tightly under her buttocks and bound to the other hand. Bloodstained bedclothing was also in the bag. The Medical Examiner declared her dead also.

The third victim was a half-nude black girl, ten or eleven years old. She was lying on her back, her legs wide apart and her pajama top pulled up under her arms. Her hands were bound behind her with thick, dark duct tape and sash cord. She had been beaten severely about the face, and the shape of the lethal instrument was readily definable on her face. It appeared to be a rectangle approximately two inches long and three-quarters of an inch wide. Wrapped around her neck were two ligatures: one was sash cord, the other an elastic bandage. Attached to the sash cord was a cylindrical object approximately four inches long made of terrycloth. It appeared that the elastic bandage had been pulled over the girl's face to make a blindfold, and the terrycloth object a carefully sewn gag. There was little doubt in the officers' minds that the girls had been raped and sexually molested.

Agent Thurman sighted through the aperture of the camera, mechanically snapping the shutter as he moved from one position to another. The dirty son-of-a-bitch, he thought. What kind of an animal could commit such an act? Just five minutes—that's all the time he would want with the bastard. Thurman suddenly realized he was angry; an anger bordering on fury. As he glanced around him, he realized he was not alone in these feelings. He had felt such anger before but never quite so intense. He almost smiled. Never get personally involved, he had been told since his first day in law enforcement. Well, he was involved in this one, not only as a criminal investigator, but as the father of a twelve-year-old daughter.

"Mike," D.A. Sid Wise said, "this young man is from the local newspaper. He can be trusted. I thought I would just have him take some back-up pictures, if it's all right with you. After all, you can't get too many crime scene pictures. Believe me, he can be trusted."

Wilkerson shrugged his indifference and the young man began snapping pictures at Wise's direction.

•

As Ted Limke killed the engine, he could see the bodies being placed in the ambulance. The sticky heat engulfed him as he left the air-conditioned car and started walking toward the group of men huddled 45 yards away. He recognized Thurman and Wilkerson, as well as District Attorney Sid Wise and Sheriff Pete Weaver. He could see Wise flailing the air in an attempt to emphasize some point that probably wasn't relevant to anything, Limke thought. He dreaded having to listen to Wise, having known him for several years. Sid Wise was honest and well-meaning. But, as many of the people who knew him said, "not the kind of guy you'd want to have a beer with." Wise overstated everything and had a flare for the melodramatic, which Limke found boring and aggravating.

Sheriff Weaver was another matter. Limke knew the relationship would be strained with this lawman he had once had to investigate, but he knew, too, that Pete Weaver was one hell of a cop. In his late fifties, Weaver appeared the stereotypical eastern Oklahoma sheriff: tall, slender, leathery tanned face. Weaver cultivated the image of a slow-talking, dry-witted, hick lawman, but underestimating Pete Weaver was a big mistake and Limke knew it.

Limke shook hands with each of the group, exchanging cordialities. The atmosphere was heavy, almost like that of a sanctuary. There was no wind; surrounded as they were by the dense woods, the air seemed thick and stale to them. Mike Wilkerson ushered Limke to the site where the bodies had been found. A large roll of black duct tape and a red-and-white 9-volt flashlight lay within a few feet of where the bodies were found. Wilkerson called Limke's attention to the lens, which was covered by a piece of green garbage-bag plastic. The plastic was attached to the lens with masking tape and a hole had been torn in the plastic so that only a small beam of light would be emitted. As soon as the pictures had been taken, the sleeping bags had been zipped up and the bodies—in the same positions as they were found—were placed in the ambulance. The Medical Examiner's office in Tulsa had been alerted and Wilkerson had been assured the case would be given top priority.

"Looks like they were carried over here, no drag marks," Wilkerson said as he pointed toward the tents, the nearest of which was less than a hundred feet away.

"Let's take a look," Limke said, and with Weaver leading the way, the group walked single file toward the tent.

Kiowa Unit, like most of the other units, was arranged in a semicircle with the top opening toward the north, and consisting of eight tents. These usually housed three to four girls, and each tent was within a few feet of the others. The tents had wooden floors, two feet off the ground, to which the canvas sides were tied. The counselors' tent was located at the southwest corner of the campsite. Tent Number 8, the victims', was the last one in the unit. The closest building to the east of it was the washroom and latrine. Tent 8 looked to be 150 yards from where the corpses were found. It contained four cots, two against each side. The southwest corner of the tent was stained and spattered with blood. The stains on the floor were smeared, as if someone had attempted to wipe them up. The cot in the southeast corner of the tent was covered with blood and a large smeared stain was apparent on the wooden floor nearby. A small soft suitcase was on the floor at the back of the tent. On the cot in the northwest corner were two raincoats, two pairs of shorts, a blue blanket folded at the foot of the cot, and a sock. Under the cot were two plastic bags. On the northeast cot was a duffel bag. Denise Milner's name was printed on its side. Alongside it was a bra, a pillow, some small plastic bags, and a ballpoint pen. Under this cot was a knapsack, a pan containing facial tissues, and a canteen.

It appeared as if someone had attempted to clean up the floor with the slipcovers and the blanket from the cot, then had thrown them inside the sleeping bags with the dead children. On the floor were two different types of footprints. Both tracks appeared to be of a tennis shoe design. Being careful not to disturb anything, the officers walked around the tent. The screw hooks holding the back flap of the tent had been unscrewed and were on the ground at the back of the tent. After the preliminary scan of the area, the officers returned to where the bodies had been discovered. They went back the same way they had entered.

Limke had earlier contacted Agent Larry Bowles, who was to meet the ambulance at the Medical Examiner's office in Tulsa and witness the autopsy. The immediate crime area was roped off to await the arrival of technicians from Oklahoma City. Fifteen agents had been summoned. Limke assigned Wilkerson to the camp cafeteria for interviews with the counselors and the children in the Kiowa Unit. A group of OSBI agents and local officers was organized to conduct a general search of the area, excluding the immediate death scene and tent area.

By 3:00 P.M. the mobile laboratory and command post, a converted 25-foot motor home, had arrived from Oklahoma City. Agents converged from all over the state. Limke was confident that he had the kind of men necessary to do the job. As one agent said, "Somebody's in a lot of trouble. I'd hate to have this bunch after me."

With the investigation of a major homicide come major problems. The first, as always, was the news media. D.A. Sid Wise, Ted Limke, and Sheriff Pete Weaver met to discuss it. Wise suggested that Pryor *Daily Times* newsman Ron Grimsley be made "press coordinator" and proposed to the two lawmen that he, Wise, should be called Coordinator of Investigation, and Limke called Head of the Investigation. He could call himself the Easter Bunny, Limke thought, as long as he kept the press off his back and didn't interfere with the case. Limke never liked talking to the press, anyway. At the same time, he warned Sid Wise that he did not want the reporter, Grimsley, to print any information in his own newspaper that the general press did not get.

"I don't know any bigger way to piss off the press," Limke warned, "than to play favorites. If you treat them all good or all bad equally, they don't have a gripe. But if you start playing favorites, they will cut your throat."

D.A. Wise, Agent Limke, Sheriff Pete Weaver, and Press Coordinator Grimsley trudged up to the main gate and were met by a mob of reporters who were already on hand. Wise introduced them and explained in what capacity he would be acting during the course of the investigation. Grimsley was introduced to a wave of grumbles from the reporters. Crowded around the men, they began firing questions, not waiting for answers.

"Who are the girls?" "How were they killed?" "Do their parents know they're dead?" "Were they sexually molested?"

Most questions were fended off by Wise and Limke. Limke told the reporters that it appeared that the little girls had been beaten to death. He said, "There was some evidence of sexual molestation on two of the girls."

As the men talked, the buses arrived to take the remaining children from the camp. Most of the childrens' parents were anxiously waiting in Tulsa, not knowing whether or not their child had been one of the victims.

God, what would it be like to be one of those parents, Limke thought, knowing only that three girls at the camp had been murdered. Limke was frustrated. He wanted to release the girls' names but the victims' parents had not all been notified. Damn, he thought, to just be waiting there wondering, hoping, terror-stricken, frustrated, and angry—very angry. Limke wondered what he would do as a parent. He clenched his teeth. What a hell of a way to make a living.

Larry Bowles looked and acted like a professional criminal investigator. He stood over six feet and tipped the scales at two hundred pounds. Bowles was the only agent of the OSBI who was a former Oklahoma Highway Patrolman. He had never regretted the switch. He and his family lived in Tahlequah, within 25 miles of Westville, where he had grown up. He knew the local people well, both white and Indian. Being one-quarter Cherokee, he was able to function comfortably in either world. He and Mike Wilkerson were hired at the same time and had worked many cases together in the intervening years.

It was a little after 12:30 P.M. when he focused his 35 mm camera and snapped the first of some 75 photographs of the three little girls as they were brought into the Medical Examiner's office in Tulsa. He had seen a lot of autopsies. It was part of the business—the smell of burning bone as the skull saw made its circle—the total irreverence toward a human being sprawled on a porcelain table, the chest cavity open from the collar bone to the genital area. Necessary, no doubt, but it always seemed to Bowles that it could be done with more respect, more solemnity, more . . . something.

Bowles's thoughts were invaded by approaching voices. Paul Boyd, the Chief Fingerprint Technician of the OSBI, greeted Bowles with a quiet smile and a nod. Boyd was accompanied by Janice Davis, forensic chemist. They had just arrived from Oklahoma City with two Midwest City police officers, Chuck Morrison and Larry Cooper. Morrison and Cooper had experimented with a technique utilizing iodine fumes and a silver plate to develop and lift latent fingerprints from human skin. They would try it here.

At 2:10 P.M. the collection of evidence began. Janice Davis took oral, vaginal, and anal swabs from each victim. The pubic area was combed and all loose hairs were collected. The tape and cord bonds were removed.

Paul Boyd had been with the OSBI for twenty years. He worked mechanically: hair, blood, fiber, fingerprints, anything that could tie the criminal to the scene, was what he was searching for. Boyd removed three hairs from a piece of tape that had bound Doris Denise Milner's hands, slipped them into a plastic bag, sealed it, then dated and initialed it.

The collection of trace evidence completed, Morrison and Cooper began fuming the bodies. On the buttock and the thigh of Milner, the iodine fumes formed a dark purple. The silver plate was carefully rolled onto the skin. As Morrison turned the plate over, those nearest him gasped. An almost perfect fingerprint—bright purple—appeared near the corner of the shiny plate. It had to be the killer's. Boyd inspected the plate. He was skeptical. It was just too good, too clear, but what if it was—what if this was the killer's print?

At 3:30 P.M. Dr. Neil Hoffman began the autopsies. First Milner, then Guse, then Farmer.

Bowles took his pictures. What if the murderer got away with it? What if they never caught this animal? Bowles felt fear moving in his stomach. Not physical fear—he had always been able to handle that—but fear that the world, his world, was threatened. Fear that nice people like his parents, who had never known true violence, could be victims of pointless, brutal, unreasoning violence that could not be understood. If these little girls could be the objects of such obvious rage, then anyone could. He thought about his young son and the unborn child his wife, Kathy, was carrying. It was incredible—for no reason—no motive. In the Thrasher homicide in Woodward, Oklahoma, three years earlier, a family of four—father, mother, nine-year-old girl, and eighteen-month-old boy—had been shot to death. More and more, what Dick Wilkerson had said about the earlier Thrasher case seemed true. "The whole damned world's gone crazy."

CHAPTER 3

GOOD PLACE FOR A HOT DOG STAND, TED LIMKE THOUGHT AS HE threaded his car slowly through the reporters at the entrance to Camp Scott. It was barely daylight and already the place was crawling with newsmen. The competition among the news media was bordering on the unbelievable. Reporters had even been caught trying to sneak into the camp area. Representatives from every major newspaper, radio, and television station in Oklahoma and many from outside the state lined the road near the entrance. And motels in the area had begun to fill as news of the slayings was broadcast and published across the nation.

With three hours of uneasy sleep behind him, Limke prepared himself for the second day of the investigation. Overnight, hundreds of phone calls had been received from all over the United States—some claiming they knew who the killer was or that they themselves were the killer. They all had to be checked out. Twenty-one of the thirty-six OSBI agents were assigned full-time to the case. All laboratory personnel were placed on twenty-four-hour call. It was an all-out effort.

What else could be done? Limke didn't know. Maybe today there would be a break, that good lead that would make it all unravel. Maybe today.

Sid Wise again met with reporters at the gate and answered questions. He seemed to be basking in the publicity. There was talk that he was using the case to catapult himself into state politics, as it was known that he was interested in the attorney general's office.

In the meantime the town of Locust Grove and Oklahoma towns and scout camps throughout the state were stepping up security. One camp in the northeastern part of the state hired armed guards and was taking precautionary measures. A spokesman for Salvation Army camps announced that their camps were actually the safest because there was one counselor for every eight children. Camp Discoveryland for Indian youths, west of Prattville, Oklahoma, explained that they had one counselor for every child and guards on duty around the clock. All of the camps conceded that the slayings would affect their summer programs. The situation at Camp Garland, a Boy Scout camp near Locust Grove, would definitely be affected. A public relations director for the Girl Scouts said that she really didn't know what would happen to Camp Scott after this.

Other camps in the state were also increasing security. Youth camps in Vian, Sapulpa, Wagoner, Oklahoma City, and Seminole were all initiating security measures ranging from having one counselor for every two children to full-time armed guards.

Shortly after mid-morning Limke received the results of the autopsies by Dr. Neil Hoffman. Doris Milner had died of strangulation. There were also indications that she had been sexually assaulted—lacerations of the genitalia and fragments of leaves and other debris found there as well.

Michelle Guse's death was caused by blows to the head, with lacerations and contusions of the brain. Her wounds were located on the back of her head, as well as the sides, leading investigators to believe that she was either lying or standing with her back to the assailant. There were also indications that she had been sexually assaulted, both vaginally and anally.

Lacerations of the brain due to blows had caused Lori-Lee Farmer's death. She too appeared to have been sexually assaulted. All tape and cord were removed from the body, not by untying or unwinding, but by cutting the ligatures away from the knots so if the knots were of a peculiar variety they could be matched later. The ligatures, clothing, and pubic hair samples, scalp hair, vaginal, anal and oral swabs, and blood were given to Dennis Reimer and Janice Davis, OSBI forensic chemists, for transportation to the Regional Laboratory at Tahlequah and the Headquarters Laboratory in Oklahoma City.

Objective, professional, to the point. There was nothing in the cold facts about terror, nothing about three little girls who had been robbed of their lives. Limke shook himself back to reality. What did he have? Lacerations of genitalia of Milner might indicate that something other than a penis was used in the assault. No sperm or semen had been found as yet, so the possibility still existed that the assailant might be a woman. All women interviewed would have to be questioned about their sexual habits. And there was that strange, carefully sewn terrycloth cylinder around Milner's throat, which appeared to Limke to be some type of phallic symbol. But the girls had been carried 75 to 100 yards, maybe at the same time. Few women could carry over 100 pounds that distance.

The agents were in general agreement that the killer had entered the tent through the back and struck the two girls sleeping on the south side of the tent, killing them. The lack of blood on Doris Milner's bed led agents to theorize that she may have been tied up in the tent, a ligature or strangulation knot placed around her throat so she could not cry out. Then she was led outside perhaps and assaulted. This theory seemed to be supported later in the day when an elastic hair band identified as Milner's was found in the middle of the camp leading to where the bodies were dumped. It was also discovered that two purses were taken from counselors in the Camp Scott area that night. It seemed that the assailant had randomly burglarized occupied tents.

Forensic chemists and crime scene technicians continued to sift through the evidence. The technicians first vacuumed the tent, using a special vacuum with a filter that would catch even the minutest hair follicle. After the tent was vacuumed, the floor was meticulously painted with ninhydrin, a chemical used to raise latent fingerprints from wood and paper. Larry Mullins and Paul Esquinaldo, OSBI technicians, were very careful not to touch the blood smears or the blood prints. That section of flooring, four feet by four feet, was removed by Agent Arthur Linville and transported to the OSBI Laboratory in Oklahoma City by Highway Patrol Trooper Charles Newton in his pickup truck.

Everything—anything—that might later become evidence was collected. Agents Joe Collins and Ed Loffi photographed and made plaster casts of a footprint found 100 yards west of the Camp Director's office. All of the children in Kiowa Unit, as well as all counselors from all of the units, were interviewed by Agents Collins, Davis, Albro, and District Attorney's Investigator Beverly Hough. Agents Wilkerson, Bowles, Linville, and Thurman inventoried the personal effects of the victims.

Spray equipment was flown from headquarters in Oklahoma City, filled with ninhydrin spray, and the entire tent was sprayed. Agents then began new searches of the kitchen and storage room area in the Kiowa tent unit. One agent noticed the outline of a hatchet on the wall but the hatchet could not be found. It had a blunt end with a rectangular shape. Ben Woodward, the camp ranger, was contacted. He said several hatchets had been stolen from the area and it was not uncommon at all for one to be missing from these kitchen areas. He showed the agents one of the hatchets and the blunt end seemed to match the wounds found on the victims' bodies. Agents began looking for a hatchet.

Eastern State Hospital is located in Vinita, Oklahoma, some 60 miles from Locust Grove—a mental institution that houses the criminally insane as well as those with minor emotional problems. A list of the outpatients with child molesting records was received by the OSBI. Agents and police officers were shocked to find that there were 17 paroled child molesters within a 40-mile radius of Locust Grove.

Ben Woodward, the ranger and custodian at the camp, was asked to take a polygraph test. He readily consented and signed a waiver to take a polygraph and have his house and any of his property searched. A search of his home and property proved fruitless. He took the polygraph examination in Tahlequah. He was asked if he had committed the crime and if he knew who committed the crime. Woodward passed the polygraph test. Palm prints and fingerprints, blood and hair samples were taken from him. That same day his wife was polygraphed to double-check the results of Woodward's tests. Her polygraph test confirmed that Woodward had been at home during the time that the killings took place. Hair samples and prints, as well as blood, were also taken from Mrs. Woodward.

On the afternoon of June 14 Sheriff Pete Weaver received a call from Jack Shroff, who owned a small farm about two miles west of the Camp Scott area. He told Weaver that his house had been burglarized and several items taken. OSBI Agent Arthur Linville went to the residence and found that the door had been kicked open. Shroff reported that a roll of black duct tape was missing as well as several bottles of Pabst Blue Ribbon beer. Cord matching that which was wrapped around the victims' bodies was also found at the Shroff residence. Outside the door of the house was a small piece of carpet used for wiping one's feet. On the carpet was the distinct imprint of a waffle-type jungle boot. The print appeared to match that found in the Camp Scott area.

Shroff agreed to look at some of the items of evidence at Camp Scott. He identified the tape as looking like the tape he had in his house but could not identify the flashlight or any other items found at the scene. Major case prints were taken from Shroff and he was now considered a suspect. Agents were working on the theory that the burglary could possibly have been a cover-up when Shroff realized that he had left his flashlight and tape at the scene and his fingerprints would be on them. He had also made a statement to officers that he thought that his tape had his initials on the inside curve of the roll. The tape at the scene did not.

A larger search of the Kiowa Unit area revealed three empty Pabst Blue Ribbon beer bottles in the southeast corner of the camp property.

Agents were now becoming optimistic. They had a prime suspect. They were linking evidence to that suspect. They had a great amount of physical evidence, including a footprint. Their enthusiasm was quickly dampened that afternoon when the Tulsa *Tribune* printed a news story saying that several tennis shoe prints, too large to belong to the girls, were discovered inside the blood-smeared tent.

Limke was enraged. "Who the hell leaked this to the press?" He slammed the newspaper down on the desk in the command post. "Some press coordinator. Some investigative coordinator. With my luck they will get us all lynched."

Limke decided Shroff should be given a polygraph test at his convenience. Shroff appeared to be a naturally nervous man, which might prejudice the results. For accurate results, the test would have to be administered when Shroff felt more at ease.

The phone in the mobile command post rang constantly. Veronica Simon, the chief stenographer, had been flown in from Oklahoma City to assist Limke. She answered the phone, took messages, made coffee, typed reports and lead sheets, and generally kept Headquarters advised. Limke ran between the mobile command post and Camp Director's office, next door. If the phone in one was busy, which it usually was, the other was used.

"Ted, it's Dick," Veronica said as she thrust the phone toward him with her left hand and reached for a cup of hot tea with her right.

"What do you want?" Limke said in mock irritation.

"How's it going, boy?"

Dick Wilkerson and Ted Limke were very close, a relationship that had developed over years. Dick had been resident agent at Tahlequah while Ted was stationed in Muskogee, less than 25 miles away. They had busted a lot of bad guys together and had never had even a mild disagreement. Dick, as Chief of Investigative Operations, was responsible for the coordination of all statewide investigations. If a regional supervisor needed more manpower or a specialized piece of equipment, he contacted Dick. The agents and other employees usually referred to him as Tricky Dick or simply Trick.

Dick Wilkerson competed with himself. As a U.S. Marine paratrooper and frogman, he had continually tested himself physically and psychologically. While taking pride in his accomplishments, he continually searched his consciousness for the motives that made the "proving" necessary. At thirty-four years of age, his five foot ten frame now carried fifteen more pounds than the one hundred and seventy pounds he had weighed at his discharge from the Marine Corps twelve years earlier.

In seven years with the OSBI, he had risen rapidly through the ranks, acquiring a master's degree along the way. He now supervised men who were at one time his supervisors. During his ascension he had attempted to heed the advice of former OSBI Director Carl Tyler: "Be nice to 'em on your way up, you may meet 'em coming down." This had never been difficult for Wilkerson, as he had always believed that professionals didn't have to be soldiered around. He liked and respected most of the agents and employees of the OSBI. He cultivated the good ole boy image. Referring to his pronounced Oklahoma drawl, he would joke, "All my life people have thought I was stupid because I talk this way and that's given me a great advantage."

"I thought I'd call to let you know how incredibly competent and dedicated we are over here," he joked to Limke.

"Bullshit," Limke retorted. "You were probably home by 5:30 last night playing with your damn horses."

The preliminary, customary chiding over, the two men, without either commenting, got down to business. "Ted, I got a couple of things, for what they're worth. Linville flew the stuff in from the scene last night. The glasses found near the bodies belong to Carla Wilhite, the counselor. We had the prescription read here and got us a list of every optometrist in the state. Kathie Blackmon, Linda DeArman, and Jan Clary stayed here with me last night and we started calling. Sure enough, we got an optometrist in Sapulpa out of bed; he checked and it looks like the glasses belong to her. Well, are you impressed?"

"Yeah," Limke said, "but then you big-time crime fighters always impress me."

"Okay," Wilkerson said. "Let me put this one on you. The 9-volt flashlight found at the scene—well, inside was some newspaper folded up, I guess so that the battery would make better contact. It was a section of the classified ads but no date or anything. Kathie noticed a typographical error; called the company who ran the ad. Anyway, to make a long story short, it's pages 5 through 12 of Section C of the April 17th Tulsa *World*. So, all you got to do is find a bad guy who is missing these pages from his newspaper and you can take the weekend off."

"Thanks a heap," Limke said dryly. "Between you, Sid Wise, and Grimsley, and these other clowns who can't say anything except, 'Hey, Ted,' I may go quietly outside and open a vein."

Wilkerson's voice lowered, "Ted, I've got some reports up here that your press coordinator isn't the only problem you have with the news media. It seems that the newspaper photographer that Wise had take the crime scene pictures may not be quite as reliable as Wise believed. I'm getting reports that he's using his position to take news photos. I even heard that he is selling pictures to the press. Better check it out. Even if it isn't true, the mere rumor that it's going on will be trouble."

"Oh, God," Limke said, trying to suppress his anger and frustration. "That's all I need. We've got two local newspapermen who are being given information that the big city news media don't have. It's a matter of time before they go for the throat, Dick."

Wilkerson's voice lowered, "Do you want some help, partner? I'll come over there if you want me to."

"Well, get your ass over here then," Limke responded. "If this crap keeps up with the photographer and the press coordinator, I'm going to need some help. Maybe just somebody to shoot the rope when the media decides to hang me."

"Okay, when Linville flies back tomorrow evening, tell him to call me and I'll come back with him the next morning," Wilkerson said.

"See you then," said Limke, and he lowered the phone.

So much, so many things; had he forgotten anything? Limke was sick of hearing everyone calling his name. He was in charge, no doubt about that. It was his responsibility. Every officer, trooper, agent, had a hot lead and wanted to talk to Limke. His mind raced and he worried. Had he forgotten anything?

On the morning of June 15 the press was waiting at the main gate to Camp Scott, approximately a mile from the murder scene. The tremendous competition for news stories continued. The Tulsa *World* headlines read, "Official Tight Lip on Girl Scouts' Killer"; the story, however, contained parts of the case that were anything but tight-lipped. District Attorney Sid Wise said that all three girls had been sexually molested. The story revealed the theory that the two younger girls were slain inside the tent while the older girl was killed outside. Wise was quoted in the article as saying, "Logic leads us to conclude the murderer is a man. A stealthy, physical, agile man." He added that the murderer worked quickly and swiftly, executing a well-thought-out plan. It began to look more and more as if Wise was running for political office or trying to get his name in the newspaper. He held three news conferences that day and all he accomplished was to create hostility among the news media.

"Why does the Pryor *Daily Times* get more in-depth stories than we do?" one reporter inquired.

"Yea," another yelled from the back. "What the hell's going on? We're out there working our butts off and you won't give us any information at all. Grimsley is printing a hell of a lot more than we are getting. Where did the *National Enquirer* get its photographs?"

Wise either did not hear the comments or chose to ignore them as he turned and walked down the hill toward the headquarters.

It didn't take long before many of the people in Locust Grove, for the first time in their lives, began to lock their doors. Guns became prevalent in the town. They could not believe that in a town of 1,090 there possibly walked a mass murderer.

The investigation was continuing at a rapid pace. Agents and local officers were interviewing people up and down the rural roads, running out leads from telephone calls, still processing the crime scene. Funds were being raised to aid the families and to help catch the killer. Community concern over the murders of the three Girl Scouts had caused eight separate funds to be set up. The Magic Empire of Girl Scouts had begun a reward drive with a $1,000 donation from the Board of Directors of the Fourth National Bank of Tulsa. The Council, through Jane Hill, the Program Director, said that they would also set up a memorial fund drive with money to be used "in an appropriate manner to be announced at a later date after consultation with parents of the three children." A reward fund was established by the First National Bank of Pryor, County Seat of Mayes County. D. E. Brown, Vice-President of the bank, said he and A. J. Southern started the fund and that the money would be disbursed by the Mayes County Sheriff's Office in conjunction with the District Attorney's office if an arrest was made. Both men had daughters who were present at Camp Scott when the three girls were slain. There were also rewards offered for information leading to the arrest and conviction of the murderer. Drug Awareness, Inc., a private fund often used for undercover narcotics purchases in Mayes County, offered a $1,000 reward. The Tulsa Retail Clerk's Union offered a $500 reward. A Tulsa woman, Gwen Vanderpool, started a Girl Scout Memorial Fund at Security National Bank. Still another memorial fund was established at the First National Bank of Tulsa for the three families. A benefit car wash was announced to be held Wednesday at a Texaco station in Tulsa.

Funeral services for the three victims were scheduled. A memorial service for Lori-Lee Farmer would be held at 2:00 P.M. Wednesday. Doris Milner would be buried on Thursday. Funeral services for Michelle Guse were scheduled for Friday in Broken Arrow.

By late Wednesday afternoon the reporters were interviewing anybody who would talk to them about the murders, from the people on the street to police officers who were less than professional. An unemployed Locust Grove man had been arrested the previous night in Grove, Oklahoma. One newspaper reported that he was considered a suspect by Pete Weaver. The drunk had reportedly been living out of his car and was arrested about seven miles from Grove in Ottawa County by the Oklahoma Highway Patrol. Weaver was quoted as saying the man might possibly throw some light on the slayings. As hungry as the media was, this made banner headlines. Sid Wise was then interviewed and said he did not consider the man a suspect at all. It appeared to the media that they were getting the runaround. One agency would say that a person was not a suspect and another agency would say the person was a suspect. One agency might be checking out the suspect's alibi and the other agency might not know the results until that night. The leaks continued and it was reported that evidence of the killer's presence had been found at the Jack Shroff residence. Jack Shroff was deluged with reporters and phone calls. He was considered the most likely suspect.

Later that afternoon three specially trained dogs were flown in from Pennsylvania to search for the route of the killer. The so-called superdogs had reportedly cracked an eight-month old murder case in Pennsylvania by picking the suspect out of a lineup on three different occasions. Later the suspect confessed.

June 16 had all the makings of a circus, complete with dogs, men with funny hats, and cameras. The morning newspapers carried stories that three excellent fingerprints were found on the bodies, as well as the footprints, and two burglaries were linked to the killer. They also said that the camp was being searched for a hatchet as a possible murder weapon. Wise again held his daily news conferences and gave his daily suppositions on how the investigation was going. The newspapers also reported that the autopsies revealed no semen. The news accounts told about the lens of the flashlight being covered with dark plastic and that a roll of electric tape was found.

The Cessna 172 broke through the dense clouds and banked to the right. The pilot, Arthur "Aupy" Linville, was as surprised as his two passengers that he had emerged almost directly over Locust Grove.

"You lucky bastard," Dick Wilkerson laughed from the right seat.

"Luck has nothing to do with it. Skill, that's what it is," Linville grinned.

Both men were pilots but neither was instrument rated. Over Tulsa they had discussed whether they should attempt to make it to Locust Grove with the heavy overcast. They had decided to try, with little or no input from Agent Miles Zimmerman, who silently occupied the back seat. Zimmerman was a new agent, fresh out of the University of Arkansas College of Law. This was his first involvement in a murder case.

Wilkerson and Linville had worked and flown together many times. For over a year they had worked undercover as partners in the narcotics division. Linville was known throughout the state for his work in narcotics investigation. He had made more than two hundred felony cases, of which none were lost at trial. He was innovative and resourceful, with a talent for anything electronic or mechanical. Linville possessed an incredibly analytical mind and was highly articulate and extremely self-confident. Standing no more than five feet six inches tall, with red hair and a deep baritone voice, a former Green Beret, he thrived on any type of challenge. Dick Wilkerson accused him from time to time of suffering from a superiority complex. His extreme self-reliance and self-confidence were often mistaken for rudeness. He was, in the final analysis, a hothead, but a gentleman.

On the flight to Locust Grove they had discussed the case. Wilkerson valued Linville's assessment of a criminal case as much as anyone he knew. Linville thought the overall operation was going smoothly. Limke was doing a good job but had too many men to be able to know everything that was going on. Sid Wise was a problem. The media was really hot and Linville believed they would do anything to get Wise, even to jeopardizing the case. The atmosphere was not good with the media, not good at all.

Did any of the suspects look good? Everybody was interested in this guy Shroff, but Linville was also curious about a convicted rapist and fugitive whose mother lived less than half a mile from the camp. He was a Cherokee Indian named Gene Hart. Linville had talked to Sheriff Weaver about him and Weaver sure thought Hart was capable, as did Agent Leo Albro, who had handled Hart on the rapes a few years before. He had first escaped from the Mayes County Jail in April 1973 and again in October of the same year. Since that time he had been a fugitive. Charges of Unlawful Flight to Avoid Confinement had been filed and the FBI had been looking for him ever since.

The investigation itself was not the center of attention after all. There was a regular dog show going on, with the dog trainer claiming that his superdogs would make the case within forty-eight hours. The trainer was quoted as saying, "There's no doubt in my mind whatsoever that Harras will produce a major break in the murder case. He's been on a hundred cases and has a hundred finds. This is going to be a hundred and one." Harras and Don Laken, the trainer, were accompanied by Butz, another German shepherd, and a rottweiler named Spartan. John Preston, a Pennsylvania State Trooper and Harras's owner, was also with them.

According to Laken, scent rises from the ground into the trees and moisture while humidity forces it down from the trees. The best times to hunt are in the early morning hours and late afternoon because the heat of the day causes the scent to rise.

Early in the morning the trainers took Harras and the other dogs to the murder site, where they were scented with an article of clothing taken from the scene. The dogs led the trainer from the scene, around the back of the counselors' tent in the general area where the glasses were found, on south approximately 40 or 50 feet, and then straight across the camp area to Tent Number 8. This, the dog trainer said, was the route that the killer took with the bodies. The dogs then took the trainer directly to Shroff's house. Several of the agents were skeptical, especially Linville.

It was too much for Linville to take when he saw the superdog being rowed out to the middle of the pond on Shroff's property. As he watched the dog hang his head from the side of the boat to sniff the water, he asked what was going on. An officer responded that the dog was sniffing the water to see if someone had thrown the murder weapon into the water. Linville looked at the officer incredulously. The officer stared back at the dog in the boat, totally serious.

At the Shroff residence Harras was scented on an old cap belonging to Shroff. The dog had taken the trainer and investigators directly back to the crime scene. This, Laken explained, indicated Shroff was the killer. He requested that Shroff be placed in a lineup and the dog scented on the sleeping bags.

Dick Wilkerson and Ted Limke sat in the mobile command post. There was too much going on; they needed more control. It was a classic case of the right hand not knowing what the left hand was doing.

Wilkerson sipped his coffee. "Ted, let's stop everything, get everyone together, find out what they have, and make assignments. If we don't, we're going to miss something."

Limke nodded. He arranged for a conference of all investigative personnel in thirty minutes in the Mess Hall.

The agents in their shirt-sleeves sat on either side of the long gray table in the Camp Scott Mess Hall. The heat was smothering and Wilkerson wanted to keep the meeting as short as possible. Wilkerson stood at the head of the table, flanked by Limke and Veronica Simon, who would record the leads and their assignments.

"Let's just start with Leo and go around the table," Wilkerson said. "Tell us what you've got and what you think."

Each agent summarized his activity and gave a prognosis as to its potential. As suspected, some agents were working on leads that had been previously eliminated by someone else. Mike Wilkerson was assigned the responsibility of eliminating Jack Shroff as a suspect. He would administer a polygraph to Shroff the next day.

The seriousness was broken only for a moment as one of the agents said that a medicine man had placed a curse on the dogs and they would soon die. With the exception of Harvey Pratt, all of the men laughed and snickered. Mike Wilkerson went on to comment, "While he's at it, tell him to change Limke into a frog." This brought a great roar from the men, especially Limke. The comic relief was short-lived as the men again channeled their thoughts toward the investigation.

Linville, flipping through the pages of his notebook, said, "I went by this Gene Hart's mother's house but there wasn't anyone home. There was a note on the door that read, 'Mom, I'm down at the river fishing. See you later,' and it was signed 'Sonny.' I guess Sonny is Hart's younger brother who is living at home."

"No, no," one of the local officers quickly interjected. "Sonny is what Hart is called by his family."

"Aup, why don't you pursue that lead," Dick Wilkerson suggested. "Clear him, or hang him, but let's resolve it." Linville nodded without looking up.

"All we need is a break," Limke announced, "so go out and make one."

As the meeting broke up, the agents began scattering to their respective assignments. Mike Wilkerson stepped from the concrete porch in front of the Mess Hall and strolled wearily toward his car.

"Hey, Mike. Hold up a minute. I want to talk to you." Wilkerson heard Harvey Pratt's voice behind him.

"Yeah, what can I do for you, Harv?"

Pratt walked up and laid his hand on Wilkerson's shoulder. "Now, not wanting to make you mad or anything," Pratt began slowly, trying not to offend his friend, "but you made a joke in there about medicine men and you may not know exactly what you are talking about."

Oh, damn, Wilkerson thought. He knew he might have infringed on Pratt's beliefs. Pratt was a Renaissance man; a Cheyenne-Arapaho caught between two worlds. Even though he had a college degree, he still clung to many of the old ways.

"Harv," Wilkerson stammered, attempting an apology. "You know I would never say anything to insult you, partner."

"No, no. You have not insulted me," Pratt interrupted. "I just think that maybe if you understand a little bit more about the Indian religion and culture you might have a better insight into exactly what medicine is."

"You got a minute?" Wilkerson asked, pointing to a large rock near a crystal clear stream. "Let's go over here and sit down."

As the two men took their seats on the rock, Pratt lighted a cigarette, exhaling heavily. He began, "Mike, have you ever heard of the old ways?"

Wilkerson nodded.

"Well, the old ways maybe can be used synonymously with the Indian culture and religion," Pratt continued. "The term 'medicine' has two meanings to the Indian. One meaning of medicine has the same connotation as magic; the other meaning for medicine is the white man's meaning. Medicine to an Indian is power."

"Yeah, I knew it was some kind of power, but I just thought it was superstition, Harv. I know a lot of people in this part of the country revere the medicine man, but on the other hand, I know a lot of people that are scared to death of the medicine man."

"Oh, for sure," Pratt nodded. "The Indians in this part of Oklahoma believe that medicine men have medicine so strong that they can change themselves into birds, or animals, or give someone else this power. There are different types of medicine men for different things."

"I don't understand," Wilkerson said, confused. "You mean there are different degrees of medicine men?"

"Yeah," Pratt nodded, sensing that he was getting his point across. "A good analogy might be karate. For instance, while there is a brown belt in karate, there may also be a brown belt or that degree of medicine man. A better analogy might be the difference in the training of a general practitioner and a heart specialist. The more skill the medicine man has, the more power he has."

"What determines whether the man is a GP or a specialist?" Wilkerson asked.

Pratt crushed his cigarette against the rock as he looked directly into his friend's eyes. "Power," Pratt replied. "I've seen a lot of strange things done with medicine. I personally believe in medicine. Yeah, I know, you find that hard to believe. I am supposedly a highly educated agent of the OSBI who believes in medicine. Well, Mike, I've seen it work. It's worked for me."

"What do you mean it's worked for you?" Wilkerson questioned.

"Do you remember the White Oak incident?" Pratt continued. The White Oak incident was a powwow that had been held in the early seventies after Wounded Knee. Indians from all over the United States had met at White Oak, Oklahoma, to determine their future courses of action. Fearing possible violence, Governor David Hall had asked the OSBI to monitor the activity. Harvey Pratt and his younger brother were chosen to observe the powwow. "Well," Pratt continued, "before I went to White Oak I went to my medicine man."

"Your medicine man?"

"Yes, my medicine man," Pratt replied softly. "I asked him for medicine that would serve as protection for my brother, myself, and another brother, not a brother of my blood, but an Indian brother. He prepared the medicine and put them into three small rawhide bags. The last thing he told me when I walked out was not to drop any of these bags on the ground. He said that the medicine came from the earth. He went on to say that if I dropped them on the ground they would return to the earth. On my way home I stopped by my mother's to talk to her and tell her about the medicine that I had been given. She asked to see it. I took the bags out of my pocket and carelessly let one fall to the ground. I grabbed it up as quickly as I could and returned it to my hand with the other two bags. I didn't know what bag had fallen to the ground but I remembered what the old medicine man had said. I went home and got some old crow-head beads to make some necklaces." Pratt explained that crow-head beads were large, multicolored ceramic beads that Indians frequently wear around their necks. "Then," Pratt continued, "I threaded the beads into three necklaces and tied the rawhide sacks onto the beads so that each of us could wear them. I kept one set of beads for myself, gave one to my brother and one to my friend. I told them to make sure the bags were securely fastened to the beads. In a few hours my brother looked down and his bag was gone. It had disappeared. I knew that it had returned to the earth. We looked everywhere for that bag. It was not to be found. I went back to the medicine man and told him what had happened. He laughed and said, 'I told you it would return to the earth,' and he gave me another bag."

Wilkerson was hypnotized. If anyone else but Pratt had told him this story, he would have laughed. "How does someone become a medicine man?" he heard himself ask.

"That's a very closely guarded secret," Pratt answered. "You have to be taken under the wing of a medicine man and he teaches you the secrets. I can tell you this: As they get older they become more powerful. They more or less serve an internship and then a residency like modern doctors do. For instance, my medicine man is going to Canada next month to trade medicine with another powerful medicine man. There are many different stories among the Indian people about medicine men, and you're right, they are revered. I don't know whether there are people that can still change their forms, but I believe that at one time they could."

"Well, Harv," Wilkerson said, "first I want to apologize if I offended your religion. I had no idea. The only thing I can do is plead ignorance and maybe stupidity. I had no idea that medicine men were a part of your religion."

"I know you didn't," Pratt waved off the apology, "and I knew that you'd listen. That's the reason I took the time to tell you. You know that I will try to explain the Indian ways to anybody who will listen. I knew you wouldn't laugh." The smile faded from Pratt's face and his voice lowered. "Mike, believe me. There is medicine being used in this case."

Wilkerson's brow wrinkled. "What makes you think so?"

"Because my medicine man told me there was. He said that there was a powerful Cherokee medicine man protecting the person that did this."

"Harv, can medicine be used for good or evil?"

"Either one," Pratt responded, "but it's only supposed to be used for good. If the medicine man is helping the killer, he's probably doing it unknowingly."

"Is there punishment for using medicine for evil purposes?" Wilkerson pressed.

"Oh, I don't know if you could call it punishment or not," Pratt mused. "One of two things will happen. Either the medicine won't work or an ill fate will befall the person who uses the medicine." Pratt quickly continued. "When we are talking about right or wrong, we're talking about red and white. We are talking about the difference between Indian law and white man's law. What may be a crime under the white man's law may be a bold and heroic act under red man's law."

"Harv," Wilkerson said solemnly, "you saw those three kids. Isn't that a crime under red man's law?"

"You bet it is," Pratt said through gritted teeth. "That's a crime under anybody's law."

"Agent Wilkerson," a voice rang through the woods. "Come up to the command post. Limke wants to talk to you."

"All right, I'll be right there," Wilkerson shouted back in the direction of the voice. He turned back to Pratt and said, "Harv, I don't want this conversation to end here. I'm very, very interested in this. Let's get together in the next couple of nights and talk some more."

"It would be a pleasure. I have a friend that you may be interested in talking with. I'll check with him and get back to you," Pratt said as Wilkerson turned and trotted toward the command post.

Pratt leaned back against the large rock. Limke was right, Pratt thought, what we need is a break.

The reward and memorial fund continued to mount. Almost $10,000 had been contributed by private citizens and organizations in northeastern Oklahoma for the arrest and conviction of the murderer or murderers.

The Tulsa Lodge of the Fraternal Order of Police had pledged $5,000 and members of the Oklahoma House of Representatives began collecting money for a reward fund. All three girls were from Tulsa County and Tulsa County legislators were leading the drive. The reward fund at the First National Bank in Pryor had reached $1,317 and the car wash had produced some $460.

The police station in Locust Grove became the center of attention for calls from people who wanted to give tips, spread rumors, unburden their hearts, or generally discuss the murders. The dispatcher there had received a call from a homosexual in Toronto, Canada. Before the conversation ended he offered the forces of one hundred and twenty other homosexuals in Toronto. He had read a news story where the slayings were attributed to a homosexual. He spoke for two or three minutes, expressed great concern and sympathy for the parents of the children. Generally, all he wanted to offer was help.

Willis Ray Thompson and Johnny Russell Colvin were squirrel hunting and they wondered why. It was too hot and muggy to do anything but lie under a fan with a cold drink. The wooded hills were quiet, belying the furious activity taking place at Camp Scott some three miles to the northeast. The two men were natives of the area and knew the woods well. As they approached a small cave, they noticed what appeared to be a flour sack in front of the cave opening. A closer inspection substantiated their observation. Suspecting that someone had been living in the cave, the two men took the partially filled sack of flour, returned to their pickup, and drove to the main gate of Camp Scott.

Highway Patrol troopers Charlie Newton and Leon Rice didn't relish the idea of tramping through the woods in the steamy heat but they had been told to check out everything. The two hunters guided them to the cave and nearby cellar where they collected a bean flip, a pair of lace-trimmed red panties, a pair of green cotton gloves, two torn photographs, two pieces of newspaper, and one pair of broken sunglasses in a beige vinyl case.

Linville dug into the box just presented to him by Trooper Charlie Newton—panties, broken glasses, newspaper, April 17 Tulsa *World*. April 17! The same date as that in the flashlight! "Where did you get this?" Linville said excitedly.

"In a cave about three miles back that way," answered Newton as he pointed to the southwest.

"Well, what are we waiting for," Linville said as he moved toward the four-wheel drive vehicle, with Newton and Rice quickly following. It took about fifteen minutes to drive to the foot of the mountain and another fifteen minutes to traverse the rocky cliffs to the natural cave.

At the site Linville found a roll of masking tape with a small piece of plastic garbage bag stuck to the end.

The tape and the piece of garbage bag, along with the items collected by the troopers, would be submitted to the lab. The pictures would also be sent to the lab. They appeared to be pictures of women but they were torn and it was difficult to tell without expert restoration.

The next morning, June 17, at 9:00 A.M., Mike Wilkerson met Jack Shroff at the District Attorney's office in Tulsa. Wilkerson already had the polygraph instrument set up in one of the investigator's offices when Shroff walked in. He talked to Shroff and asked him if he would mind taking a polygraph examination, explaining to him that he would just be one of several who were taking the test and assuring him that he was not a prime suspect in the case.

A polygraph or lie detector test measures a person's breathing patterns, galvanic skin response (skin's ability to resist a slight electrical current), blood pressure, and pulse rate. The subject is placed in a chair, pneumograph hoses are attached to his stomach and chest, flat metal finger plates are attached to his left hand, and a blood pressure cuff is attached to his right upper arm. The subject's responses are recorded on chart paper that flows through the instrument at a speed of six inches per minute. The two main types of questions used in a polygraph test are "control" and "relevant" questions. A control question is also called a probable lie or a known lie question. It is a question to which the subject will lie or probably lie. An example of a control question is, "Prior to the age of twenty, did you lie to someone who trusted you?" The examiner will set up the control question by almost demanding a no answer. For example, the examiner might say, "There are people in this world who are so sorry that they would lie to people who trust them. You are not one of those people, are you?" The reaction that the subject has to this control question is compared with his response to the relevant question. If the subject's response to the control question is greater than that to the relevant question, he is considered nondeceptive. The theory of polygraph is that the subject will channel his fear toward that question that offers the greatest threat to him. An innocent person will channel his fear toward the control question because that is the question to which he is lying. A deceptive individual will channel his fear toward the relevant question because that is the biggest and most threatening lie.

A trusting rapport was established between Wilkerson and Shroff. Wilkerson was confident that a reliable polygraph test could be run. Shroff was asked if he had attacked the girls and if he had been in the general area that night. The test showed that Shroff had not been in the area on the night in question, nor had he attacked the girls.

Wilkerson took down a statement of Shroff's activities on the night of the murders so that it could be verified even though the test had cleared him. Shroff was very concerned about whether or not anybody would find out that he had taken a polygraph test. Wilkerson assured him that neither he nor anybody else at the OSBI would publicize the fact. He warned Shroff, however, that he could not speak for the other law enforcement people but he would do what he could. He asked Shroff if he would sign a waiver of search of his residence there in Tulsa. Shroff declined and was on the verge of becoming hostile. He did, however, give Wilkerson hair samples from his head and pubic area.

Wilkerson took the polygraph charts and met Chief Polygraph Examiner Tom Puckett in Oklahoma City. Puckett reviewed the test questions and the charts of the test and concurred with Wilkerson's conclusion that Shroff was not implicated in the murders.

Wilkerson dialed the number of the command post at Camp Scott.

"Hello," Linville's familiar voice answered.

"Aupy, this is Mike. Just got through polygraphing Shroff and he looks okay," Wilkerson said.

"Well, you and I are probably the only ones in the state of Oklahoma that believe that," Linville said. "A while ago the superdog picked Shroff out of a crowd. Laken is running around here saying he's the killer, he's the killer, and it's got everybody worked up. So, needless to say, your news is going to be met with less than enthusiasm."

"Damn," Wilkerson responded, already feeling the pressure and the loneliness of a member of the polygraph profession. "Well, Aupy, it's kinda like this; you can either go by my judgment or you can go with the damn dog. What I'm telling you is that I don't believe the man committed the murders. Now, if those people down there feel like they have to go along with a dog, they're going to have to fight me."

"Hell, I believe you, Mike. I never had any faith in those damn dogs anyway," Linville replied. "We're scenting the dogs on articles taken from the Shroff house, the cap, the tape, etc. What in the hell do we expect. Of course the dogs are going to pick out Shroff, the articles are from his house. I've felt like a dumb ass ever since they got here. We've been following a dog around and listening to a trainer interpret his movements. But let me tell you, partner, it's going to be lonely for a while around here for you. The whole damn bunch, with the exception of the OSBI, is going to be ready to lynch you. If you had said that he was guilty, they would have had first degree murder charges filed on him by now."

"Well, just tell Limke the results if you would, Aup, and I appreciate your support. As far as loneliness, I can put up with that. As far as other officers being down on me, I can damn sure put up with that too. I don't need that kind of friendship. We're down there trying to catch a person or persons who killed three little girls, not trying to bum-rap a farmer. When I left him, the man looked like he was bordering on a nervous breakdown. How did he act when he got down there?"

"Nervous," Linville responded. "Of course, I would have been nervous too if I had just got through taking a polygraph examination out of the blue. It didn't help the atmosphere with Laken walking around saying 'He's the man, he's the man. File charges on him.'"

"Well, I'll see you down there in a couple of hours, Aupy. Tell Limke that the newspapers may be getting ready to lynch him, but law enforcement is about ready to lynch me."

Before Wilkerson could return to the Tulsa area, the Tulsa *Tribune* was already on the stand. One-inch headlines on the front page read, "Lie Detector Test Given Here in Girl Scouts' Slaying."

Wilkerson would later visit Shroff in Tulsa's Hillcrest Medical Center where he had been confined after a physical and emotional breakdown. Wilkerson was led into the room by Mrs. Shroff. Mr. Shroff sat on the side of the bed and reluctantly grasped Wilkerson's outreached hand. "How are you, Mr. Shroff?" the agent greeted him softly, detecting the hate in the man's eyes.

The silver-headed man tearfully told the agent, "See what you've done to me. You promised that you wouldn't talk to the newspapers."

"Mr. Shroff, I told no one but the proper authorities," Wilkerson interjected, watching Shroff's face turn cherry-red and the veins protrude from his forehead as if some terrible pressure were building within.

"Now, honey," Mrs. Shroff gently chided, laying her hand upon her husband's shoulder. "You know that reporter said he didn't get his information from the police."

"Do you know what my friends and neighbors think of me?" Shroff continued, oblivious to his wife's words. "Do you know the awful telephone calls I've gotten?" His fingers and hands shook terribly as he reemphasized his loathing for the agent. "Someone is going to pay, I promise you," he spat.

Wilkerson tried to reason with the man, but his explanations were ignored. After ten minutes Shroff's doctor came into the room. Wilkerson walked into the hall with Mrs. Shroff as the doctor took Shroff's pulse and cautioned him to calm himself.

"I'm sorry Jack treated you that way," Mrs. Shroff apologized. "This thing has just eaten him up. He believes everyone thinks he killed those children. It's those awful phone calls he gets. They say the most awful things. The reporters are hounding him to death. He'll be all right soon. He really doesn't hate you, it's just that he has to strike back at someone."

"Yeah, I know," Wilkerson responded. "Jack's a victim. Sometimes I think we're all victims."

CHAPTER 4

ARTHUR LINVILLE DEVELOPED MORE THAN A HUNCH THAT GENE Leroy Hart should be considered a suspect. Oh, this guy is a prince, Linville thought as he thumbed through the twenty-odd sheets of legal-sized pages he had accumulated on Hart. His first conviction had been more than ten years ago. In 1966 Hart had been tried on charges of kidnapping and rape and found guilty. From the accounts of the victims, Linville could reconstruct Hart's crime.

Joan and Barbara had been best friends since junior high school. Now they were both nineteen, both married, and both pregnant. Tonight they had gone out together alone, like they used to, since their husbands were away on a fishing trip. They were in the parking lot of a favorite bar, trying to decide what to do next.

They could see the dark man sitting behind the wheel of the 1958 Chevrolet. Joan got into the passenger side of their automobile and Barbara slid behind the wheel. As Barbara was about to close the door, her peripheral vision picked up the dark man getting out of his car. She started the engine and turned around in her seat to back out. At that moment Joan's door opened and a large Indian wearing dark-rimmed glasses glared into the car and said, "I think I'll go with you." Joan, thinking he was drunk, pushed him back and exclaimed, "You've got to be kidding."

As she tried to close the door the man produced a small nickel-plated revolver. "I said I'm going with you," he repeated.

Joan instinctively slid over to the driver's side and gasped, "My God, Barbara. He's got a gun."

The man looked at Barbara and said, "You go back into the bar and wait there fifteen minutes. If you don't, I'll kill this one," pointing at Joan. The impact of what was happening riveted through Joan like an earth tremor. She began to sob uncontrollably.

"Don't leave me. Oh, please, don't leave me, Barbara. He'll kill me. Please don't leave," she cried as she seized Barbara's arm.

He must have sensed that she was becoming irrational and realized his plan was disintegrating, because the dark man told Barbara, "Okay, you stay. Now you shut up," he said, pointing at the sobbing Joan. "Give me your keys," he ordered. "Now get into the back seat." Barbara crawled awkwardly into the back seat and the man slid in next to Joan. They could both see him now. He was tall, athletically built, and about twenty years old. He was dressed in faded jeans, black slip-on shoes, and a short-sleeved sport shirt.

He took a deep breath, sat back in the seat, and said, "Give me the car keys."

Barbara handed him the keys and told him, "Take the car if you want."

"We're going to sit right here," he said, as he seemed to be trying to gather his wits. After a few seconds he ordered them out of the car. The two women scrambled out of the car and the man pointed the gun toward the trunk of the 1958 Chevrolet.

"Over there," he said, collecting their purses.

The women walked to the back of the Chevrolet and the man raised the trunk lid. "Get in," he ordered.

Barbara replied timidly, "No, we won't."

Joan began to cry again. Pushing the gun into her ribs, the man repeated, "I said get into the trunk."

The sobbing, shaking young women crawled into the trunk space. Before he could close the trunk, a man and a woman walked around the side of the building adjacent to the parking lot. With his gun hand, the man grabbed Joan by the hair and shoved her back into the trunk space, allowing the trunk lid to close as much as it could. The girls could hear the couple laughing as they walked to their car and in a few moments they heard a car engine as the automobile pulled out of the parking lot. The man let go of Joan's hair, the pistol barrel leaving an imprint on her temple. The horrified girls watched as the light from the parking lot disappeared and the trunk lid slammed closed. A terrible darkness engulfed them as they clung to each other. They wondered what would happen. Were they going to be killed? Were they going to be raped? Where was he taking them? They both noticed fresh newspaper placed meticulously on the floor of the trunk.

My God, Joan thought. He's planned this thing. He's not drunk. He's planned this. Was the paper to catch blood or to make them comfortable or what? They didn't know and they wondered. They could hear the man rummage through their car, then walk back to the trunk, stop, and then walk back and get into the car. They hugged each other tighter as the engine started and they pulled slowly out of the parking lot. The tailpipe scraped as they went over a dip that separated the parking lot and 11th Street and exhaust fumes filtered into the trunk space.

The old Chevrolet rumbled along for about twenty minutes before stopping. The man walked back to the trunk and opened it. He smiled as he saw the two girls clinging to each other. He looked at Barbara. "Get out," he said softly.

Joan would not let go of her girl friend. "Oh, please, don't hurt us," Joan pleaded, thinking that the man was going to kill them. It was pitch dark but she could still see city lights and hear the oil pumping stations and she knew that they were somewhere near Tulsa. She looked at the man's hands searching for the gun. She couldn't see it. She thought about running but was afraid that she would be caught and killed or the man might kill Barbara. Hell, she thought. She and Barbara couldn't outrun a turtle in their conditions.

"Let her go," the man ordered, looking at Joan. They reluctantly released each other and Barbara got out of the trunk. The trunk again closed like a coffin around Joan. She began crying, and the exhaust fumes, coupled with her fear and her pregnancy, were making her ill.

Barbara was shoved into the front seat by the driver's side. She slid over to the other side of the seat. The car again pulled back on to the street. "Get onto the floorboard," he ordered.

"Please don't kill me," she whimpered.

"Shut up and get onto the floorboard," he repeated. She slid down between the seat and the dash, her pregnancy making it a most difficult task. She could barely breathe.

"Please, I can't sit like this. I'm five months pregnant. You'll hurt me and my baby."

He looked down at her with a disgusted look and told her to get back up into the seat. They drove for a few more minutes without speaking, the man occasionally glancing down at the baby Barbara was carrying. "I didn't want to take you anyway," he mumbled as he pulled the car off on the shoulder of the road.

She couldn't tell where they were now. There were no longer any lights or cars. She was almost sure, though, that they were still on a major highway. He killed the engine, stepped out of the car, and told her to get out. My God, she thought. He's going to kill me.

"Oh, please don't hurt me. Please, my baby," she begged.

"Get out, I said." She began crying again and Joan, hearing her cry, began screaming from the trunk. "Shut up and get out or I will kill you. I'm just going to put you back in the goddamn trunk," he said, reaching into the car and grabbing her by the arm. It was at that moment she realized how strong the man was. His grip was like a vise and all she could do was go with him as he pulled her from the car. She fell as she got out of the car and skinned her knee on the sharp white gravel that covered the shoulder. He did not wait for her to get completely out but half-dragged her screaming to the trunk. With his free hand he opened the trunk. Joan had pulled herself into the upper right-hand corner of the trunk where she crouched like a frightened animal. The man reached into the trunk and grabbed her by the arm, pulling her out.

"No, please. Oh, please, no," she screamed.

"Shut up," he demanded as he shook her.

She tried to hush her terror as Barbara was pushed back into the trunk and the trunk lid again closed. They walked around to the driver's side of the car and she was ordered onto the floorboard of the passenger side.

"I'm sick," she said. He ignored her. Again the car pulled back onto the road, only to stop again after a few minutes. Joan could tell it was a service station of some kind.

The man got out of the car and stood by the door. "If you make a noise," he said in a low voice, "I'll kill you both. Three dollars," he said to the attendant.

Joan's mouth was as dry as a desert's sand and she was nauseated. "Could I have something to drink?" she said softly. He glanced at the pitiful young woman on the floorboard and disappeared from view for a moment. Where did he go, Joan thought. Now is the time to run. Her muscles tensed as she started to get off of the floorboard, but when she was halfway out she heard footsteps returning to the car. She slid back onto the floorboard. The man got back into the car with two bottles of pop. He handed one down to her and placed the other between his legs. The light of the service station disappeared as the car pulled back onto the highway.

Twenty minutes passed before the car pulled onto a dirt road. Another five minutes while it twisted and turned down the road. The car pulled off the dirt road into a dense wooded area that seemed to engulf the whole countryside. He turned off the engine and looked at Joan as she lay petrified on the floorboard. "What are you going to do?" she asked.

"Get in the back seat," he ordered.

"Oh, no. Please, please, no. Don't do this. Please don't do this," she pleaded, knowing what was to come.

The man reached down and pulled her by the hair. "Get up, I said," he told her calmly.

"I won't let you do this," she insisted.

"Then you'll die here," he told her. He opened the car door and grabbed her by the arm and dragged her out of the car. He opened the back door and physically threw her slight body into the back seat. Barbara could hear what was happening and knew that her friend was either going to be raped, killed, or both.

He jumped into the car on top of her, his two hundred pounds squeezing the breath from her. He began kissing her neck and face and his hand tore at her blouse. His pelvis began moving up and down on her legs. One of his arms held her down while the other pushed up her dress and began groping at her body.

"Please. Please don't do this to me," she begged, tears streaming down her face as she twisted to free herself.

The man began to grunt and snort like an animal as his hand hooked her panty hose, pulling them down to her ankles. She screamed as loud as she could as he pulled her panties down to her knees. He unbuttoned his trousers and pulled them down to his knees. His belt buckle cut into her shins as he pushed her legs apart.

Barbara lay crying and screaming in the trunk as she heard what was going on. She grew physically ill as the car rocked from side to side. As Joan screamed, the man emitted a strange animallike sound. After a few minutes he emitted a final grunt and the car quit rocking. The only sound Barbara could hear was Joan crying. The sweating man slid off her and stepped onto the ground. He pulled his trousers up and told Joan to get out of the car. She slid out, trying to cover herself and retain at least some semblance of dignity, not really caring whether the man killed her. Now that he had gotten what he wanted, she thought, he would probably do just that.

"You can straighten yourself up," he said.

She reached down and pulled up her panties and panty hose and straightened her bra and blouse.

"What's happening?" Barbara screamed from the trunk.

He walked to the trunk and opened it. "Shut up or I'll kill you." He slammed the trunk lid back down and turned to Joan, telling her to get back into the front seat. He slid behind the wheel, reached down under the seat, and pulled out a roll of black tape. He pushed the girl back onto the floorboard and wrapped the tape around her head so that it covered her eyes. She was in a state of shock and offered no resistance. The automobile again pulled back onto the dirt road. After another fifteen minutes or so, the car again stopped. He pulled Joan from the car and dragged her to the back of the car and opened the trunk.

"Get out," he ordered.

Barbara saw Joan's condition and said, "Oh, honey," and tried to embrace her. The man grabbed her and wrapped black tape around her eyes, neck, and head. He then shoved a dirty grease rag in her mouth and wrapped tape around her face and mouth and taped her hands behind her. He grabbed Joan, put a rag in her mouth, and taped her eyes, mouth, and hands. As he taped Joan, Barbara discovered that she could see from under the left side of her blindfold. She looked down at the tag and memorized ME 8042.

After the taping was completed, he took them by the arm and started walking into the darkness. The terrified women found it almost impossible to traverse the rocky terrain blindfolded. They fell many times, cutting themselves on jagged rocks and brush. The man merely snatched them back to their feet. Both girls were almost suffocating because their mouths were taped and their mucus-filled noses were not providing enough oxygen for their exhausted bodies. They walked down a rough incline in the terrain and suddenly they stepped into water. The ice-cold water jolted Joan out of her somnambulistic state. Both tried to pull away, straining and screaming through their gags; both were helpless. It was almost like a dream. They were in total darkness, muted by their gags, and they could not resist because of their bound hands. The water had risen to their knees as they walked.

My God, Joan thought, he's going to drown us. The water rose past their waists and crept up to their shoulders. Only nasal squeals from the women indicated the true terror of the moment. Joan tripped on a rock and was momentarily completely submerged, flopping helplessly in the dark water. She knew that she would be dead in a few moments but the man pulled her to the surface. The water started getting more shallow and the women began to feel a ray of hope that their ordeal was about over. They finally stepped out of the water onto dry land.

At last their captor stopped. "Lay down," he ordered as he punched Joan with his finger. She shook her head, whining and straining against the tape. He's going to kill us now, she thought.

"Uh, you will lay down whether you want to or not," he muttered as he pushed her to the ground. "If you move I'll kill you."

He took Barbara by the arm and led her stumbling into the brush, finally stopping only to throw her to the ground. She could hear him unfastening his belt and unzipping his trousers. She felt his hand push up her dress and pull her panties down. She tried to roll as she emitted a muffled scream but she was helpless. He crawled between her legs. Her pregnancy had already made her extremely tender, and coupled with the dryness of her vagina, the pain was almost unbearable. She began to choke on the handkerchief as she writhed in pain. The man stopped and said, "Does it feel good or am I hurting you?" She responded with more muffled screams and choking. She could hardly believe it when she heard him stand up, pull up his trousers, and walk toward Joan. Joan could hear him coming. She pulled herself up into a ball and hoped the darkness would hide her. He reached down, pulled her panty hose, panties, and shoes off, and threw them into the brush. She could hear him drop his trousers as he stood over her.

"Not again, oh, please, not again," she tried to scream through her gag. Why is he taking so long? Maybe he's not going to rape me again, she thought, clinging to a hope. Still the silence continued. He may have killed Barbara and now he's going to kill me.

He reached down and turned her over on her stomach and pulled her buttocks up off the ground. His penis brushed against her buttocks and she could tell that he had applied a lubricant to himself. Her muffled screams rang throughout the night as he committed sodomy upon her until he ejaculated.

Her body was so wracked with pain and her mind so filled with total degradation and humiliation that she barely noticed when he turned her over on her back and again raped her until he again ejaculated. All that her frenzied mind could perceive were the long animallike sounds that the man emitted.

Finally finishing with her, he stood up. Joan lay half-conscious on the ground. He reached down and pulled her legs together and wrapped tape around her ankles. He then wrapped sash cord around her ankles and through the tape. He attached the rope to her wrists, looped it tightly around her neck in a slip knot and then back to her ankles. The slightest movement caused her to strangle. He took the tape and again wrapped it around her face, this time covering her nostrils. She did not resist. She welcomed the sweet unconsciousness of asphyxiation.

He walked over to Barbara, bent her backwards, and tied her in the same fashion. Then he told both of them, "If you move at all, the noose will choke you to death. I'll be back for you later." He covered both girls with brush like an animal covering his prey or a little boy hiding what he'd done.

They could hear him walk toward his car, get in, and drive away.

Joan could feel her head becoming light as she grew closer to unconsciousness. She decided to end it all in that moment. She pulled at her wrists and the noose tightened around her neck, cutting off the flow of blood to an already oxygen-starved brain. With superhuman strength she struggled at her bonds. All of a sudden her wrists came free from the adhesive tape. Quickly she freed the other hand and tore the ropes from her legs before she lost consciousness. She tore the tape from her mouth, spit out the rag, and drank in the freshness of the night air. Almost immediately her brain began to clear and the pain returned to her body. She heard a weak moan and realized that Barbara was still alive. Then, pulling the tape from her swollen eyes and ankles, she kicked the brush off and jumped to her feet, only to fall back to the ground. Her ankles would not support her weight.

Joan crawled in the direction of the moan and found it coming from under a pile of brush. She tore at the brush and found her friend, while she ripped the tape from Barbara's nostrils and mouth and jerked the handkerchief from her mouth. The gurgling sound that came from the young woman indicated that she was choking to death. She turned her over on her stomach and her numb fingers fumbled at the hard knots in the darkness. After a few long seconds the rope came loose and she, too, gulped in the clean night air. Joan finished untying her and both lay back for a moment to recoup their strength.

"Joan, did he hurt you?" Barbara asked.

"Oh, Bobbie, what he did to me." She started to cry again. Barbara put her arms around her shoulder and embraced her. "But the bastard is going to get his. I got his license tag," Barbara said as her humiliation gave way to rage and the thought of sweet revenge. "We better get out of here. He said he'd be back."

Joan felt around and found her shoes and the girls crawled on their hands and knees through the brush. They were afraid they might be seen if they stood and ran. Cut, bruised, and tattered, they crawled to the road. They tried to wave down several automobiles but none would stop at 4:00 A.M. Finally, a car stopped and took them to the residence of a local highway patrolman.

The young Indian sat with his head bowed in the Sheriff's office of the old Mayes County Courthouse. The tall, balding County Attorney, Carl Longmeyer, walked briskly into Sheriff Pete Weaver's office carrying a tape recorder, slowing only momentarily for a glance at the young man. As he walked into the Sheriff's private office, he said, "Pete, let's get this statement on tape."

"Gene," the Sheriff yelled. "Come in here and sit down and maybe we can get this mess cleared up."

The young Indian rose slowly and walked into the room where the Sheriff and County Attorney were already seated.

"Sit down there," the Sheriff pointed, his hand holding a Camel cigarette and indicating the chair directly in front of the desk. The young Indian slowly looked around the room and only then did he notice the two men dressed in suits sitting at the back of the room.

"Those are OSBI agents," the County Attorney grunted as he stood up, walked across and sat on the edge of the Sheriff's desk, and studied the young man sitting before him.

"All right, now. Your name is Gene Leroy Hart and your address is Route 1, Box 119 K2 in Locust Grove, Oklahoma, and you're twenty-two years old and you own a 1958 Chevrolet, turquoise and white, and your tag number's ME 8042." The County Attorney's voice drifted into a monotone as he explained the young man's constitutional rights. "You know that you can have an attorney with you and there's a great possibility that one of three, or all three, serious charges will be filed against you. You do understand that?" Hart nodded and seemed to be bored.

"Now, Gene," the County Attorney continued. "I'll let you explain what happened Friday night so that we can get the complete picture. It's my understanding that you didn't work at Flint Steel in Tulsa Friday night but that you just drove around most of the evening."

Again Hart nodded. The County Attorney knew that he had already fallen into the Indian's trap of letting the white man do the talking while he merely acknowledged whether the statement was correct. He knew from experience that Hart would show no emotion and getting a statement from him would be difficult.

Pete Weaver silently drummed his fingers on the desk. The statement was a formality. The girls could identify him. Tape and cord matching that used to bind the girls had been found in his car. Weaver was confident that the OSBI lab would microscopically match the tape used to bind the girls with the roll found in the car. Weaver listened as Longmeyer painstakingly led Hart through the events of the night of the crime. Hart recounted essentially the same details as had the girls, however, he adamantly denied possession or use of a gun.

"Did she help you or did she put up any fight or anything?" Longmeyer asked.

"She helped me more than anything," Hart answered.

"Did she say anything while it was going on?" the County Attorney asked.

"No," Hart grunted.

"Did either one of them object to it?" Hart was asked.

"Didn't look to me like they was," he answered.

"Were they tied up at the time?" Longmeyer asked.

"Yeah, they was. They were both tied," Hart answered as he squirmed in the hard wooden chair.

"Did you untie them to have sex with them?" Longmeyer wearily asked.

"No. They were tied around in front and I untied them and retied them around the back," Hart answered.

Weaver took a long draw on a Camel cigarette. Yeah, because they didn't say anything, they helped you; tied up hand and foot with a dirty grease rag stuffed in their mouth they didn't object, he thought. Weaver gazed out the window and wondered if before the statement was over Hart would convince himself that the whole thing was the girls' fault and that he, rather than they, was the victim. Weaver heard Longmeyer ask where Hart had gone after leaving the girls and listened incredulously as the young Indian told of running his fishing lines and boasting of having caught four.

I don't believe it, Weaver thought, shaking his head and again gazing out the window. I just don't believe it.

•

On October 14, 1966, Hart was sentenced to three ten-year terms concurrently after pleading guilty in Mayes County to two charges of Kidnapping and one charge of First Degree Rape.

On March 19, 1969, after serving twenty-eight months, Hart, on unanimous recommendation of the Pardon and Parole Board, was paroled.

Officer Heather Campbell had worked at the Tulsa Police Department until 2:00 A.M. that morning, June 7, 1969. It had taken her only five minutes to reach her one-room efficiency apartment. It had been a long night and she was tired as she unlocked the door and pushed it open with her foot. She flipped the light on as she closed the door behind her. As her eyes adjusted to the light, she relocked the door and laid her purse on a small table. As she wearily undressed, she turned on the police monitor near her bed and placed her .38 special revolver on the nightstand. After turning off the light, she slipped between the cool sheets, lay back on her pillow, and listened to the police calls in the darkness.

In the twilight between sleep and consciousness she was aware of a scratching sound at the door. "The wind," she thought as the police monitor continued its staccato rhythm. There was a click, not loud, familiar, but foreign. The lock, the door lock! Heather was sitting up now. She turned the monitor down. She was straining her eyes. "The door, it's opening," she gasped as the creaking door inched slowly open. She slid her hand under the pillow where she usually kept her gun. "Damn," she cursed the darkness. "Damn," as a shadowy arm appeared through the cracked door, "this is not really happening."

"You better shut that door," she commanded, her voice almost breaking. In the darkness she groped frantically until her hand felt the cold steel of the pistol on the nightstand. Now, now, you bastard, she thought. He must be crazy. Instead of retreating, the guy was coming through the door. She brought the pistol to eye level, the sound of the cocking hammer echoing through the still, dark room, the unmistakable sound of impending death. The large dark figure froze. Heather's voice, now cold and confident again, commanded, "I said shut that damn door or I'll blow your head off." The figure slid back out the door and closed it, the lock engaging.

Heather sat on her bed in the darkness with her gun still trained on the door and listened. After a few minutes she lowered the gun, stepped from the bed and walked unsteadily to the door, opened it cautiously, and peered outside. Unable to see the man, she closed the door, making sure it was locked, fumbled in the darkness for the telephone, and called the police department. By the time she had given the dispatcher the information and slipped on a pair of pants and a blouse, two police officers knocked on the door. As Heather briefed the officers, they heard the sound of a jiggling doorknob coming from the second-floor apartment directly above them. One officer started to the east stairway where he could see a man now walking swiftly away from an apartment. He ran to the stairway toward which the man was walking and waited. The man came scampering down into the officer's waiting gun.

"Don't move. Put your hands on your head and walk toward the wall." The man offered no resistance as he was searched. In the light from the second floor the officers could tell the man was an Indian. "Do you understand English?" an officer asked. The man nodded affirmatively. "What's your name?"

"Gene Hart," the man answered.

"Do you have a car?" asked the officer.

"No, I came in a cab, that's all I'm saying."

Hart was transported to the city jail and booked on a burglary charge. He was searched; $90 in cash, a brown leather wallet, two sets of car keys, and a small amount of change was found. As he was being booked, he told the officers that he thought he was at the Conquistador Apartments located a short distance from Heather's apartment house. He said that he was trying to find a buddy who lived there. The officers checked both local cab companies regarding a fare they had taken to the area of Heather's apartment. Neither company had delivered a fare to that area. Hart was led back to a cell with a steel bed and no mattress.

At 8:00 A.M. Detectives C. E. Gatlin and D. E. Morris were assigned to the case. Gatlin went downstairs to the jail and brought Hart back up to the burglary squad room. As they walked, the young Indian tripped several times and said to the detective that he could not see very well. After entering the squad room, he was introduced to Detective Dennit Morris, a former University of Oklahoma football star. Both of the detectives were soft-spoken, and to the young Indian it seemed that they posed little threat. Morris softly read Hart his Miranda rights and asked him if he understood them. Hart nodded affirmatively and said that he wanted to see an attorney. Gatlin handed him a phone book and told him to call anyone he wished. Hart thumbed through the yellow pages and asked Gatlin to dial a number for him. Gatlin dialed and handed the phone to Hart. The attorney told Hart to keep quiet and he would be at the police department in forty-five minutes. Hart hung up the phone and told the detectives, "I'm not going to talk to you."

"That's fine, Gene," Detective Morris said. "We'll wait till your attorney gets here before we question you. By the way, what were you doing at the apartment house anyway?" Morris asked, trying to be friendly and make conversation, or so it seemed to Hart.

"I was looking for a friend," Hart replied.

"What was the friend's name?" the detective asked, as if he didn't care whether Hart answered or not.

"I can't talk to you about that," Hart replied.

"No problem, Gene, you want a cup of coffee?"

He nodded that he did. Gatlin left the room and returned with the coffee and handed it to Hart. Because of his poor eyesight, the young Indian misjudged the distance of the cup and spilled some of the hot liquid on his hand.

"Did you burn your hand?" Detective Morris exclaimed, overly concerned.

"No," Hart replied, smiling at the detective's concern for him. "Thanks," he said to the kind smile of Detective Gatlin. The man sipped the coffee as the friendly detectives made small talk.

"Oh, Gene," Detective Morris said, as if he had just remembered something. "Where'd you park your car? We'd better go pick it up before it gets towed away or stolen."

Hart suspected nothing as he said, "It's a couple of blocks south in a parking lot. A 1963 white Chev."

The attorney arrived a few moments later and the detectives left Hart and him alone for a few minutes. The attorney knew that his client had already made some very damaging statements to the detectives and advised Hart to cooperate. Quietly and almost sheeplike, he did everything that the detectives asked. He admitted that he went to the policewoman's residence to burglarize it, but could offer no explanation why he stepped into the apartment after the woman told him to close the door.

He gave the detectives permission to search his automobile. In the trunk they found a white straw purse containing the identification and property belonging to Ronnie and Susan Furrh, Eugene Latham, and Steven Stewart. These people were contacted by the detectives and they identified their property.

The Furrh residence had been broken into while they were sleeping in the early morning hours of June 1. The burglar had removed the window screen at the front of the apartment, pried open the window, and crawled into the apartment without waking anyone. All he took was a white straw purse that contained some personal papers and a checkbook. They did not report the burglary.

The Latham residence was also broken into in the early morning hours of June 1. Apparently someone had entered the apartment through an unlocked door and had taken his billfold while he slept. He didn't report the missing billfold because he thought he might have misplaced it.

The Stewart apartment was broken into in the early morning hours of June 2. The thief probably entered the apartment through the unlocked door while Stewart slept. A white-handled paring knife was taken from the kitchen and Stewart's billfold was taken from a nightstand approximately six inches from his head.

All of the burglaries were in the same area and all took place while the occupants were at home sleeping.

The detectives returned to the police station and told the suspect what they had found. Doing as his attorney told him, he readily admitted to the burglaries and gave the officers a complete statement. Gatlin cringed as Hart told them of taking the paring knife from the kitchen, then walking into the bedroom and taking a billfold that was almost touching the owner's head.

Hart was arraigned on June 10 and bond was set at $10,000 for each charge of First Degree Burglary After Former Conviction of a Felony.

Veteran prosecutor Ben Baker was assigned to the case by District Attorney David Hall. Hall himself would later become the Governor of Oklahoma. After his term he was convicted of bribing a state official and sentenced to a federal prison.

Baker offered to let Hart plead to all four charges while letting the sentences run concurrently. This meant that if he were sentenced to ten years on each charge, the total time he would receive would be ten rather than forty years. Hart refused to accept the offer and elected to go to trial.

On September 25 he went to trial for the Heather Campbell burglary. He sat expressionless as the state paraded witness after witness to the stand. One day later a jury found him guilty and he was sentenced to thirty to ninety years in the State Penitentiary.

Again Baker offered to let him plead to a much lesser sentence than he would receive from a jury. He again offered to allow the sentences to run concurrently. Again Hart refused. On October 20

Hart's defense attorney made application to the court to withdraw from the case but the court refused the request.

On October 21 Hart was tried for the burglary of Steven Stewart's residence. The jury listened intently as they were told about a man carrying a knife into a bedroom and stealing a billfold that was a few inches from its owner's head. Hart was again found guilty and sentenced to forty to one hundred and twenty years.

Hart still refused to compromise and, as one lawyer said, "He seemed content to sit in the courtroom and take his lumps." Two days after the Stewart trial his lawyer was granted permission by the court to withdraw from the case and a public defender was assigned.

On December 9 Hart was tried for the Latham burglary. He was found guilty and sentenced to fifteen to forty-five years.

On January 20, 1970, Hart was tried on the last of the four charges, found guilty, and sentenced to fifty years in prison.

Hart had received sentences of thirty to ninety years, forty to one hundred and twenty years, fifteen to forty-five years, and fifty years, all sentences to run consecutively. This meant that he would have to serve one sentence before the other began. It also meant that if he were paroled from one sentence, he must immediately begin the next sentence.

In a few days Gene Hart was sent to the Oklahoma State Penitentiary at McAlester to begin his first sentence.

On April 25, 1973, Hart was transferred from McAlester to Mayes County Jail so he could appear for post-conviction relief involving the rape-kidnapping charges imposed in 1966. Five days later Hart and another inmate, Larry Dry, escaped from the Mayes County Jail by sawing through the bars. Five days after that, two Second Degree Burglary charges were filed against Hart, although he was still at large. On May 25, 1973, Hart was captured and charged with Second Degree Burglary after allegedly breaking into a home in Strang, Oklahoma. He was also charged with Possessing a Sawed-off Shotgun. On September 16, 1973, Hart again escaped from the Mayes County Jail along with Dry and another inmate. The other two were captured but Hart remained at large.

No righteous thief would fall for First Degree Burglary, Linville thought. In Oklahoma that requires breaking and entering in the nighttime of an occupied dwelling. Any thief worth his salt would make sure the house was empty. It sounds like a rapist M.O., and then there was the tape and sash cord.

This little sweetheart has one hell of a pedigree. He might just be good for something as crazy as this whole thing. His mother lives within one-half-mile of the scene and he's very familiar with the area. He's a confessed, convicted rapist with a history of breaking into occupied dwellings. He has used tape and sash cord before. Linville shook his head and smiled as he read a notation by a staff psychiatrist who had examined Hart in 1966 prior to sentencing. He was found "not suffering from psychotic disorder."

Linville almost chuckled. No, nothing wrong with him. Nothing at all.

CHAPTER 5

"Okay, here's what we've got out of Oklahoma City," Limke said as he addressed the dozen agents seated in the Mess Hall at Camp Scott. "The lab is reasonably certain that one set of tracks on the floor of the tent were made by a Wing Athletic Shoe, Model No. B5855. The shoes usually come in gold and they've got three chevrons on the side. They're usually sold by Payless Shoe Stores. In this area there are five stores in Tulsa and one in Bartlesville. It's a relatively new style that's only been on the market two or three weeks. They're making comparisons now and it looks like it's one of the girl's. We still don't have anything on the waffle-stomper print.

"The piece of plastic that Linville picked up at the cave is of the same type used to cover the lens of the flashlight. The pieces of newspaper at the cave are from the same section and the same date, April 17, 1977, of the Tulsa *World*. The end of the roll of masking tape matches identically with one of the ends of the tape used to tape the plastic around the flashlight. The hair from the tape used to tie the Milner girl is of Mongoloid characteristics so we are looking for an Oriental or an American Indian."

"Major breakthrough," someone moaned sarcastically from the rear of the room.

Limke nodded and continued. "The pictures that were found there were taken at some kind of party. There's one picture—I've got some copies here that I will pass out—of a dark-haired girl in a party dress sitting down and the other one is of two women, one standing and one seated at a piano. We need to see if we can identify them.

"Thurman just got back from Arkansas, and Susan Emery, one of the counselors, has positively identified the broken sunglasses from the cave as hers. So we've obviously got a definite link between the cave and the crime scene. The chemists want us to go to Tulsa and talk to the families and get hair samples, both head and pubic, off of every member of the families so they can eliminate them from those that they found in the sleeping bags. Mike, why don't you and Larry do that. Take your inventory of the girls' belongings and see if there's anything missing.

"For you guys who have been entertained by the fingerprints on the body, I have news." Limke paused, taking a long draw on his cigarette. "There were no fingerprints on the bodies." The agents looked puzzled. "The silver plate used to take the prints was manufactured at Tinker Air Force Base," Limke continued. "Paul Boyd had it checked out and in keeping with our policy of strict adherence to Murphy's law—that is, anything that can go wrong will—he found that the prints belong to the Midwest City officer who picked up the plate at Tinker."

"Sensational," Linville groaned. "Now the press will accuse us of covering up evidence that doesn't meet our needs."

Coleman Townsend leaned back in his chair. "You guys ever heard of O'Toole's law?"

Limke smiled. Townsend never lost his sense of humor.

"Murphy was a goddamn optimist," Townsend explained. Affirmative nods and chuckles of agreement interspersed with comments of "no shit" continued until Limke returned the group to the sobriety of the issue at hand.

"That does not mean we are going to stop fingerprinting people. We still have palm prints on the cots from the tents and some ridge detail on the flashlight."

Limke discussed the new information with the agents and made specific assignments for follow-up investigation.

At about midnight the conference broke up and Limke walked slowly back to his car. It had been a long day. It had started to rain that morning and he had hoped the rain would bring the scent down from the trees so the dogs could be of further assistance. Limke had always thought that rain destroyed the scent but, according to the dog trainer, the moisture would bring the scent down from the trees where the dogs could track more effectively. The previous day a crop-dusting airplane had dumped hundreds of gallons of water on the woods surrounding Camp Scott.

The investigation was now ending its sixth day and Limke was bone tired as he turned south on Highway 82. He smiled as he thought about Linville, who immediately upon seeing the photographs of the solitary woman had excitedly announced that she looked just like Gene Hart's ex-wife, whom he had interviewed the day before. Like a bulldog with a rat, Limke thought. He's gonna worry that lead to death. One way or another, Linville will resolve it.

Mike Wilkerson and Larry Bowles spent that Friday, June 20th, with the families of the victims, taking inventory of the children's personal property.

The two agents stopped first at the Guses'. Dick and GeorgeAnn Guse and their thirteen-year-old son Mike live in a two-story house in Broken Arrow, a suburb of Tulsa. Mr. Guse is a corporate credit manager for Froug's Department Store and GeorgeAnn is a high school math teacher. Mrs. Guse sat on the floor and carefully went over each item. She stopped for a minute as she picked up a stuffed autograph dog that Michelle had taken to camp. As she examined the things scattered about the room she talked to the agents about Michelle. She had been a scout since 1974 and had been to camp the previous year. She was a healthy, sturdy girl, who was active in sports and a member of a local soccer team. The last time the Guses saw Michelle was when they waved good-bye to her as the bus pulled out from the Girl Scout headquarters in Tulsa.

Bowles and Wilkerson then drove to the Farmers' residence, a two-story home in Tulsa's stylish south side. Dr. Charles Farmer, a Tulsa physician, and his wife Sherri showed the agents into a large living room. The Farmers were angry and frustrated. Fearing a lawsuit, the Girl Scout Administration was refusing to give them any information about the security procedures at Camp Scott. Dr. and Mrs. Farmer cried as they talked about their daughter. She had been advanced a grade and was a year younger than the other children in her class. When Lori had gone camping for a weekend a month before, she got homesick and had called out for her mother. Nevertheless, she and a friend had made plans to go to Camp Scott together. The friend changed her mind at the last minute and Lori would know no one at camp. Mrs. Farmer had told her that she could wait until the following week when her younger sister, Misti, would be going, but Lori had decided to go ahead. Saturday would have been Lori's ninth birthday and the Farmers had planned to celebrate it with her at Camp Scott.

Mrs. Milner, Denise's mother, was under light sedation. As she went through her daughter's personal effects with the agents, she told them that Denise had been excited about camp but had had to be reassured that Sunday morning. She hadn't wanted to be away from her grandparents or her five-year-old sister. Mrs. Milner had even climbed onto the Girl Scout bus to let her daughter know that she could always call if she got lonely. Denise had been a straight-A student. Mrs. Milner showed the agents some of the awards she had won.

The families could find nothing missing from their children's things. The agents had taken hair samples from the victims' families to be compared with those found at the crime scene.

At the end of the day Wilkerson and Bowles were emotionally drained and physically exhausted.

Wilkerson wished he hadn't met the parents or found out anything about the children. For years he had been able to remain aloof during homicide investigations. He never got close to the victim's family. But now his psychological defense had been removed by the few things he had learned about these three little girls.

One week had passed since the murders and the strange leads kept filtering in. A local man was interviewed by agents because he allegedly tied his wife to a bed and forced her to submit to unnatural acts. Hair samples and major case prints were taken.

Two other men from the Locust Grove area were interviewed who, according to an anonymous caller, had been seen in the area on the night of the murders. One of them had reportedly run into the local Laundromat in Locust Grove with a bundle of bloody clothes and thrown it into a washer. When the man was interviewed, and his story verified, it was found that the allegation was pure fabrication.

Another dog was flown in from Pennsylvania to replace the rottweiler that had died on Saturday of heat prostration.

Forensic chemist Janice Davis temporarily dampened Linville's enthusiasm for Gene Hart as a suspect when she reported that a very real possibility existed that sperm was present inside the victims. She said that the sperm appeared to be fragmented or deformed, but she hastened to add that she was using a new staining technique and could not state positively that sperm was present although the indications were very strong. Linville had found during his investigation that Hart had previously had a vasectomy. He had also learned that while an individual with a successful vasectomy will produce seminal fluid he will not produce sperm.

On June 21 Highway Patrol troopers notified the command post that there had been a burglary the previous night at a small rural grocery store at Sam's Corner near Locust Grove. Agents Townsend and Gosser arrived at the scene and noted that only foodstuffs, insect repellent, cigarettes, and a flashlight with batteries had been taken. The scene was processed for trace evidence and fingerprints.

Limke, Wise, and Weaver discussed the possibility of initiating a large search extending over several square miles although they knew that with the personnel on hand this would be logistically impossible. It was ultimately decided, over Limke's objection, that civilian volunteers would be asked to participate in the search. Wise announced publicly that he would accept applications for participation in the search. No guns, weapons, or dogs would be allowed. Women, children, and members of the news media would be excluded from participation. The media were given telephone numbers that volunteers could contact. Only those preregistered and told they would be needed would be allowed in the area.

The Governor authorized the utilization of approximately fifty National Guardsmen, the majority of whom were medical corpsmen and support personnel. Several large National Guard vehicles with 250-gallon water tanks would be sent to the area. Response to the plea for volunteers was overwhelming. Half an hour after the announcement, telephone lines were jammed.

"I hope that old medicine man never gets hacked off at me," Agent Coleman Townsend reflected.

The agents had just received word that Harras, the superdog valued at between $10,000 and $20,000, had been struck by a car and killed as he crossed the Pennsylvania Turnpike while he and his owner John Preston were returning home. Preston had gotten out of his car to get a soft drink and the dog had followed him.

Director Jeff Laird, Deputy Director Tom Kennedy, and Dick Wilkerson finished conferring with Limke over the telephone. Agents had had no luck in identifying the women in the photographs. It wasn't much, but it was all they had. It had been decided that Laird would call a 3:00 P.M. press conference and release the pictures to the newspapers and television and ask for public assistance.

•

It was almost 9:00 P.M. when Harvey Pratt slipped quietly out of the mobile command post and moved slowly toward a small creek approximately 100 yards north. He had not announced his departure to the other agents huddled inside the motor home. His mission was not secret, but it was probably better that it remain private. At the edge of the stream, Pratt halted next to a small cedar tree. He took a deep breath of the sticky night air and gazed through the trees into the cloudless sky. Harvey Pratt, Cheyenne-Arapaho warrior. Harvey Pratt, ex-combat Marine. Harvey Pratt, OSBI Agent. Harvey Pratt, father of a pre-teen daughter. Harvey Pratt, artist, sensitive, a compassionate and dedicated man, was in a quandary. This wasn't the first time in his law enforcement career that his loyalty to his profession had conflicted with his loyalty to his heritage. No one who raped and murdered babies was his brother, but would he try too hard to prove that it was not an Indian? Would he try too hard to prove it was? Could he be objective? Pratt shook himself as he began snapping small branches from the cedar tree. After stripping a quantity of the boughs, Pratt turned to see three figures approaching through the darkness.

"That you, Harv?" Pratt heard a familiar voice ask. "What are you up to?"

Pratt tried to appear nonchalant as he recognized Agents Coleman Townsend, Charlie Wellman, and John Gosser. He shrugged his shoulders and replied unconvincingly, "Aw, just catching a little night air."

"Come on, Harv," Gosser began incredulously. "What are you up to? What's that in your hand?"

"Cedar boughs," Pratt answered matter-of-factly.

"Little too early for Christmas," Townsend quipped. "What are you really up to?"

Pratt looked slowly into the sky and pondered his answer. His gaze returned to the three white men before him and he began slowly, almost methodically. "Fellas, I came here to pray. I came here to practice my religion and cleanse myself with the smoke of the cedar tree."

Pratt's eyes narrowed as he watched for any hint of amusement in the three agents' faces. The men were nervous. They felt like interlopers or peeping toms. If the words just spoken had come from anyone other than Pratt, they might have been amused. But they respected Harvey Pratt and they respected his beliefs.

Townsend glanced at the ground and half stammered, "What do you mean 'cleansed by the smoke'?"

"It's just Indian medicine," Pratt replied. "We burn cedar branches and let the white smoke cleanse our bodies of any evil thoughts. I wanted to be purified. I wanted to be completely objective on this case. I thought that if there was ever a case that deserves objectivity this would be the one."

The agents exchanged glances. In unspoken agreement, they stood there for perhaps thirty seconds. Finally, Townsend broke the silence. "Harv, could we join in your ceremony?"

Pratt's chiseled features gave no indication of his surprise. These were white men. He had prayed for and cleansed many people during his lifetime but never a white man. These were men to whom he would entrust his life and the lives of his family, but they were white men.

Pratt made his decision quickly. "I would be honored," he said quietly. His voice then changed to a firm coldness as he warned, "Let me caution you about one thing. If at any time during the ceremony you laugh or make light of what's going on, that will be the end of it. Do you understand?"

The three men nodded in agreement and watched transfixed as the young warrior gathered a bundle of twigs, which in short order he transformed into a small crackling fire. Pratt instructed the men to strip to the waist and seat themselves around the fire. The green branches sizzled and hissed when Pratt laid them on the fire, causing a rich white smoke to billow straight up into the breezeless night.

"Are you a medicine man, Harv?" Gosser asked respectfully.

Pratt smiled and replied softly, "No, John. I'm not a medicine man. I simply practice my religion. As you will see, it correlates much with the white man's religion."

Pratt took a small feathered fan from the leather medicine bag that hung from his shoulder. He had received the fan from his medicine man. It had been used by the Native American Church during a peyote ceremony.

The men stared into the small fire and white smoke, mesmerized by the mood of the moment. "Now, if you will stand and line up," Pratt softly instructed as he took a small branch from the fire. He held the sizzling bough next to the agents' bodies and fanned the smoke around them.

"As the smoke flows over your bodies, you will become purified. The smoke will cleanse your body." The billowy white smoke clung to the sweat of the agents' warm bodies, giving off an eerie, specter-like appearance. They stood quietly, solemnly, as Pratt fanned the smoke about them.

He continued his prayer. "Let you seek only things that are true. Do not seek falsehood, but seek purity and truth. Have an open mind and do what is right. I pray that you will not falsely accuse anyone of this crime. I pray we may have complete objectivity in all that we do regardless of the pressures that are put upon us. May our hearts remain true. I further pray that we will receive the help of good men because we seek goodness and justice."

Pratt put the fan temporarily in his medicine bag, exchanging it for a filtered cigarette. As he tore off the filter he continued, "Gentlemen, we do not have a pipe, but we will smoke the smoke of truth." He lighted the cigarette with the fire of the burning cedar branch, took a long puff without inhaling, and blew it into the thick night air. He handed the cigarette to Townsend, who mimicked his friend and then passed the cigarette to Wellman. Although Wellman did not smoke, he also took a puff. Gosser finally took his turn and returned the cigarette to Pratt. Pratt again produced the peyote fan. Taking deep puffs, he blew the smoke on each agent's body and again prayed for purification. He then knelt at the side of the fire and took a small buckskin bag that hung around his neck.

"I'm going to tell you a story," he began. "One time while I was at the bureau, a police officer came by and saw this very same necklace and sack hanging around my neck. He asked me what it was and I told him it was medicine. He asked me if it helped me get pussy." Pratt paused, wanting to quote himself exactly. "'You have offended me,' I told him. 'I will not discuss it any more.'" Pratt shook his head and looked at his three friends. "I will share my medicine and belief with anyone as long as they do not ridicule or offend me.

"Now then," he continued. "I have something in this bag and it's called medicine." Pratt opened the small bag and poured what appeared to be a mixture of grass and sand over the fire, causing even more smoke. As he poured the contents of the bag onto the fire he said, "I know this medicine works, because I have used it. It is the medicine of truth. If you put this medicine on someone, he will help you. If you put it on several people, they will help you. They are going to like you and they will do things for you. I am putting it on the fire and this very smoke will settle upon someone, somewhere, who knows something, and they will tell us. Now again, we will smoke."

Lighting the remaining cigarette, Pratt again fanned the smoke around the agents' legs and backs and over their shoulders. Pratt kneeled by the fire and bowed his head for a moment. He then stood and said simply, "It is over."

The agents remained solemn. They knew that they had experienced something that had been shared with very few white men. They were appreciative. Whether they believed or were skeptical, they had one thing in common. They respected Harvey Pratt. Not speaking, they extinguished the fire and walked quietly back to the command post, each feeling oddly moved by what they had shared. As Pratt stepped inside the motor home, his watch read 10:05 P.M.

Dick Wilkerson had just seen the pictures of the mystery women on the ten o'clock news. The news media had given them good coverage and unless the women were from out of state, by morning they should be identified. It was now 10:15 P.M.

"Oh, shit," Wilkerson groaned as the telephone in the bedroom rang. The telephone ringing all night was part of his job but he had always resented the uninvited invasion of his private thoughts. He forced a hello and heard a familiar voice with a pronounced Oklahoma accent whine, "Tricky, this is Jerry Sunderland." Sunderland was an ex-OSBI agent and now the Warden of the Oklahoma State Reformatory at Granite.

Wilkerson liked Sunderland. He was a good person and Wilkerson was always glad to hear from him. His mood changed instantly.

"How are you, boy?"

"Tricky, I just got a call from Paul Morris, Probation and Parole Officer at Mangum. Those pictures that were on the ten o'clock news —he says he knows two of the women. I got his phone number here. Why don't you just call him and talk to him direct."

It had been a long night and June 22 was going to be a long day. Dick Wilkerson sat in his office mulling over the events of the night. Paul Morris had identified the woman in the solitary photograph as Judy Petzold West, formerly of Mangum, Oklahoma, and presently of Clinton. The woman sitting at the piano was Peggy Walker, a piano teacher from Mangum. Inspector Al Abernathy and Agent Frank Brady had been sent to Mangum to interview Morris and to locate and interview the women. They had talked to Ms. Walker and she could not remember when the pictures were taken. They were still looking for Ms. West.

"There is a Mr. Looper on the phone who says the pictures in the paper are of his wedding," shouted Jan Clary from her desk just outside Wilkerson's office.

Wilkerson snatched the telephone from its cradle and identified himself. A man's voice introduced himself as Benny Looper, a high school teacher from Byng, Oklahoma. Looper explained that the pictures were of his wedding on May 25, 1968. He identified the woman standing at the piano as Ann Blackmore, formerly of Canute, Oklahoma. He verified the identification of Ms. West and Ms. Walker. Looper explained that a Mr. Lindsey from Granite, Oklahoma, was the photographer. Twenty-two photographs were made. One copy went to Looper's mother-in-law and he and his wife received one copy. Looper could account for all photographs and the negatives. He was told that an agent would contact him some time that day.

About fifteen minutes had passed since Wilkerson's conversation with Looper. Deputy Director Tom Kennedy and Dick Wilkerson were trying to figure out where to go from there when the secretary stepped in the door and told Wilkerson that Warden Sunderland was on the line.

"Tricky," Sunderland began. "My Deputy Warden can identify those women and he says the photographer was Louis Lindsey. He's a retired records officer here at the reformatory. He did a lot of moonlighting as a photographer and he developed all his pictures down here. This Hart guy that Linville called me about the other day —he worked for Lindsey as a darkroom technician from December 7, 1966, to March 19, 1969, when he was paroled."

Wilkerson felt his face flush. "We've got the son-of-a-bitch," he mouthed across the desk to Kennedy as he snapped the pencil he held in his right hand. "Jerry, I need a certified copy of Hart's work record as soon as you can get it here, and how can I get hold of Lindsey?" Wilkerson drawled, trying to suppress his excitement.

"He's living with his daughter in California," Sunderland said. "I can check his retirement records for the address and get back to you."

"Do that as soon as you can, Jerry, and thanks, partner." Wilkerson slammed the receiver down. "That son-of-a-bitch did it, Tom. Hart, Gene Leroy Hart. I bet you money, marbles, or chalk he developed the pictures and kept them because one of them looked like his ex-wife."

"Let's get Ted on the phone," Kennedy grinned.

Before Limke could be located, Sunderland called back with a phone number and address in Westminster, California, for Lindsey. Lindsey could not be contacted by phone so Wilkerson called the Westminster Police Department and asked them to locate Lindsey and request he call Wilkerson at OSBI Headquarters as soon as possible.

At approximately 1:15 P.M. the long-awaited telephone call came. Lindsey confirmed that he had taken the pictures and that they were developed at the Granite Reformatory. While he could not remember specifically the date, or the pictures, or even that Hart had developed them, he said that if the records showed that Hart worked for him during that time, he would have been the person who processed the film. Lindsey said that while he had never authorized Hart to remove any prints, it would have been relatively easy for him to do so. Finally, he assured Wilkerson of his continued cooperation.

Ted Limke was excited—as excited as he had been in a long, long time. He tried to remain calm as he briefed Sid Wise and asked him to file First Degree Murder charges against Gene Leroy Hart.

"What about the sperm, Ted?" Wise asked, pawing the air with his hands.

"What about it?" Limke responded. "A large percentage of vasectomies are not successful. We have got to get the bastard in custody before we can establish whether or not he produces sperm. It's obvious that no one's going to just stumble onto Hart. He's been a fugitive too long. Everyone's going to have to start looking for him. If he doesn't produce sperm, then I'll apologize, but the bastard owes the state three hundred and five years."

Lawyers, Limke thought. They are so concerned about their batting average, not about justice or what's right, just whether or not they can win. Limke had seen, during his career, felons walk free because a prosecutor was afraid to bring them before a jury and roll the dice. He knew it was a calculated risk but how else could it be resolved?

With the combined efforts of Limke and Weaver, Wise acquiesced and filed the murder charges.

CHAPTER 6

WITHIN HOURS OF THE FILING OF THE CHARGES, IT SEEMED AS IF THE entire community of Locust Grove and Mayes County rose up in defense of Hart. He was remembered as a soft-spoken football star. The crime, Limke reflected, is so grotesque, so hideous, maybe the people want to believe that some terrible alien monster committed it. Maybe it's too much for them to believe that one of their own, someone they knew, was capable of such a thing. During the next few days the media would capitalize on the fear.

A Tulsa newspaper's headlines said "Locust Grove Residents Remember Hart—Their Football Hero." The subtitle read "Man Charged in Triple Murder Called 'Good-Looking Kid.'" The picture under the headlines was taken from a high school annual, and showed a handsome, clean-cut young Indian of seventeen years of age. The article quoted Locust Grove citizens defending their football hero.

"It took five guys to bring him down," said one citizen. Another man said, "He was a fullback—gained 2,200 yards for the team." The article continued:

> Many of those who "knew him when" expressed doubts that authorities were looking for the right man. ". . . I think it's crazy," said 21-year-old Miller Johnson, one of Hart's half-brothers. "Every time something goes wrong the law always goes to him—no matter what."
>
> ". . . When the killing first happened a lot of people said that poor ole Gene will get it . . . that they'll blame Gene. I don't be-

lieve he did it," she [another interviewee] said. "And most people around here don't believe he did it."

Down the road a woman seated outside a mobile home said, "It was a set-up. They just want to get somebody in jail," she said. "I seen it happen before. I seen it happen to Gene. . . ." Classmates described him as a quiet good-looking boy . . . a woman who dated him said he was "always a gentleman."

Another Tulsa paper said:

> A half-brother of Hart interviewed Friday said authorities blame Hart whenever something happens in the area, and a cousin says she believes Hart was named in the charges, because he is an Indian. . . . Kirby Vaughn, 18, also scoffed at the charges against Hart. "I guess (Sheriff) Pete Weaver just doesn't like him," Vaughn said.
>
> Ted Stamper, who once employed Hart as a farmhand, said the suspect was "intelligent and not half as bad as they make him out to be. I don't think he did it," Stamper said. "He's not sexually oriented to that kind of business."

Other people quoted on radio and television said, "He's just a scapegoat." "It's Pete Weaver's way of getting even with him for escaping from his jail." "It's Sid Wise's ticket to the Attorney General's office." The phrases "pressure was on the investigators to find a suspect," "public opinion was demanding that they find a suspect," and "Gene Leroy Hart was simply a convenient suspect," seemed to be on everyone's lips. It seemed to the agents that every time one of these people made a statement there was either a microphone or a tape recorder in front of them.

Larry Bowles sat in the Camp Director's cabin, wadding up pieces of paper, flipping them into a trash can. It was 5:30 A.M. and he had worked all night for the second straight evening in a row. The other five agents who had been with him had bedded down at the first aid station a hundred feet north. Bowles was tired, bone tired. His body ached and his dark eyes were bloodshot. He turned in his chair as he heard someone walk up the steps of the cabin. It was Mike Wilkerson, who had left Tulsa at 4:00 A.M. He walked through the door and said, "What are you doing up so early, partner?"

"I haven't been asleep yet," Bowles grunted, his tone indicating irritation.

Mike had known Larry for a long time and could tell when there was something eating at him. He knew that when something troubled

Bowles he had trouble sleeping. Pulling a folding chair directly in front of Bowles, he sat down. "Partner," he said, "what's bothering you?"

"Nothing," the Indian agent again grunted.

"Hoss, I've known you too damn long. There's something gnawing at you. Now spit it out, 'cause if you don't you'll eat out everyone's butt that gets in your way."

Bowles looked up, forcing a smile that quickly faded as he groped for the words to express himself. In a slow bitter tone, he began. "Mike, I'm a criminal investigator for the State of Oklahoma. I probably belong to the most efficient criminal investigative organization in the world—for its size. Because of this, I like to think that I was hired, as were the rest of you, because I'm something special. Right or wrong, I think of myself and the rest of the agents as being a little more efficient, a little more honest, and a little more principled than the other officers."

"What are you trying to say, Larry?" Mike queried.

"Just this," he said, his voice trembling with pent-up emotion. "Where to hell does the goddamn news media get off challenging our integrity? This crap I read and hear makes me sick. Look at this shit," he said, grabbing a newspaper lying on the floor. "They're making it sound like we charged a man because of public opinion and any evidence we have has been planted. I take that as a personal insult. When they intimate that the OSBI could be a party to this, they insult me and my family."

"Damn it, Larry. They're not even saying that about the OSBI. They are just quoting people who say that's what Sheriff Weaver is doing."

"Bullshit," Bowles said, his voice rising. "By saying that Pete is railroading Hart, they're inferring that we are going along with it. Do they think for a minute that if any of us had the slightest suspicion that anyone was fabricating evidence, we wouldn't arrest the whole damn bunch?"

"Well," Wilkerson continued, "we're all working under a handicap. We can't keep the District Attorney from jumping in front of the TV cameras, and everyone says he's using the exposure to run for Attorney General. The press is pissed at Wise for playing favorites. And then there's Sheriff Weaver who is hated by every thief and drunk in Mayes County. But most of all, the press is creating controversy where there is none. What it boils down to is that the public buys news about murder, rape, and innocent people being railroaded.

It makes a great story—an Indian who has eluded the white gestapo pigs for over four years, and an even better story to intimate that he is an innocent young Indian football star who once again has been made a scapegoat. This little rural state has three things that it can brag about: Indians, football, and oil. Boy, when you got a football-playing Indian, he makes the greatest hero since Jim Thorpe. This bastard is enjoying the present belief that an Indian can do no wrong and that they are the victims of the white man's prejudice. You see, the public is not ready to throw away their image of the stoic, dignified Indian for that of a child-murdering escaped rapist who is hidden by every thug in eastern Oklahoma."

"But, Mike," Bowles interrupted, "I'm Indian, you're Indian, and we're both proud of that fact. But most of all, Mike, I'm an honest man. I wouldn't railroad or be a part of railroading anyone. My job is to catch the scum who killed three babies, not simply to make an arrest." Bowles's voice broke and tears of frustration welled in his eyes. "I guess what I want the world to know is I give a damn about them—all the sensation-seeking, irresponsible press and publicity-grabbing politicians included. I don't want their children to be killed and I will do everything that an honest man can do to catch the man."

Wilkerson stood up and poured him and his partner a cup of coffee. "Honesty and integrity aren't good copy. Mistreated minorities, Oklahoma football, and crooked cops are."

Bowles shook his head at the coffee and said, "Yeah, I guess," feeling better that he had gotten it off his chest.

"Now, get your can to bed. You're tired."

"Yes, I am."

Wilkerson started out the front door as Bowles dialed the phone to call home.

The search that was originally planned to look for clues in the several-square-mile area around Camp Scott was now a manhunt. Limke did not like what was happening. He had law enforcement officers coming from all over the state in order to participate in the search. Most, however, were trained police officers and he decided to let the search go on.

On June 23 Victor Auxier, who lived a couple of miles from the Girl Scout camp, called the command post at Camp Scott and reported that while checking fences on his property he had seen a man sitting in a cave located southwest of his residence. Not wanting to startle the man, Auxier proceeded as if he had seen no one. He didn't have a telephone at home so he had driven to the nearest one. OSBI agents met Auxier at his residence. He volunteered to take law officers back to the cave.

Agents Pratt, Wellman, and Thurman, accompanied by Auxier and several police officers, retraced Auxier's footsteps to what the agents called Cave Number 2. A quarter of a mile from the cave, Pratt, Wellman, and about half the officers split up from Thurman, Auxier, and the remaining officers so they could approach the general area of the cave from opposite sides. This would at least cut off two avenues of escape. After fifteen minutes of climbing through the dense blackjack trees, Wellman and Pratt arrived at the cave. Silently, Pratt waved Wellman to the left side of the entrance while he stepped to the right. Pratt cautiously looked inside. The cave was empty. Wellman climbed to a ledge area above the cave only to be greeted by the barrel of a .357 magnum in the hands of Cary Thurman. As Thurman reholstered his gun, he said, "Charlie, I almost blew your head plum off. Mr. Auxier and I could hear the noise coming down from below the cave and the first thing I thought was that that stinker was still here. Damn, son, make some noise so I know it's you." Wellman smiled and nodded, thankful that Thurman wasn't trigger-happy.

Pratt examined the area in front of the cave closely. He picked up a piece of tattered cigarette butt that had the filter torn off. Medicine, he thought to himself. Hart is using medicine.

Pratt noticed the remnants of four tiny fires. Four; medicine number, Pratt equated silently. Four fires denote the four winds or the four seasons. White denotes north for white snow, south, green for spring, east, red for sunrise, and west or black denotes the sun is going down.

Pratt's concentration was broken as someone shouted, panic-stricken, "Goddamn. They're all over me!" Pratt turned to see police officers frantically jerking their clothes off and throwing them to the ground. The half-nude men were covered with thousands of ticks. They pulled out their pocket knives and scout knives and cut the carnivorous little blood-suckers off by the hundreds.

"Someone get a fire started! We'll have to put some heat on them!" an officer exclaimed.

"We got to get the hell out of here!" shouted Thurman. "These things are going to eat us up!"

Pratt looked down and saw that his hands were covered with ticks.

Unperturbed, he crawled back into the cave directly behind the four fires. There were no ticks to be found! Not a single tick! He did find two things—cigarette butts without filters, and strands of long black hair. He used the medicine to ward off the ticks, Pratt thought. He remembered talking to an old Indian in the area who said that Hart was counseled by a powerful medicine man who had given him the ability to turn into either a cat or a bird to elude his captors. As a twentieth-century man, he should scoff at the idea, but now a certain uneasiness was creeping into his consciousness.

That's the reason Hart always said that he could see the men while they were chasing him. "He was looking down on them," the old Indian had told Pratt. Pratt had thought that the statement meant that Hart had been hiding in a tree looking down. Absurd, he thought to himself, completely absurd.

"We better get the dogs up here," Pratt shouted, "and see if we can pick up a trail."

Later that evening the men returned with a tracking dog. The yelping dog was turned loose and immediately struck a trail. The men did their best to follow the dog down the side of the mountain, but were soon outdistanced while the barking of the dog faded into silence. Some fifteen minutes passed when the dog returned battered, bruised, and cut. It appeared that someone or something had beaten the animal terribly. The men retraced the dog's fresh trail. It led them to the middle of an open field only to vanish as if the person who had made the tracks had been lifted skyward.

"He's doubled back," the dog handler reasoned.

Yeah, that has to be it, Pratt pondered, feeling the uneasiness returning.

Meanwhile, the massive search of the area started on schedule. Over one hundred police officers were present, as well as dozens of CB radio operators who pulled their cars onto the search perimeter and turned their headlights on to keep the subject from passing outside unnoticed. Officers were stationed at intervals of a quarter-mile apart around the area. About twenty tracking and attack dogs were also involved in the search.

The officers and other searchers seemed excited. The dust was almost choking as they all ran up and down the road in their cars, creating great dust storms. As night fell, the search was called off with no results. It was estimated at final count that somewhere between three and six hundred people had eventually been involved.

Although Hart had been connected with the crime scene, the fact that sperm had been found during the autopsies seemed on the surface to discount him as a suspect.

Hart had been married in 1963 and his wife soon became pregnant. They made their home in Locust Grove, where his son was born the following year. During the early years of his marriage he seemed to be a happy, affectionate husband. For some reason, however, he began to have long periods of depression. At times he seemed to resent his son and on several occasions told friends that if he had not been forced to get married, he would have gone to college on a football scholarship.

According to a friend of the family, Hart was suspected of having molested a minor relative on at least one occasion. The incident took place shortly after the child's second birthday. The mother had gone shopping and had left her mother with the child and Hart. As the grandmother was hanging out laundry, she heard the baby scream from the house as if he were in pain. She ran into the house and found Hart lying on the floor and the baby sitting on the sofa crying. She walked over to the child and examined him to see if there were any marks to indicate whether the child had been abused. There were none, but the child was obviously in pain. Soon after, the child developed diarrhea and pain in the rectum. The child's mother took him to a physician in Fort Smith, Arkansas. After an examination the doctor asked her about the possibility of the child sitting on a foreign object, inserting something into his rectum, or if she had given the child an enema with a syringe that was too large. The mother said that she had not and asked the doctor whether the damage done to the boy's rectum could have been caused by a penis. The doctor nodded his head and said, "That's exactly what could have happened."

The agents already knew that Hart had been a member of a gang in high school. According to local sources, the gang had a reputation of raping high school girls in the surrounding communities. No criminal charges were ever filed.

Mrs. Hart was interviewed by the agents and she confirmed that Hart had had a vasectomy. She said that she had personally accompanied Hart when he had taken a semen sample back to a doctor's office in Tulsa. She was present when the doctor told Hart that he was sterile.

Further investigation revealed that the doctor who performed the vasectomy was Dr. C. S. Summers of Tulsa, Oklahoma. At the time the agents interviewed Dr. Summers, he was eighty-seven years old, which would have made him approximately seventy-eight when he performed the vasectomy. He confirmed that he had performed a vasectomy on Hart and his records indicated that Hart had brought in his semen sample and had it tested for sperm. The tests were negative and he told Hart that he could not father a child. The doctor said that he had followed standard medical procedure, which consisted of clipping the tubes, binding the severed ends back, and sewing them together. He said that possibly two or three patients had to come back and have the operation again, but after the sperm count was reduced to zero, he had never had a reversal. At that point there was permanent sterility and, in his opinion, that would have been the situation with Hart.

Consulting physicians theorized that the old doctor could have made a mistake, or the severed tubes could have grown back together and fertility restored. It was also theorized that if the sperm were forced through a very small opening where the tubes had grown back together, this could account for the deformed sperm.

OSBI forensic chemist Ann Reed determined that the hair from the tape used to bind Doris Milner's hands, the hair from her pajama top—as well as hair recovered from the floor of Tent Number 8 and Cave Number 2—all had the exact same microscopic characteristics. She was of the opinion that all of the hair could have been and probably was from the same person.

Another report was received from OSBI that forensic chemist Janice Davis detected blood group H (O-type blood) from four cigarette butts found in the second cave. It's generally recognized in the scientific community that 80 percent of the population secretes a hormone in their saliva from which a blood type can be determined (secretor). The cigarettes were smoked by a person with O-type blood. A check of Gene Hart's medical records from the penitentiary revealed that he had O-type blood.

Ms. Davis had flown the swabs taken from the victims to the Southwestern Institute of Forensic Scientists in Dallas, Texas. The swabs were treated with a special dye to make the sperm more readily detectable. This treatment, known as the "Christmas Tree" staining technique, was performed by Dr. I. C. Stone, Ph.D., and Serologist S. B. Williams. They determined that although no intact spermatozoa were found, what appeared to be decomposed or deformed spermatozoa were observed on a vaginal swab from Doris

Milner, and on an anal swab from Michelle Guse, and on a vaginal swab from Lori Farmer. Acid phosphatase, indicative of seminal fluid, was also detected on a vaginal swab taken from Doris Milner and on an anal swab from Michelle Guse. Williams detected human blood group H (or O-type blood) on a vaginal swab from Doris Milner and on oral swabs from both Michelle Guse and Lori Farmer.

Euwell Tharp, the co-owner of the T & H Grocery at Sam's Corner, outside of Locust Grove, identified a Vienna Sausage can found by the agents in Cave Number 2 as having come from his store because of the unique price-marking.

It appeared to the investigators at this point that the capture of Hart was the only way to positively identify whether he was the killer. Hair samples had to be taken. It had to be determined whether or not he was a secretor. It had to be determined whether or not he was, in fact, sterile, and if he was not sterile, did he produce fragmented sperm.

CHAPTER 7

"FEDS," COLEMAN TOWNSEND SNARLED, "THEY CAN'T EVEN FIND THE courthouse, and they're going to show us how to find an Indian in these hills. Of course, with their press agents," Townsend's mood lightened, "maybe they can keep Hart from getting elected Governor or going in the first round of the Pro draft next year."

Limke didn't interrupt as the other agents interjected their own sarcastic comments. It was June 26 and they had just left a meeting with a dozen FBI agents. The authority for their entering the case was based on an Unlawful Flight to Avoid Confinement warrant issued on October 29, 1973. OSBI agents and deputies were bone tired. They had been on the case with only intermittent rest for almost a solid two weeks. After so much hard work, they had identified a suspect and felt they had been slapped in the face by the news media and general public. As one agent said, "Even a dog needs a pat on the head every once in a while."

The FBI had insisted that they reinterview all of Hart's friends and relatives. Limke had reluctantly agreed to pair an OSBI agent with a Federal agent for the recontacts. It was a waste of time, Limke knew, but he had his orders to cooperate. Limke's men would do their job, would be professionals, but in private maybe they were entitled to bitch a little.

There were several reports that Hart had been seen in the Locust Grove-Muskogee-Hulbert and Sallisaw areas. Police in Texas had arrested two Indians who were trying to sell their blood. This immediately brought an outcry from the American Indian Movement (AIM) who claimed that the Indians were being harassed because of the Oklahoma murders. An AIM representative from Rapid City, South Dakota, arrived in Oklahoma and began monitoring the activities.

The representative said he had come to Oklahoma at the request of Tulsa AIM members who were concerned that there might be vigilante committees sent out to bring in Hart dead or alive.

"If they follow the white man's law, that will be all right," said the Indian. He also sent a veiled warning to law enforcement and citizens in the area, claiming that he could call in a hundred warriors on a day's notice.

Law enforcement officers had no illusions about a quick capture of Hart. The FBI had been looking for him for four years. They knew what kind of terrain they were up against. Even traveling a short distance over any part of the area around Locust Grove involved crossing a multitude of cliffs, valleys, ridges, and all the officers knew they could pass within a few feet of Hart and not see him. The area could be compared with the jungles of southeast Asia or Africa, complete with poisonous snakes and carnivorous insects.

Ticks were the major nuisance and concern of the searchers. These were not the normal dog ticks that attached themselves to canines in the area, but rather what the natives called seed ticks. This name was given to the insect because it was no bigger than a pin head or a small seed. Its size belied its poisonous quality.

All of the searchers had at least one remedy to keep the pests off them. These ranged from kerosene-soaked ankles to taking a bath in sulphur soap, but none of these methods seemed the least bit effective against the ravenous little insects. After the victim discovered that the pest had attached itself to his skin, there was little that could be done. The insect could be plucked from the body or made to detach itself by placing a cigarette against its body. The bite, however, became inflamed and caused the flesh to decay around it. The itching was all but unbearable, and usually lasted for weeks and sometimes months. All one had to do was walk into the dense woods and brush against a tree to have literally hundreds of imperceptible little creatures on his clothes. On one occasion, Bowles and Limke ran into the command post and frantically began tearing their clothes off. They were covered with hundreds of ticks. The other agents ran to help them, brushing the ticks from their backs. Only after five minutes of frantic brushing and picking did they notice the two female secretaries in the room.

It was rumored that the ticks did not bother Indians because they had a natural immunity. Larry Bowles's observation best summed up the viability of this theory. "Bullshit," he said. "You can see how immune Indians are," pointing to the bites on his body. "These little buggers are equal opportunity blood-suckers."

The officers also knew that hidden among the seed ticks was another very deadly species of tick that caused Rocky Mountain spotted fever, a disease with a very high mortality rate.

Generally, agents of the OSBI and special agents of the FBI were met with hostility by Hart's relatives and friends. Most of them denied that they had seen Hart since his escape and none knew his whereabouts. The Indians who did talk intimated that Hart might possess some supernatural powers that were given to him by a very powerful medicine man. Information, however, indicated that many of these people had harbored Hart at various times during the preceding four years, including his mother, Ella Mae Buckskin, who had hidden him up to one week before the homicides.

It was learned that Hart was schooled in the old ways. He could live off the land indefinitely, eating herbs and wild animals; however, he depended mainly upon other people in the area—usually his relatives—for his subsistence.

Sid Wise was also dispirited by the local people who refused to believe Hart could do such a thing. Before national television he said, "For those do-gooders who want to make a Sunday school teacher out of Mr. Hart, let them ask the victims of the rapes he pleaded guilty to in 1966 when he forced two pregnant women into the trunk of a car and violated them. That man stood before God as his judge and said, 'I am guilty because I did commit those acts.'" Wise was beginning to become very emotional. Obviously, he believed in what he was saying. "I'm saying the man we're looking for out there by the name of Hart is no exemplary citizen and should not be considered a football star."

The searches continued in the general area of Locust Grove. Several agents, however, were pulled off the case. Although the FBI reportedly had forty agents on the case at one time, this number quickly dwindled. Now only a few agents were staying at a motel in Pryor. Three FBI agents were known to have stayed for over a month in a house trailer belonging to Mayes County Deputy Sheriff

A. D. David. They had kept a twenty-four-hour surveillance on the residence of Ella Mae Buckskin located a short distance away. Tactical teams of Oklahoma Highway Patrolmen still combed the area in and around Locust Grove looking for Hart; however, these were unorganized operations and all proved fruitless.

To the lay person, it would seem that the most foolish thing Gene Leroy Hart could do was to stay in northeastern Oklahoma. Many of the officers also doubted that he was still in the country when no verified sighting could be made of him after four years. However, it was well known that people could hide indefinitely in these hills, as well as the Cookson Hills, south of Tahlequah. This had been the legendary hideout of many of the nation's most colorful outlaws from Jesse James to Pretty Boy Floyd.

Another problem worried investigators. Hart had not been seen or photographed in approximately four years. At thirty-three years of age, his size and features could have changed a great deal. It was reported through informants that Hart now had shoulder-length hair.

During the massive search on Friday, Michelle Guse's father came from Broken Arrow. He talked to many officers, shook their hands, and told them he appreciated the job they were doing. He let it be known that he held no ill feelings toward the killer, who would have to make his peace with God. To all around him, Mr. Guse was a gentleman, a perfect gentleman.

To try to combat the problem of the heavy terrain and dense foliage, an airplane equipped with a heat-seeking device was brought in. The airplane was used by the U.S. Customs Service to help detect illegal aliens. The device was theoretically so sensitive that it could tell the difference between humans and animals; however, it was admitted by officials concerned that a person could defeat the device by hiding in caves, under rock ledges, and so forth. SWAT teams moved into the junglelike area. Over one-half inch of rain had fallen late Friday and early on the morning of July 25. Temperatures rose over 90 degrees and the humidity was over 80 percent. The woods turned into a seething sauna, adding to the discomfort caused by the insects. All the searches were fruitless.

The agents had received word that the processing for fingerprints had also been generally fruitless. There were no fingerprints on any of the cans stolen from the T & H Grocery at Sam's Corner or any identifiable prints at the other scenes. There were some fingerprints taken from inside the death tent. The agents were told by technicians that the fingerprints could be as much as a year old, depending upon weather and other variable conditions.

The rolled terry cloth tied around Doris Milner's neck was sewn with very neat stitches. They might be surgical stitches. To ascertain whether they were, the agents contacted a doctor at the Osteopathic Hospital in Tulsa. Such stitches, particularly the continuing suture, resemble a buttonhole stitch frequently used in sewing. The doctor explained that in case of an interrupted suture, each of the stitches would be tied off with usually four or five square knots. No surgeon would ever use a granny knot. He furnished samples of all varieties and types of suture materials used in a hospital. These were compared with the rolled terry cloth and none of the stitches or threading matched.

Limke figured that the man most likely to know Gene Leroy Hart's escape habits was Larry Gene Dry, also a Cherokee, who had escaped from the Mayes County Jail with him twice. He called Agent Tom Puckett of the Lawton Office.

Puckett was a ten-year veteran of the OSBI and was recognized as one of the Bureau's most competent agents. Prior to joining the OSBI, he had served as an Army CID (Criminal Investigation Division) Agent for twenty years.

Puckett went to Granite Reformatory where Larry Dry was serving sentences for Auto Theft, Escape, Injuring a Public Building, and Second Degree Burglary, from Mayes County. Dry seemed eager to talk to Puckett. He said that in September of 1973 he and Hart escaped from the Mayes County Jail.

Since both men had grown up in Mayes County and had fished and hunted extensively there, they knew the area very well. Initially, their plans were to hide out in the woods for a period of three months, or until the search waned, to accumulate money and then to flee to a large city like New York where they could get lost in the crowd. They had been furnished food by many of Hart's relatives. Dry said that he recognized the photographs in the paper as those that were in Hart's possession during the time they were fugitives together. Hart had not had the pictures when they escaped and Dry assumed they had been at a relative's home. Dry claimed that he was willing to assist in apprehending Hart with no stipulations other than reasonable protection.

Puckett was skeptical of parts of Dry's story. He might be trying to use this to get paroled. A check of his prison record, however, revealed that Dry had only about a year left in jail and that his criminal record was relatively minor. Maybe he could be trusted.

Agents of the OSBI had met with special agents of the FBI who had also interviewed Dry. He told them essentially the same story, except that he elaborated on some of the places where he and Hart had hidden. It appeared from his descriptions that they had hidden in the cave where the pictures were found (designated Cave Number 1), and in Cave Number 2, where the canned goods, foodstuffs, and hair were found. But it also seemed that Dry was withholding information and it was decided to wait a while before deciding to use his help. Investigators became more and more confident that they were tracking the killer of the three Girl Scouts.

Agents slowly began piecing together Hart's movements after his escape. One of Dry's relatives told them that Hart and Dry had come to his home two or three weeks after their 1973 escape. It was nighttime. A car driven by Hart's cousin drove by the house several times. After the lights went off in the house Hart and Dry burst through the door. They wanted the people to take them to Tulsa but were refused. After Hart and Dry escaped the second time, the same relative had seen them at his aunt's house in Locust Grove, and had received an anonymous call telling him where they were. They had tried unsuccessfully to persuade Dry to surrender. He and Hart were hidden in an old cellar about a quarter of a mile to the rear of his aunt's house. This was found to be within 50 yards of the cave where the pictures and other evidence were collected.

Other information showed that Hart had spent five months at a residence north of Hulbert, Oklahoma, in a community called Lost City, approximately 40 miles from Locust Grove. Some time prior to the Christmas of 1976, Hart came to the residence. The only name that he was known by was his family nickname, Sonny. He told his host that he had been discharged from the Army but gave no reason why he wanted to stay there.

Hart had no unusual habits. He cooked all his meals and cleaned the house. His normal routine was to rise early in the morning, cook breakfast, and go hunting or work around the house. He never went to town, nor did he ask to be driven to town. In the evenings he usually watched television. He never talked about himself or any of his friends.

Hart was remembered as being approximately five feet ten inches and one hundred sixty-five pounds, with short, straight black hair, brown eyes, and a slender build. He usually wore thick black-frame glasses.

Hart left the residence in March or April of 1977 without telling anyone, leaving his personal belongings. A relative had come into the house after a drinking spree and had an argument with him. He had not been heard of since. This was about two months before the murders.

This seemed to be the most reliable information about Hart. He could now be placed in northeastern Oklahoma within two months of the slayings and not in Canada as many informants had been saying.

It was learned that Hart had originally gone to the Lost City residence when his mother, Ella Mae Buckskin, approached the people at a singing at Snake Creek Church near Locust Grove. Mrs. Buckskin, although she had already been approached by FBI agents, was interviewed by OSBI Agent Leo Albro concerning the whereabouts of her son. She said the last time she heard from Gene was in the form of a letter from Canada which she had received on November 25, but she couldn't recall the year that it was sent. She said that she took the letter to her attorney in Pryor, Oklahoma, and to the best of her knowledge the letter was still there. She said that she had lived at her present residence for eight years and that Hart had not visited her there. She went on to say that she hadn't seen him since the jailbreak. Pete Weaver had refused to allow her to visit Hart after he was arrested the second time because he thought that Mrs. Buckskin had previously taken a saw blade into the jail in a bible. Mrs. Buckskin gave Albro permission to pick up the letter from Hart held by her attorney.

The OSBI received information that someone named Norman Carey had supposedly visited Hart at Ella Mae's residence a few days before the murders. Carey was found in Pryor, Oklahoma. He said that he was the nephew of Ella Mae and that the Careys frequently visited the Buckskin residence. They knew that Gene had been staying with Ella Mae at different times following his escape, and it was common knowledge among the family that Gene was staying at the residence most of the time. Carey said that on the Saturday before the homicides he went to Ella Mae's residence to visit Hart. He went there because Friday night, while sleeping, he had what he considered a dream or vision of Hart surrounded by law enforcement officials. Carey felt Gene should be advised of the dream and be permitted to accept Christ. Carey, a lay preacher, also wanted to talk Gene into turning himself in.

He and another Cherokee, Jimmy Beck, stopped by the Buckskin residence that Saturday morning on their way to their fishing location. Beck visited with Ella Mae while Gene and Carey went outside where Carey told Gene about his dream. He tried to pressure Gene into accepting Christ and turning himself in. But Gene told Carey he was not interested in anything he was saying, and that he did not feel that people should go to other people's houses and try to push their religious beliefs off on them. After this slight confrontation, Carey left amicably.

Later that day, Carey and Beck returned to Locust Grove from fishing in the Peggs area to fish in a pond a short distance from the Buckskin residence. Janie Carey, Norman's wife, came to the Buckskin residence at 5:30 or 6:00 P.M. for Norman. When she got there, she visited with Gene and Ella Mae. Gene directed her to the pond where the men were fishing. While they were there, Gene picked up their two-year-old daughter and carried her around the house. Both Norman and Janie Carey said they did not want to testify because they feared for their safety.

Jimmy Beck was interviewed by agents and verified the story Mr. and Mrs. Carey had told. He said that he had never met Gene Hart before, but when he went to the residence Hart was introduced to him as Gene Leroy Hart. He described Hart as weighing approximately one hundred and ninety pounds and wearing a pair of glasses with black frames and square-type lenses.

It seemed now that pertinent facts were being developed regarding Gene Hart. Reports were coming in from everywhere. One report put Hart in a bar in Tahlequah, while another put him in a pool hall in Tahlequah. Two teen-aged boys were supposed to have seen Hart in Tulsa. Inmates in the penitentiary were talking about Hart.

It was also determined that Hart's eyes had progressively deteriorated as he got older. He was described as wearing different kinds of glasses at different times by different people. His personality, agents thought, seemed to change with the loss of his eyesight. One relative said that he thought that, if captured, he would commit suicide.

To add fuel to the fire of discontent, the rumor had been circulated by the press and various periodicals that the pictures found at Cave Number 1 had been planted by Pete Weaver, despite the fact that the squirrel hunters had found the pictures, brought them to highway patrolmen who, in turn, took OSBI agents to the cave before Weaver had ever seen the pictures.

As one agent observed, "If Pete planted the pictures then how did a piece of the same newspaper that was in the flashlight get there? How did Susan Emery's glasses get there? How did the masking tape used to tape the garbage bag on the flashlight get there? If someone believes Pete planted the pictures, then they would have to believe Pete committed the murders."

It was reasoned that the pictures had to be planted because Weaver took all personal belongings from the inmates when they were booked into his jail. The inventory sheet that enumerated Hart's possessions when he was checked into the Mayes County Jail did not reveal that he had the pictures in his possession at that time, nor were they on the inventory sheet at any of the state penitentiaries.

Limke could think of no logical reason to continue working out of Camp Scott. Large searches were still taking place around the Camp Scott and Locust Grove area but they were manhunts, after all, not fugitive investigations. The reward fund had swelled to $14,000 by this time and Limke, Weaver, and Wise figured that ultimately the money would cause someone to inform on Hart.

On June 30 another crime was taking place in another state that, for the moment at least, directed Oklahoma's and the nation's attention away from Locust Grove.

In Sarasota, Florida, a fifteen-year-old Girl Scout named Charlotte was dragged screaming from her tent in a state park by a heavily built man as her sister and another scout screamed in terror. According to newspaper accounts, the man ripped open the back of the three-person tent in the 468-acre Oscar Scherer State Park about 6:00 A.M. The assailant seized the child by her long brown hair and dragged her into the short, pointed palmetto shrub.

After sealing off the area of the camp, a one hundred-man posse searched the park throughout the day for the girl, but the search was curtailed by nightfall. The only sign of the abductor and his victim was a set of footprints that vanished into a pasture about half a mile away.

Charlotte was described by teen-age friends as outdoor-oriented; a pretty, slender girl, five feet four inches, ninety pounds, with braces on her teeth. "She's very strong but a little sensitive," said an acquaintance who had known Charlotte through a church fellowship group at Nacomis for the past five years. She was in a group of eight Girl Scouts accompanied by an adult leader on the first night of the campout.

Searchers found a trail of footprints leading northward away from the ripped tent. The prints were of a man's sneakers and the bare feet of a child. Indications were that the girl had been dragged first, then carried, and then forced to walk. The trail led for half a mile through the brush and into a pasture where it disappeared 100 yards short of an abandoned plant nursery.

OSBI agents immediately contacted the Sarasota County Sheriff's Office to get firsthand information on what had taken place. They were told by officials there that they thought the publicity over the Oklahoma case may have given rise to a copycat type of crime.

Through the night, authorities and relatives played a waiting game. Authorities issued a composite photograph believed to resemble the man who dragged the girl from the tent. The photos depicted a man with dark, stringy hair and a stubble of whiskers on a thin face. The man was about six feet tall, one hundred and seventy pounds, with a dark complexion. He was supposed to be driving a medium blue or green two-door car, possibly a Gremlin, and wearing a dull-colored Windbreaker, dark jeans, and deck shoes.

An interview with one of the occupants of the camp revealed that on Thursday they had heard rustling in the underbrush around the campsite all night. "Charlotte," she said, "was really bad, really jumpy. I don't think she slept at all." The three girls stayed up late playing cards and listening to the radio and mentioned the murder of the three Girl Scouts at the camp in Oklahoma. One of the children said she tried to calm Charlotte down when they heard something outside their tent. She told her that "nobody in their right mind would be out there at 4:00 A.M. Why don't we just try to fall asleep."

Just before dawn, Charlotte woke the other two girls to tell them, "It's back!" At that moment the mosquito netting at the rear of the tent was ripped apart and a dark figure burst into the tent, grabbing Charlotte by her waist-length brown hair.

"Oh, my God. It's got her!" a girl screamed.

"Please," Charlotte cried, "don't take me!" as the man dragged her away. In a nearby tent the noise awakened two more children.

"The screams, I'll never forget them," a child said. "They were terrible."

The kidnapping had the State of Oklahoma, as well as the nation, wondering if this were the same person. If so, it had been a white man and not an Indian who had murdered the girls.

However, the waiting game played by the authorities in Florida paid off. On July 1 Charlotte called home about 10:00 P.M. and told her anxious parents that she was free after more than fifty-two hours of captivity. She called from Siesta Key, a beach area off Sarasota and only about thirteen miles from the park where she had been camping.

A suspect, apprehended shortly afterward in the same area of the beach, was brought to the sheriff's office slouched in the back of a patrol car with his hands cuffed behind him. He was thirty-three years old and was over six feet tall. The man was expressionless as he was hauled out of the car and hustled through a door into the jail.

After Charlotte was home, the story began to unfold. She had been tied up, locked in a room, and left alone in the suspect's house Friday morning, but somehow had managed to break free and reach a telephone. When she called her father, the detectives had urged her to flee quickly. She protested that she didn't have any clothes. Her father told her to grab something and get out of there. She had thrown on a shirt and bolted out the back door, crying and screaming hysterically. Her call home had sent police rushing to the island near Sarasota. The two drawbridges were ordered raised to block any possible escape of the suspect. The suspect was caught backing out of his driveway in a 1972 Ford. He was charged with Involuntary Sexual Battery.

It was determined that there was no way the Florida man could have committed the murders in Oklahoma because investigation revealed he was in Florida during that time.

For lack of any other logical avenues of investigation, the OSBI decided to put undercover agents in the Locust Grove area to frequent the places that Gene Hart was supposed to have visited during the past ten years. The two men who volunteered for the job were Agent Harvey Pratt and his brother, Midwest City Police Detective Tony Pratt, the stereotyped portly, dark Indian. They were Cheyenne-Arapahos and knew the Indian ways.

Before going into the woods, Harvey Pratt contacted his medicine man in Oklahoma City. "He is using medicine, sir," Pratt told the elderly Indian man with the strange eyes. "They say he has the ability to change himself into a bird or a cat, and that is why he has not been found." Pratt found it hard to say these words without smiling, but the old medicine man's eyes never hinted of surprise, suspicion, or doubt.

"If this is true," the old man said slowly, "he does indeed have a powerful medicine man. If he did kill those children he is misusing his medicine and he has a terrible fate waiting. I would not want to be him."

"What I need, sir, is medicine. I need medicine powerful enough to combat his medicine. I want medicine that will make me be there when he is caught. I want medicine that will protect me. I want medicine to guide my bullets. If I get close enough, I don't want to miss. I'm taking my brother with me and I do not want him hurt."

"It can be done," the old man said. "Come back tomorrow night."

The Pratts returned late the next evening. They knew that the best medicine was made in the late evening or early morning hours.

"Harvey, let me warn you," the old man began softly, almost fatherly. "If his medicine is that powerful, you could be in great danger. You see, his medicine could come from any direction. He could put it on an animal and have it come to your house and you would not know that you were in danger until it was too late. But I have protection for you." He handed Pratt two small rawhide bags. "This medicine will protect you from danger. If Hart walks between you he will not be able to see either of you. You will be invisible to him; but this could only happen as long as you are separated. He will be able to see you if you are walking together."

He handed Pratt another small sack of what appeared to be herbs. "This will make you invisible if you follow my directions. You turn sideways and hold this sack facing you. You have to have this medicine in your hand, you cannot have it in your pocket. If you are walking, you must carry it in your hand. Here is one for your brother too. He must use his the same way that I tell you to use yours. You know what happens if you do not use the medicine properly."

Pratt nodded.

"Now then," the old man said, "each of you give me four of your bullets."

Pratt took the .357 from his shoulder holster and ejected four of the large bullets, handing them to the old man. His brother in turn did the same. Taking the bullets, the old man crossed the room to a small bowl that contained a potion. He rubbed the bullets in the potion, dried them, and returned them to the young warriors. "You cannot miss with these bullets. You carry these bullets and keep them all wrapped up. Just carry them. You don't need to load these bullets, but just keep them wrapped up and in your pocket. I wouldn't be too afraid of the man being able to 'out-woods' you. I don't think this man can see well. If you will be very still, I don't believe that he will be able to see you."

He handed Pratt another small packet. "If you get on his trail or you see him and he runs from you, give him some of this medicine. Sprinkle this medicine on the track, reach down, and grab the track. You can either put it in your pocket or throw it on you. As long as the medicine is on that track he cannot run far enough or fast enough to get away. That is all I can do for you. For you are right and he is evil. Go with God, Huntchkin," the medicine man said, choosing to use Pratt's Cheyenne name, which meant "going to be Chief."

Pratt and the old medicine man had a mutual respect for one another. Pratt believed in the wisdom of the old man and the old man believed in the solemn goodness of his two Cheyenne warriors. The two Pratt brothers felt good as they left the suburban Oklahoma City residence.

It's a nice night for a warrior, Tony thought to himself. He was an Indian and was proud of it. An old Indian man who hated the whites and their ways had once asked Tony why he would ever become a police officer and enforce the white man's law. Tony pondered for a moment and told the aging Indian, "When I put on my gun and gun belt, I'm putting on my loincloth. When I put on my badge and the rest of my brass, these are my ornaments, my necklace, or my war paint. When I put on my cap, this is my war bonnet. This is the only way in my lifetime that I will ever be able to be a warrior and go on raids or the warpath as my forefathers did. I am just as right doing what I am doing and feeling as good as my forefathers did. I am a Cheyenne warrior." At five feet ten inches and one hundred and ninety pounds, Tony was indeed an imposing warrior.

The following day the Pratts found themselves at the base of one of the mountains outside of Locust Grove. It was their intention to search the area described in intelligence information that had been gathered from all low-enforcement sources. They spent most of the day stretching tiny thread fibers across worn trails to see if anyone would pass. As deep as they were in the woods, they believed that if anyone did break one of the threads, there was a chance it could be Hart. They rechecked the threads many times during the week.

The brothers set up camp on top of the rock plateau immediately above Cave Number 2. They built a small fire and both sat cross-legged, Indian fashion, with their arms across their chests. This was the symbolic way that Indians sit but it also had another purpose. Their right hands rested on the magnums that hung from shoulder holsters under their left arms. Neither talked. They had infinite patience. They watched and listened. Only the crackling of the small fire broke the stillness of the night.

Under normal conditions they would not have had a fire. They knew that a fire could be seen for some distance, and they felt Hart might take an opportunity to visit two young Indians who were camping.

Both men were startled for a moment as an owl hooted a few yards away. Harvey's mind wandered as he watched the fire. The hoot owl was a talisman for the Cherokee people. There was the legend of the white Stageny, the Cherokee medicine owl. At the turn of the century a great medicine man was supposed to be able to turn himself into this great white owl, which roosted only under the cedar, the medicine tree. Pratt remembered talking to one of Hart's young cousins who had said that he believed Hart was the Stageny because Hart had told him once that when the snow falls he sleeps under the medicine tree.

The little fire began to fizzle out until only a hiss was left with an occasional flame shooting up to break the monotony.

Harvey Pratt had almost dozed off when out of the darkness sprang a screaming, white-fanged black cat. It struck him full in the chest, causing, he believed at the time, his heart to almost stop. Automatically his pistol came out of his holster, but by the time he had regained his composure the cat had scampered screaming like a banshee into the woods. They stood there looking at each other in total disbelief. Each knew what the other was thinking. Both men were unnerved.

The search continued. Every possibility, every chance, anything the agents' imaginations could conjure up was tried. A good lead—that's what they needed—just one good lead.

CHAPTER 8

THE CONFESSIONS OF THE INSANE, THE MENTALLY INCOMPETENT, and the attention-seekers continued. They varied from the very simple to the extremely elaborate. One man said that he had killed the girls after he had escaped from the State Penitentiary. He indicated that after his escape from prison he had "degutted" a man in Kansas City. Newspaper accounts indicated that there was only one entrance to the camping area; however, he said there was another entrance located at the rear of the camping area. The man drew agents a map of the area where he claimed the crimes took place. He said that he had planned the murders with one of the counselor staff members at the unit. His signal to move in was when she told the little girls to be quiet, that it was time to go to bed. He and the counselor allegedly took the three girls from the tent and dragged them approximately 150 yards from the tent. He claimed that when he took the girls from the tent, all were fully clothed in their sleeping bags. At the same time he contradicted the newspaper articles, which had claimed all the girls had been sexually assaulted. Only one of the girls had been sexually molested after he had observed her nude and became aroused.

The murder weapon, he contended, was a tire tool. He beat one of the girls to death and strangled the other two. After the girls had been killed, the staff member took the tire tool and threw it in a dump which was relatively close to the areas where the counselors slept. He went on to say that the particular dump was located between the staff members' sleeping area and the tree where he was hiding prior to enacting the crimes. He said that the newspaper articles indicated that a size 8 footprint was found in the area where the bodies were located—and he wore a size 8. He also recalled that Hart wore a size 9. He further said that he knew Hart because he was in the State Penitentiary with him. He thought it silly that officers could think one man could drag all three girls from the tent in the area where they were murdered.

After the murders he walked to a farmhouse and met with the individual who had hired him. When he got to the farm, he changed clothes, as he was carrying an extra change. He washed a cotton shirt and double-knit trousers soaked with blood in the pond at the farm. The owner of the farm had a car and he was taken out of the area.

Nothing in the man's story checked out.

A mental patient in Norman, Oklahoma, had confessed to the killing of the Girl Scouts to several people. He was arrested in his home and taken back to the hospital where he became incoherent and couldn't be questioned further.

Still another convict in the Tulsa County Jail confessed to the crimes. When interviewed by agents, he said he had to serve forty-five years and simply didn't want to go to the penitentiary. He wanted someone to check out his story so he could stay out of the penitentiary a little longer.

Another man, in western Oklahoma, who also confessed to the crimes was given a polygraph examination. Afterward he admitted he had lied and had fabricated the entire story. He just wanted someone to listen to him.

Sometimes it seemed to the agents that half the population of the United States were either psychics or soothsayers. In the daily mail there was always someone who had had a vision. They proclaimed they knew who committed the crimes and promised to use their psychic powers if they were either sent money or given a plane ticket to Oklahoma. Others, however, simply gave their information in the letter and these, too, were checked out on the remote possibility that one could be the killer and this his way of confessing.

One such letter began, "In the murder of those three Girl Scouts near Camp Garland, look for them here in Tulsa—a sixteen-year-old with a car and probably two buddies. One or more of those involved have been to Camp Garland. They know the girls real well. Knew where the girls were and when. . . ." The letter went on to say "if this helps, I would appreciate the reward in cash, no publicity. Let the dogs have the credit."

Another letter said, "Those three men you're looking for who killed those little girls in the Scout Camp last week are driving a four-door sedan, blue in color, that looks old. At present they are hiding out near Robber's Cave in Wilburton, Oklahoma, in a dense wooded area. They are heading toward the Talihina Mountains. I am studying ESP. I saw these men June 13 at 4:30 P.M. No, I am not nationally known, but I have seen other things."

Other self-proclaimed psychics sent detailed descriptions of the individual who had committed the crime. Some even provided the investigators with sketches to illustrate their descriptions. Yet another well-intentioned person sent a copy of the *National Enquirer* that contained an article about a national psychic crime squad. Several other letter writers blamed the killings on their ex-husbands.

All, even the most farfetched, were checked out.

During the next few months it seemed everyone in the State of Oklahoma would get a crack at capturing Gene Leroy Hart. Members of the Twelfth Force Reconnaissance Army Group of the Tulsa Reserves searched the area known as Bryan Hollow east of Peggs, Oklahoma, and observed an Indian male in his early thirties. They said that he wore a three-quarter-length jacket, shoulder-length hair, and was walking along whistling. Dogs were brought in but were unable to trace the man because, the men said, he kept circling back on them. The Sheriff's office, however, retrieved cigarette butts and several empty cans of tobacco.

The leader of a team of ex-Vietnam veterans who called themselves the Spooks said that his group could capture Hart within a week. Officers snickered at their naiveté but consented to their request. The jungle team emerged from the woods several days later, tired, hungry, and covered with ticks and chiggers. Their search, too, had been fruitless.

The inmates of the state penitentiaries also wanted their chance at trying to find Hart. The OSBI received letters almost weekly from convicts who said they didn't know where Hart was now, but if they could camp out with an agent near the Camp Scott area, they could certainly find him. They usually claimed to have known him when he was in the penitentiary and knew his hiding places well. Others would write from the penitentiary saying that they had been boyhood friends of Hart, knew his hiding places, and could find him.

During the next few months, even though the investigation appeared to be slacking off and the publicity dying down, the reward fund continued to grow. The people in the small agricultural town of Leesburg, in central Florida, raised $3,000 reward money for the capture of the murderer of the Girl Scouts. They had raised the money $500 at a time selling fresh, boiled, and salted peanuts on street corners. But that wasn't enough. One weekend they held a public auction and auctioned off dozens of items donated by merchants. Over one hundred fifty-five bidders showed up on a rainy afternoon to buy the merchandise. The band was playing for free and an auctioneer had driven 50 miles to provide his services at no charge. The final tally from the peanut sales, cash contributions, and the auction was over $3,000. The Leesburg community then created the Leesburg Protect Our Girl Scouts Committee, comprised of local businessmen. This raised the reward for Hart to over $20,000. All the money was kept in a Pryor bank.

On July 9, at the Associated Press Oklahoma News Executive Annual Meeting at Western Hills State Lodge, outside of Tahlequah, Dr. Robert Phillips, a clinical psychologist, who for twenty-five years had treated criminals and the criminally insane, gave a psychological profile of the kind of person who would commit the Locust Grove murders.

Phillips said that while not legally crazy, "he survives on such a savage animal-level it would be impossible to change him. He does not have a chronic psychosis. He's calculated and plans his deed in a cold-blooded manner. He took the tools he needed to do the terrible deed and then escaped. But in the process of committing the crime, the passion took over. After one kill, he returned to the tent for another and another. He couldn't leave the bodies alone. He was caught up in his deed and lost all control. In a demonic way, he carried the girls outside and continued to violate them. And at that second, he was completely mad. A monster. An animal. Then something happened which brought him back and alarmed him. Like an animal, who scratches the ground trying to cover up his tracks in an almost ritualistic way, he then tried to cover up what he had done. He put two girls back into the sleeping bags and tried to wipe up the blood. A man with complete disorder in his life, the killer was trying to create order."

Dr. Phillips described the killer as being "very dark and depressed. He hates life and feels very inferior. He is terrified of rejection, especially by women, and he's a very angry person. The sadist part comes through in his anger at life. Sex means something; it symbolizes something to him. He violated these girls because he hates happiness, innocence, decency, and the best way to degrade those and himself was by sex. Usually, sex is life-giving but in this case it was life-taking. He hates being alive, and in killing he is taking revenge on a world that he believes has mistreated him. Something happened during this man's life to make him feel extremely inferior and to build up passion and hatred in him. I believe it would be impossible to help such a person or ever release them on society. The killer has gone too far, he has crossed the line. He is an animal."

A local newspaper had talked with five attorneys who had represented Hart. None of them were surprised that Hart had been charged with the deaths. "He was a very bitter and hostile man," said one Tulsa attorney. "It was like he was Geronimo and had declared war on the white world." According to two of the attorneys, Hart freely admitted the burglaries to police officers but denied them at trial. He strongly denied the rape, even after he had served time for the crime. This seemed to coincide with Hart's prison record and his psychological testing at Eastern State Hospital in Vinita.

Using the doctor's data as a guideline, the agents checked into Hart's background to see if he fit the description. Gene Leroy Hart was born on November 27, 1943, at the Claremore Indian Hospital. His father, Walter Hart, never came to see Gene when he was a child. All that was ever known of the elder Hart was that he died of a heart attack. No one knew where or when. Hart regularly attended Locust Grove schools with his best grades being in the manual field, such as shop, where he had a B average. Otherwise, his grade average was C. In high school his I.Q. was listed as 100. He was said to be congenial with his fellow students and teachers, and generally his conduct was described as good. He was an outstanding athlete in high school in both football and basketball. He was offered several scholarships to major institutions but instead he chose to get married and his wife gave birth shortly thereafter. Not long after the birth of his son he confessed to the rapes of two Tulsa women and was convicted of Kidnapping and First Degree Rape. After his incarceration, his wife divorced him and had the name of her son changed. According to his former wife, Hart hated his father and blamed him for everything that had happened to him.

On June 28, 1966, he was sent to Eastern State Hospital in Vinita for psychological testing to determine whether he was sane under the Oklahoma rules of law. He told the psychiatrist that he was innocent of the rape; that he had met the girls outside of a nightclub in Tulsa and had talked to them for a while before accompanying them to Locust Grove. He told the psychiatrist that he had made love to one that night and then, the next morning, to the other. While he was making love to one girl, the other was asleep. Hart said that after the girls were dropped off they probably got mad for some reason and notified the authorities.

Hart underwent several psychological tests. His I.Q. was set at 96. The doctors said that his basic abilities and potential were higher than indicated by the I.Q. score. His general knowledge was good, and he had a large vocabulary. However, he was found to have some difficulties in abstracting and generalizing. His rote memory was poor, as he was only able to correctly recall five digits in a forward direction and four backwards. The Bender Motor Gestalt Test indicated some underlying anxiety, a need for structure, and possibly some basic insecurities.

He spoke in glowing terms of his mother, but said he didn't know his father.

While in prison, Hart seemed to withdraw from the people around him. He wrote to the classification officer at McAlester State Penitentiary, "Due to difficulties of a personal nature I feel it would be best for all parties concerned if I should have everyone removed from my mailing and visiting list except my mother." This request was granted.

Hart later wrote again to the classification officer, bitterly requesting his mother be removed from his mailing list, because he had received only a "short half-page letter" during the year and she had not visited him in three years. He accused his family of sitting on their "duffs" and acting as if they didn't know him. He concluded by saying that there was "a breaking point for anyone and anyone can take so much."

Larry Dry, who escaped on two occasions with Gene Hart from Mayes County Jail, said, "Gene was not the person that he used to be—that the people in town remember him to be. When we escaped he was unbelievably bitter. On many occasions he planned to go kill his son and his wife. He felt like the whole world had betrayed him and he was going to get 'em back."

Leo Albro looked like a Baptist preacher, a quiet, soft-spoken man in his fifties with gentle blue eyes. Albro was one of the senior agents of the OSBI. He had been stationed in northeastern Oklahoma for his entire career, and enjoyed a reputation of knowing everyone in that part of the state. He had known Gene Hart and his family for a long time. Any time he was in the area he would drop by and visit with Ella Mae. He had always been met with at least a civil reception. Albro approached the old house one August morning for his periodic visit. As he pulled into the yard, Mrs. Buckskin and a younger son were seated on the front porch. As Albro stepped onto the porch, the old woman, still seated, erupted. "Don't ask me any questions, Albro," she shouted. "You are a lizard. You go away."

"What's the matter, Ella Mae," Albro stammered, taken aback by her hostile greeting.

"You lied to me," she shouted, shaking her finger. "You're a bounty hunter. You tell Pete Weaver everything I tell you. You are only trying to send my boy back to the penitentiary."

"I'm not a bounty hunter," Albro began. "Who told you that?"

"A friend of mine told me about Albro," she screamed.

Albro could see the old woman was becoming more and more agitated. Suddenly she sprang to her feet and ran into the house shouting, "I'll show you." Seconds later she reappeared and Albro found himself staring down the barrel of a .12-gauge shotgun. "Get out!" she commanded.

Albro smiled, shook his head, and stepped from the porch.

"Why don't you shoot me?" she screamed after him. "Go tell Pete come after me."

Albro would later laugh about the incident. He knew he should have arrested her but as one agent commented, "What if you had had to shoot the mother of a living legend?"

Occasional searches into the mountains and cliffs around Locust Grove continued. On August 1 a cave was discovered about one and a half miles from Camp Scott. On the wall, in what appeared to be a felt-tip marking pencil was written: *The killer was here. Bye-bye fools* with the date 77-6-17. The arrangement of the date—year, month, and day—was used almost exclusively in the state penitentiary.

The news of the discovery spread quickly. Pete Weaver was implored by reporters to take them to the site so that they might photograph the writings. Amused by the prospect, Weaver agreed.

A couple of days later he led a group of the reporters to the cave. Weaver enjoyed the trip. For the first time, the reporters saw the terrain that the searchers had to contend with. They discovered the heat, the humidity, ticks, thorns, jagged rocks, snakes, cliffs, chiggers, and the utter exhaustion that was experienced traversing the terrain. After an hour the reporters, carrying photographic equipment, covered with ticks, virtually collapsed in front of the cave. "How the hell can anyone be found up here?" one reporter gasped. Weaver smiled as the reporters picked ticks from one another and gasped for air.

"If this cave wasn't so remote, if it wasn't so difficult to get to, I might believe some prankster wrote it," Weaver said, pointing to the cave. "But why would someone come way up here to write a message that was only found by chance? No," Weaver told the reporters, "I think the killer wrote it. I'm sure of it. If this is the killer, he's taunting us, telling us he'll never get caught, but he will."

On August 3 the Tulsa *World* ran an appeal on the front page urging Hart to surrender. The article read,

> An Open Letter to Gene Leroy Hart.
> The Tulsa *World* has been told you fear for your safety if you should surrender to law enforcement officers. If this is so, we would offer you our help in seeing that you are able to give yourself up without harm. We also have assurance of Governor David Boren that he will use the power of his office to help assure your safety.
> Governor Boren has authorized this statement: "I will use the authority of the Governor's office and will take any steps necessary to assure his security and a fair trial if he will give himself up."
> We have talked to Mayes County District Attorney Sid Wise, Co-ordinator of the investigation in the death of three Girls Scouts near Locust Grove June 13. He has authorized the Tulsa *World* to serve as an intermediary in bringing about your surrender without harm. Wise has told us that he will see that you are placed in a jail or federal prison outside Mayes County if that will add to your feeling of safety. You could surrender to a law enforcement agency of your choosing, county, state, or federal. We are not trying to judge whether you are innocent or guilty of the June 13 crime but we have been told that you deny any guilt and your only opportunity to prove that will be in a court of law.
> If you wish to have your day in court, the Tulsa *World* will make reporter Doug Hicks available to you in arranging your surrender. He will be willing to meet with you or any person you designate at any time or place. He can be reached at Tulsa *World* office . . . and further contact arranged. . . . We believe Governor Boren and Sid Wise are sincere in promising their aid in assuring your safety and opportunity for a fair trial. Your fears are understandable. You are in a desperate situation but this may be your

best chance to get a fair shake. We hope you will take it. Please let us hear from you.

The Tulsa *World* never heard from Gene Leroy Hart.

Limke flipped the page on the desk calendar in his office at the Tahlequah headquarters. It was late September, almost three months since the murders at Camp Scott. Larry Bowles appeared in the doorway where he stood silently.

"Good morning." Limke broke the silence.

"I need to talk to you, Ted." Bowles sounded remote.

"Come on in," Limke responded.

Bowles stepped into the small office, closing the door behind him. He dropped onto the soft chair directly across the desk from Limke. Something's wrong, Limke thought. Bowles just didn't have private conversations. He was close to no one save his family and Mike Wilkerson. Limke liked and respected Bowles but he had never been able to read him.

"Something wrong?" Limke asked as he leaned forward on the desk.

"Yeah, I guess. I mean, I need to bounce something off you, Ted, maybe not officially, but about official business." Bowles chose his words. "I think I can find Hart, but I need some help with a policy matter."

"You got it," Limke responded. "What's the problem?"

"I've got an informant that can find Hart. I've promised him that no one will ever know his name except me . . . and Ted, I will keep that promise."

"Oh, boy," Limke groaned. "I see the problem."

The OSBI had a very strict policy as to the identity of informants and while it was generally on a need-to-know basis, the administration was always informed. Limke was sure that Dick Wilkerson and Deputy Tom Kennedy would respect this promise of confidentiality, but the Director was a retired FBI agent and a stickler for policy.

"How reliable is the snitch?" Limke asked.

"I'll stake my life on him," Bowles immediately responded.

Limke nodded his head slowly. Well, I guess that says it all, he thought. "How about our jobs?" Limke grinned.

"That, too," Bowles said, returning Limke's smile.

"Okay," Limke said, "what have you got?"

Bowles leaned forward, almost touching the desk. "On the 27th of August, the snitch was at a stomp dance in Sequoyah County, down by Marble City, you know?" Limke nodded without really knowing the location. "There's this medicine man," Bowles continued. "His name is William Lee Smith. He makes and sells medicine, and takes care of both physical and spiritual ailments. Well, the informant was standing near the ceremonial fire and Smith comes up to him and points out this older Cherokee in overalls on the other side of the fire. The medicine man says Hart is staying with the old man somewhere in the Cookson Hills. Hart has come to the stomp dances but he always stands off in the shadows and never comes near the fires where the religious ceremonies are held." Bowles leaned back in his chair. "What do you think?"

Limke sipped his coffee slowly. "Can the informant stay on top of this?"

"That's the great part." Bowles was almost excited. "Hart's family, the medicine man, everyone, trusts the snitch. If we just don't get in a hurry, we'll get him."

"Okay. I'm going to call Oklahoma City and talk to them," Limke smiled. "Wish me luck."

As Bowles strolled out of the office, Limke dialed the phone.

Lean on the medicine man, Limke thought. He might give it up, but if he doesn't we're right back where we started. No, the best plan is to see what else the snitch could turn up, just be cool—wait and hope.

Dick Wilkerson and Tom Kennedy were proud of themselves and surprised by the relative ease with which Jeff Laird, the Director, accepted Bowles's terms. He hadn't liked the idea at all but the two men had convinced him that Bowles would be fired before he would break his word. They had reasoned that the loss of a good agent, and with him a chance at finding Hart, was too great a price to pay when the Director could waive the policy this one time.

On September 22 the parents of Lori Farmer and Denise Milner filed a three-and-half-million-dollar lawsuit against the Girl Scouts.

Bowles talked to the informant almost daily.

In October 1977, Hart's mother contacted Smith, the medicine man. He told her that he had visited with Hart at his hideout. He felt that Hart was being careless by hunting and fishing in the woods where a hunter might see him and tell the authorities. Smith described Hart's keeper as an old man who sells firewood. The old man liked Hart and Hart readily performed all the domestic chores. Bowles felt good about Hart's host's alleged statements regarding Hart's domestic abilities. The people Hart had stayed with at Lost City had said virtually the same thing.

It was late fall and there were still no substantial leads as to Hart's whereabouts. The refusal of law enforcement and prosecution to comment on the facts of the case frustrated and angered the press. Criticism of the investigation grew as did admiration for Hart. The enigmatic and mysterious young fugitive became somewhat of a celebrity, someone to say you had known. His friends and relatives were interviewed daily. Gene Leroy Hart—burglar, fugitive, rapist, accused murderer—had become a folk hero.

In November 1977, Hart's mother was told by the medicine man that Hart would have to be moved from his hideout because the heat was too great. According to the informant, Buckskin formulated a plan by which Hart would be secreted out of Oklahoma to the Cherokee reservation in North Carolina. Hart's brother-in-law, Jim Littledave, was chosen to drive Hart to the reservation. The time chosen for the operation was the Thanksgiving holiday weekend. The only thing that could stand in their way was lack of money. It was decided that Littledave would attempt to borrow the money from a local lending institution.

Bowles determined that Littledave owned two cars, a white Volkswagen and a 1968 Chevrolet. He would probably use the larger car, which he drove to work, so Hart could be concealed in the trunk. The OSBI would have to mark the car so that it could be followed easily.

Aupy Linville dropped silently to the concrete and gravel surface as the Dodge van chugged across the large, chain-link-enclosed industrial parking lot south of Pryor, Oklahoma. The icy November wind cut through his clothes like a knife. In the brightly lighted employee parking lot he snaked his way between the cars toward Jim Littledave's 1968 Chevrolet. As he slid under the rear of the Chevy, he searched in the blackness until his hand identified the mud-encrusted four-inch cross member of the frame. Linville clawed the dried mud almost frantically as he tried to quiet his breathing. He silently cursed as pain shot up his right hand. He had broken a fingernail and his cold numbed fingers ached. After an eternity the mud crust broke away and Linville's fingers moved over the smooth, cold steel. Lying on his right side, he reached inside the light jacket and removed a small four- by six-inch black box. With his left hand resting on the freshly cleaned metal as a guide, Linville raised the black box toward his left hand until the heavy magnet seized the cross member with an audible snap which to Linville sounded like a thunderbolt.

"Havin' trouble?"

Linville's head snapped to the right as he gasped audibly. A large pair of work shoes supported khaki-clad legs just at the rear of the car. Linville slid his body across the rough surface. As he peeked from under the car, he was greeted by a large, burly, unshaven man in khakis, wearing a baseball cap. In his right hand he carried a black lunch pail.

"Havin' trouble?" the large man repeated.

"Naw," Linville swallowed hard. "I was just checkin' these shocks. I think they're okay."

"Well," the man continued, "if you do, just holler. We got a flat over here so we'll be here for a while."

Linville, still on his back half under the Chevy, glanced to his right. Feet! Feet everywhere! The whole parking lot was full of people! There's not supposed to be a shift change until 7:00 A.M., he thought. It's just now two. Littledave works from eleven to seven; must be a six-to-two shift. Linville struggled to his feet.

"Can I help you with the flat?" he asked.

"No, thanks," the large man answered. "I think we can handle it."

The big man raised his left hand as he turned toward his car 20 feet to the north.

Linville took a deep breath and leaned against the Chevy. What if Littledave has changed shifts? Linville thought. If he comes back with those guys still here, the big guy will tell him about me foolin' with his car. Linville decided to hang around the Chevrolet. If Littledave did show up Linville would start talking to him as if he knew him; then maybe the guys with the flat wouldn't get suspicious.

Minutes passed which seemed like hours. The flat tire was almost fixed. Linville slipped a small ratchet drill from his right hip pocket and stepped toward the left taillight of the Chevy. With four short strokes he drilled a one-sixteenth-inch diameter hole directly over the bulb in the taillight lens. The car could now be easily followed at night, even in heavy traffic. The hole would produce a bright white light surrounded by the dull red of the lens.

"See you now." Linville waved to the large man and his friends as they drove past him toward the gate. The parking lot was almost deserted now.

Linville dropped to the ground and scooted on his back under the car. He blindly slid his hand over the box, verifying its security, and flipped a small switch on the side.

Agents Pat Wilkerson and Gary Rogers sat silently in total darkness almost a half-mile south of the parking lot. A makeshift console sat on the floor between the two men. Suddenly a green light flashed on the strange instrument resting on the console, accompanied by an irritating beep. Both young men straightened in the seat. Six seconds later, the light and the beep were repeated. Linville had been successful; the bumper beeper was in place and operating. They could now track the car without ever coming in sight of it.

Pat Wilkerson lifted the microphone of the radio to his lips. "Bird dog is operational," he whispered.

Ted Limke and Dick Wilkerson breathed a sigh as the youngest Wilkerson's voice broke the silence. Twenty-one agents in ten cars were scattered around the small community. Cary Thurman had scaled the six-foot fence of the Locust Grove athletic field and was occupying the press box, which gave him a clear view of the rear of the Littledave home about a half-mile to the east. With the bumper beeper in place, Limke felt comfortable relieving half the agents so they could return to Tahlequah to rest. Twelve-hour shifts were established and Littledave's every movement would be monitored.

Pat Wilkerson lay silently on the frozen ground staring at the Littledave residence. The thermal underwear, thermal coveralls, heavy coat, boots, and ski mask so restricted his movement that he could do little else but stare straight ahead. He had been dropped three hours earlier on the side of the road, made his way into the woods, and found a vantage point that enabled him to watch the front of the Littledave residence. He was equipped with a walkie-talkie and a night scope, a $10,000 piece of equipment that could turn the inky darkness into midday. Every hour Cary Thurman would check on him by radio.

It was a cold, boring, miserable assignment. He wondered if he had been stuck with it to prove that he received no special treatment because of his two brothers. He had long since found out that having a brother who was a wheel was anything but a blessing. He had never detected any animosity or heard any allegations about receiving preferential treatment because of his blood relation. On the contrary, he was well-liked and very popular among the agents. Most of the agents referred to him as P.J. or Patty Joe, which had always been reserved for his immediate family.

The blanket of darkness engulfed everything around him; the silence was overwhelming, broken only occasionally by the sound of some small animal wading through the dry leaves. He smiled as he envisioned himself a modern-day Grizzly Adams, becoming so much a part of the forest that the birds would perch on his head and the raccoons would come to be petted and stroked while the white-tailed deer nuzzled his face. He was alone, all alone, with his fantasies in the comfortable twilight between consciousness and sleep.

"P-e-e-e J-a-a-a-y. P-e-e-e J-a-a-a-y."

He froze, terror stricken! The haunting voice was right behind him! His gun was underneath all those clothes. A shudder of icy chills ran up his spine.

"You there, P.J.?"

The radio! That damn Thurman. He fumbled for the walkie-talkie, trying to regain his composure. He whispered slowly into the radio, "You just scared the living shit out of me."

Limke and Dick Wilkerson would make arrangements with Cecil Hammon of Hammon's Flying Service in Tahlequah to have an airplane on twenty-four-hour standby to assist in the surveillance. Littledave would be followed to and from work, to his children's school functions, and to the grocery store.

On the morning of the third day of the surveillance, Littledave left his home and drove to Pryor where he entered a savings and loan bank. Agents theorized that he was attempting to borrow the money to finance his trip to North Carolina.

The area of Hart's suspected hideout, according to the informant, lay between Tahlequah and Sallisaw in the Cookson Hills.

As Littledave left Pryor, agents lost visual contact. Jack Lay, "the A. J. Foyt of the OSBI," and Linville followed the bumper beeper signal south toward Tahlequah, informing the other agents of their movement. The agents believed Littledave was on his way. All agents were mobilized and dispatched to their preassigned points. No arrest or contact would be made until after the suspect vehicle was on Interstate 40 traveling toward Arkansas. Limke, in the airplane, would coordinate the operation.

The signal was followed through Tahlequah and continued south. Near I-40 in Sequoyah County, the signal began to fade.

Lay and Linville began to pick up speed. The engine of Lay's 1976 Pontiac had been refined to the point of perfection. The car was capable of speeds in excess of 140 mph. As the vehicle shot past the arrest teams stationed on I-40 on the east side of Sallisaw, Linville radioed Limke in the airplane that Littledave had evidently been able to slip through their perimeter undetected. Limke ordered two units to return to Locust Grove while the remainder followed Linville into Arkansas.

Jack Lay shoved his right foot to the floor as the needle of the speedometer passed 120 mph and continued upward. Eight cars roared down I-40 into Arkansas. Halfway across the state Limke began to lose radio contact with the lead car. Linville assured him he was still receiving a strong signal indicating the suspect vehicle was just ahead. It became apparent to Limke that neither the other ground units nor the airplane would be able to keep pace with Lay and Linville. He strongly suspected that a mechanical malfunction was causing a false signal in the bumper beeper. Limke advised Linville to go no farther than Memphis, Tennessee, while the rest of the agents would return to Locust Grove.

As Limke sighted Sallisaw on the return flight, Agent Darrel Wilkins's voice blasted from the radio. "The bird is back in the nest."

"You mean he's home?" Limke asked incredulously.

"Ten-four," was the response.

"I don't believe it," Limke thought in frustration. "A million dollars in equipment, twenty college graduates, and we can't track one little Indian two hundred miles." Limke shook his head in frustration. "You're something, Limke," he mused. "Big-time state agent—who couldn't find a white horse in a one-acre burnt-off pasture."

By morning all the agents had returned to Locust Grove or the motel in Tahlequah. They were tired, frustrated, embarrassed, and irritable. Limke ordered them to rest at the motel while he and Dick Wilkerson, in two different cars, maintained a rolling surveillance of the Littledave residence.

About noon Littledave and his wife left their home and drove to the residence of Ella Mae Buckskin south of Locust Grove. Several other cars were parked around the house and it appeared to Limke and Wilkerson that a major conference was in progress, possibly the planning of a trip. As Limke watched from his hidden vantage point, two familiar cars drove slowly past.

"Oh no, no," Limke moaned, "the Feds, the damn FBI."

Moments later the conference began breaking up.

Two hours had passed since Limke had watched the FBI units cruise by the Buckskin residence. Bowles had just talked to his informant who verified that after seeing the FBI cars, it had been decided that the time was not right to move Hart.

"Let's clean it up, Ted," Dick Wilkerson sighed. "Aupy, Bud, and I will retrieve the bumper beeper tonight when Littledave goes to work, then we'll go back to Oklahoma City. Day after tomorrow's Thanksgiving. Let's let the thing cool off for a while. Larry can contact the snitch after the holidays."

On the day before Thanksgiving, six-year-old Michael Martinez was found stabbed to death. He had then been placed on a railroad track and run over by a train in Vinita, Oklahoma. His mother was Bonnie Martinez, who had allegedly hidden Hart and Dry after they escaped from the Mayes County Jail. The agents assigned to the case were told to check for possible connections between the Martinez death and the Locust Grove murders. No logical connection was found and a Vinita man with a history of mental disorders was arrested for the murder.

"Hart is living with an old man who cuts firewood as part of his living."

This was the word from the informant. Everyone within a 20-mile radius of the Smith residence was checked for stacks of firewood. Agents roamed the dirt roads and the woods searching for an old man who cut wood for a living. Many nights were spent in the woods wrapped in blankets, in sub-zero weather, observing suspects' houses. Time-lapse cameras that snapped pictures every thirty seconds were set in the woods and focused on suspects' houses.

Toward the end of January 1978 the informant contacted Bowles. He said that in early December Ella Mae Buckskin's sister was told by an unknown female employed at a police department that she overheard some officers talking about planting an electronic transmitting device in a vehicle belonging to a member of the Buckskin family. She warned Buckskin's sister to caution all of Hart's family to keep all their vehicles and homes locked. She assured her that she would contact the family and warn them if she received any other information concerning Hart.

The agents were continually amazed that Hart had so many relatives and friends—that they could actually get inside a police department and find out what was going on. It was decided to share no more OSBI information with anyone except Pete Weaver.

Bowles decided to ask the informant to telephone the Smith residence on the pretext of wanting firewood. Smith's wife answered the phone and the informant, speaking in Cherokee, asked if they had any wood for sale. She said they didn't and the only person she knew who sold firewood in the area was also named Smith and lived down the road from them.

When Bowles next met with the informant he was told that in February Ella Mae Buckskin was at the Smith residence talking to the medicine man about her son. An unidentified neighbor ran into the house breathing heavily and announced that the FBI was in the area searching for Hart. Smith turned to his wife, saying, "Get in the pickup and run up the road and tell Gene to stay in the house."

"Up the road." What could up the road mean? In rural Oklahoma it could be as much as 20 miles or as little as 100 yards. Limke decided that they would check with the rural mail carrier in the area and see if there was an old man who lived alone and chopped wood.

Jeff Laird, Director of the OSBI, resigned in January to run for State Senator. Tom Kennedy, the Deputy Director, was named to succeed him. Dick Wilkerson was promoted to Deputy Director and Ted Limke replaced Wilkerson and was designated Chief Inspector. Mike Wilkerson was elevated to Limke's former position as Inspector-in-charge of the Northeastern Region.

It seemed that everywhere the agents moved they were running across Hart's friends and relatives. They began to think that the whole world was related to either Smith or Hart or both.

Bowles again met with the informant, who told him Ella Mae Buckskin had gone to Smith's residence on the evening of February 25 accompanied by a daughter and a longtime friend. She took with her some of Hart's favorite foods, which included canned beets and assorted jellies and jams. The medicine man told her that she might be able to see her son at the stomp dance on May 25. Before she left, Smith cautioned her that when she came to his residence she should make sure she wasn't followed because he had seen a blue Pontiac with a whip antenna drive past his residence and knew that it belonged to an officer.

Bowles smiled. The car he described was his.

"Mike, could you come in here, please," Director Tom Kennedy asked.

"Sure," Mike Wilkerson said as he received his new identification from the Director's secretary which denoted his promotion to Inspector-in-charge of the Northeastern Oklahoma Regional Office. The youngest inspector-in-charge of a regional office in OSBI history, he thought. Dick is the youngest Deputy Director in the history of the Bureau. Not bad for two ole boys from Atwood, Oklahoma. He turned and walked into the Director's office, sat down in the soft leather chair, and looked across the large walnut desk at Tom Kennedy.

Kennedy was in his middle forties with unruly brown hair and graying temples. His clothes hung loosely on his five foot eleven inch, two-hundred-pound frame. Kennedy had been with the Bureau just about a year longer than Mike Wilkerson. He had come to Oklahoma from Junction City, Kansas, where he was Chief of Police. Prior to that he had been Chief of Detectives in Victoria, Texas.

Kennedy leaned back in his chair, put his hands behind his head, smiled, and said, "Mike, are you going to catch Gene Leroy Hart for me?"

"If investigation will catch the man, yes, I will catch him for you," Wilkerson replied.

"Well, I haven't been satisfied with Limke," Kennedy pronounced in mock dissatisfaction. "I haven't been satisfied with him at all. I think there is more that can be done. Now, if I have to go down there and catch him for you all, I will."

"Well, in Limke's defense," Wilkerson said, "he's been under a lot of pressure from Laird. He was the Dreyfus for the state of Oklahoma. Laird closed the Tulsa office and moved the Northeastern Regional Office to Tahlequah for political reasons. Limke bought a new house and then Laird wanted him to move to Oklahoma City. Limke knew Laird was out to get him. They hated each other's guts. You know that when your decisions are being so closely scrutinized and you realize that the slightest mistake can get you fired, transferred, or reprimanded, you tend to make slower, more calculated decisions." Wilkerson was a little ashamed that he had not defended his friend with more vigor, but he also knew that this was Kennedy's way of motivating.

"Well, I have not been satisfied with Limke or Bowles," interjected Kennedy sourly.

"Let me tell you what I think of Bowles," Wilkerson said. "I know that you are not going to agree with me, but if you took all the qualities that it takes to make a good agent, Bowles would grade out higher than anybody in this bureau. His expertise in investigation is unsurpassed. His demeanor and ability are second to none. The man would grade out at a 99 percent."

"Well, I don't agree with you. I don't agree with you at all," Kennedy said, somewhat irritated. "I just know one thing. If we don't catch Gene Leroy Hart, it's the end of our bureau."

"Do you really believe that, Tom?" Wilkerson questioned. "Do you really believe it's that important that we catch him?"

"You bet it is. If the FBI or the Highway Patrol or the locals catch him before we do, it will be the death of our bureau. Roger Webb [Commissioner of the Department of Public Safety] wants to put a trooper up in the woods to catch Hart. Do you have any idea what would happen if a trooper stumbled onto Hart after all our investigation? We'd have so much egg on our face that it would be the end of us. It can either make or break us. We have come a long way, but we need this arrest and we need it badly."

"Tell the Commissioner to keep his troopers out of our investigation," Wilkerson interjected, "but what about the FBI?"

"To heck with 'em," Kennedy barked. "I've mended fences with them and we promised that if either of our agencies got a break, the other would be in on the arrest."

"If we find out where he is, are you going to let them in on the arrest?" Wilkerson asked, knowing the answer.

Kennedy smiled wryly and said, "Sure. Just like they'd let us assist them. The one that catches this guy is the one who's going to have the credit. We need the arrest, the FBI doesn't."

"I couldn't agree with you more. Remember when Puckett told them where they could find the only woman to ever make the Most Wanted List. They wouldn't even let him go on the arrest. Besides we still owe them for burning us on the surveillance of the Littledave residence. All right. I'll tell you what. If you want me to catch Hart you're going to have to help me a little bit," Wilkerson said. "Now, I'm a motivator, that's the way I work. First of all, I want another case assignment made. We've got a case assignment on the murders, but I want to make a fugitive case assignment."

"Who do you want it assigned to?" Kennedy said.

"Bowles," Wilkerson said.

"Well, I don't agree with you, but if that's what you want," Kennedy replied, lighting a cigarette.

"He is the logical choice. He does have the informant and he is the most experienced. That's not to take anything away from Thurman, but he is about eighty miles away," Wilkerson responded.

"Well, for what it's worth, Mike, I don't believe in Bowles's snitch. I think you are going to have to go another avenue," Kennedy said, exhaling cigarette smoke.

"No, I think the avenue is to go with Bowles's snitch. He's been right on too many occasions. I think what we are going to have to do is to make some quick decisions and make them decisively. We are going to have to run hard and put pressure on everybody. I also want Bowles transferred out of Tahlequah and back to Tulsa. You know that he is not happy there. He's been a whipping boy long enough."

"You want a lot," Kennedy responded.

"That's right, but I know how to motivate men. I also need more help. I would like to have Harvey Pratt's intelligence unit. They are all good, experienced men who like to run all night."

"You've got it," Kennedy said.

"Oh, by the way, I'm going to ask one last thing. If we catch Hart through Bowles's work, I want him to get the Director's Medal of Honor."

"All right, but I wouldn't put too much hope in his informant. Mike, are you going to catch Gene Leroy Hart for me?" Kennedy repeated—his way of getting an affirmative commitment.

Again Wilkerson said, "If investigative work will catch him, we will catch him."

Bowles, Chrisco, Thurman, and Pratt's intelligence unit were assigned full-time to the fugitive investigation with complete freedom to do as they wished, subject only to the supervisory decisions of Mike Wilkerson.

On April Fool's Day, Bowles was contacted by the informant.

Buckskin had been driven to the medicine man's home the previous Saturday night by her daughter. She had taken some money for her son. While never specifically identifying the man Hart was staying with, Smith, the medicine man, talked generally about him. He was elderly and lived alone in a shack at the top of a hill. He had at least one brother who lived within walking distance at the bottom of the hill. One of the old man's brothers had died during the winter. The brother living at the bottom of the hill, on being notified of the death of the third brother, started up the hill to tell Hart's friend. When Hart saw the flashlight approaching the house, he ran out the back door into the woods. After the old man became aware that it was only his brother, he went into the woods searching for Hart who he found half-frozen. The medicine man mentioned that Hart's mentor was his wife's uncle.

The agents received their assignments from Wilkerson and fanned out over the three-county area. Agent Bud Ousley went to the Sequoyah County Clerk's Office in Sallisaw to check the marriage records for William Smith. The records showed that William Lee Smith and Eva Pigeon were married on September 6, 1949. Both Smith and Pigeon gave the address of Bunch, Oklahoma, in Adair County. Having the maiden name of Smith's wife, Agent Ousley went to a funeral home that performed most of the Indian funerals in the area. Three different relatives of Eva Pigeon had died during the winter, a Stovall, a Roberson, and a Wallace. All three families seemed to meet the criterion of having two brothers who lived next to each other, although it appeared that only Roberson had one who lived on a hill with a brother living below.

Agent Bowles contacted one of the rural mail carriers for the Vian route. He delivered mail to Route 2 which covers 80 miles and 220 stops. The mail carrier was unable to remember anyone living on his mail route who fit the description of the man harboring Hart.

The agents then contacted Vian High School to check the records of Sadie Smith, William Smith's daughter, to see what days during the winter she had missed school. It was theorized that if she missed the date that her great-uncle died to attend the funeral, the agents could pinpoint the name of the uncle in this manner. It was found that the only days she had been absent were January 10 and February 27 and 28 due to illness which had been verified by the principal.

The maps of all the mail routes leading in and out of Vian were studied, with the name of each person on the mail route placed by their respective house. The task seemed monumental, but the agents had been chasing Hart for eight months and their excitement was now heightened to an almost feverish pitch. They knew they were close. They were frustrated, but they knew they were close. They plotted the Stovall position on the map; they plotted the Roberson position; they plotted the Wallace position. It was determined that out of the two hundred and twenty families on the mail route, Hart was probably kin to at least ninety-one.

On April 5 the agents began checking the obituaries for the previous five months in the towns around Vian and Tahlequah, with no luck. There were just too many people related to the Pigeon family.

CHAPTER 9

On March 15, 1978, OSBI Headquarters in Oklahoma City received a letter from Larry Dry, in the Granite State Reformatory. He said that he had not heard from the OSBI since he was interviewed by Agent Tom Puckett. He wrote that he could find Hart, and did not want anything for his service. The catch was that he wanted to hunt Hart his way without OSBI supervision.

Ted Limke and Dick Wilkerson now agreed that it appeared that Dry was ready to cooperate. Wilkerson contacted the Department of Corrections, which arranged to have Dry transported to Oklahoma City where he could be interviewed by Limke. Limke suggested that if it were decided to let Dry look for Hart, Agent Sid Cookerly should accompany him. Cookerly was a tough, streetwise cop who had been a police officer since he was eighteen years old. At six feet three inches and two hundred and fifty pounds, wearing dark aviator's glasses, supported by dark slick hair with ragged sideburns, he could easily blend into the most sinister background. At forty years of age, he had over five hundred felony convictions to his credit, mostly as an undercover agent. Limke knew Cookerly to be a gentleman, a consummate undercover man, and, most of all, probably the most dangerous man he knew. Limke telephoned Cookerly to arrange for both of them to meet with Dry in Oklahoma City the next day.

Granite Reformatory guards were waiting in the Director's office when Limke returned from lunch with Cookerly. Limke told the guards that he would talk to the prisoner while they went to lunch. Limke took the khaki-clad young Indian by the arm and led him down the hall to an interview room, Cookerly following close behind. Dry was a tall, slender, handsome young Cherokee. As they walked down the hall, Limke asked Dry if he had eaten. Dry grunted affirmatively. They entered a small office at the end of the hall. He told Dry to have a seat and pointed to the chair located directly in front of the desk. Limke sat down in the chair behind the desk and Cookerly positioned himself in a chair almost directly behind the convict. Limke reached into his inside coat pocket and produced the letter that Dry had written.

"You said in your letter you can find Hart, is that right?" Limke asked.

"If I can't, no one can," Dry replied, his hand nearly cupped around his mouth, obscuring his decaying front teeth.

"Well, Larry, depending on what you can tell me in the next few minutes, you may get your chance. The man behind you is Agent Cookerly." Still sitting, Cookerly extended his hand and Dry shook it.

"Can I smoke?" Dry asked.

"Sure," Limke replied. "Now I'm not really interested in how you and Hart escaped from the jail. I want to know where you stayed, who you stayed with and so on. I'm not going to make you any promises. However, I assure you, you will be treated fairly."

"I don't want anything for my help, I just think it's time Gene Hart was in custody," Dry said, looking at the floor rather than Limke.

Limke knew that Dry was lying and that he fully expected something in return for his help.

"Good," Limke said, keeping his thoughts to himself. "Now, Larry, after you and Gene escaped, where did you go and where did you get food?"

"We always went straight for the woods south of Locust Grove," he replied, finally lighting his cigarette with handcuffed hands.

Limke nodded to Cookerly who produced a handcuff key, unlocked the cuffs, and laid them beside his chair.

Taking a deep draw of the cigarette, Dry continued. "There are a lot of caves and overhangs in them woods where a man can hide forever. The cave we stayed at most often was by an old cellar."

Limke's heart quickened but he remained silent, letting the convict talk at his own pace.

"To get supplies we'd usually burglarize places. Sometimes houses, sometimes stores. We'd take stuff like canned goods because we didn't know how long it would be before we'd use 'em. We didn't take bread too often, but we'd take crackers. Others things we'd take was guns, ammunition, money, clothes, and medical supplies."

"Where would you take this stuff after you stole them?" asked Cookerly.

"Well, the things we didn't use right then we took to areas we'd pick out beforehand to hide stuff. These places were always deep in the woods where we were familiar with the area, you see. In case we had to run from the laws we could run to one of these places and stay until the hunt was ended or the cops came too close. Ole Gene figured that by doing this, along with his burglaries and help from his relatives and friends, he could stay in the woods forever."

"Was Gene's eyesight bad then?" Limke queried.

"Funny you should ask that. Gene was night-blind, and was constantly looking for glasses. Every burglary we done, you could see Gene tryin' on glasses. That's reason why I said that article in the paper was bullshit about Gene being such a good shot. He couldn't see good enough to be a good shot."

"Did Gene drink?" asked Limke.

"Very little," replied Dry. "He rarely drank whiskey. 'Bout the only thing he would drink was beer."

"You mentioned that friends and relatives helped you both when you escaped. Did they know that you two were escaped felons?" asked Cookerly.

Dry covered his mouth and laughed. "Hell, yes, they knew we were escaped, but that didn't make any difference. All they know is that we escaped from a white man's jail for breaking white man's law. That almost makes you a hero. We stayed with Hart's friends who hated whites. Other times, we stayed with his mother, his aunt, or sister. The people would meet us in an already selected spot every evening if there was no laws around. They'd bring us food and cigarettes, as well as magazines and newspapers. This way we could keep up with news about our escape. Usually the person who brought this stuff was Hart's cousin. The place we usually met was Twin Bridges."

"Larry, I know you've talked to the other agents about Hart's sexual activities, but I'd like to talk to you about it. Did Hart ever want to rape anyone or commit any unusual sexual acts in your presence?" Limke asked.

"I told the other men about him wanting to rape the little girl down at Twin Bridges. Hell, I had to threaten him with a shotgun to keep him from it. Another time, we was walking through the woods going to the cave by the cellar when we came upon this clearing, and there was a small house with a woman hanging out clothes. We didn't see her until we were already in the clearing, and we had to run back in the woods. We sat there panting and looking at the woman hang the clothes out. I looked over at Gene and he was looking real strange at her. He looked over at me with a wild look in his eyes and said, 'We might as well go ahead and rape her now. There's no one else around. There's no reason not to.' I told Gene that this was bullshit, and we wasn't going to rape anyone. Gene turned back toward the woman and stared and sulked. In a little while, the woman went back into the house and we left. She'll never know how close she came to being a victim."

"Was Hart content to stay in the woods?" Cookerly asked.

"Sure," Dry said, becoming much more relaxed and talking to Limke and Cookerly as if they were old friends. "Hart's at home there. He don't need nothing else, except maybe sex. He likes to wood carve and is happiest when there is a piece of wood and a knife in his hands. Gene knows that his complexion makes him blend into the general Indian population. You know, one time ole Gene was standing in Spring Creek down by Camp Scott fishing when a sheriff's patrol car pulled up and asked him if he caught anything. Gene turned his back and told the deputy no and kept right on fishing."

"How did you and Gene get around at night in the woods? Did you use flashlights?"

"Yeah," answered Dry.

"Weren't you afraid someone would see the light and call the police?" Limke asked.

"Now, you see, we would cover the lens with plastic off a trash bag and cut a little hole in the plastic so only a small amount of light would come out. Shoot, you can walk almost anywhere without getting caught with a light like that."

Limke looked at Cookerly, who returned his glance. Limke went on, "Larry, how did you attach the plastic to the lens?"

"With tape or rubber bands," responded the young Indian.

"Did Hart ever have any pictures with him?" asked Limke.

"Yes, he had those that was in the newspaper," answered Dry. "I recognized them when I first saw them. He had them with him all the time we were in the woods. One of the women in the pictures looked like his wife. Boy, he wanted to kill her for divorcing him and changing his kid's name. Boy, that's when Gene would get strange. He'd start talking about his kid and his old lady and really get violent. I think he hated everyone else's kids because he didn't know his. You know, I think he killed that Martinez kid in Vinita. I got an anonymous letter a couple of months ago—I know it was from Gene. It said that if I help the cops my kid would wind up like the Martinez kid."

Limke was skeptical of the last revelation. "Where is the letter now?" he asked.

"My wife has them in Salina," Dry replied.

"We'll want those," Limke said, staring at Dry, who was again staring at the floor. "Now then, back to the woods; what did you do for cooking utensils?"

"We had a bunch of tin cups, pans, and a coffee pot. Some of the stuff we stole, some were given to us by Annie Ballew, Hart's relative. We carried this stuff with us from cave to cave. Water never was a problem because of the creeks, ponds, and wells around there. Every now and then we would have to take water from a dirty pond, but when we did we'd boil it in the coffee pot."

"What was your eating schedule?" Cookerly asked, fishing for anything.

"Well, we just eat when we's hungry. Usually we'd eat the evening meal at Annie and Bo Ballew's house. The way we'd get there without getting caught was simple. We'd just lay up there on the side of the hill the better part of the day and watch the house. If nothin' suspicious happened, we'd go on down and join the Ballews and eat a real good meal. We'd spend the rest of the evening just talking, smoking, and socializing. Almost all of Gene's relatives knew where we were hiding and knew where the meeting place was and would help us whenever we needed it."

"Did you all ever pick up tape or rope during your adventures?" asked Limke.

"Yeah, we always needed tape and had all kinds and shapes and sizes like adhesive tape, masking tape, and electrical tape. We used the tape and cord when we could find it to tie the bundles we were carrying."

"What kind of tools did you use in your burglaries, and how did you break into these places?" questioned Limke.

"The only burglary tools we had was a screwdriver we used to pry up windows and pry open doors. To keep from leaving fingerprints we took off our socks and put them over our hands."

Limke and Cookerly listened intently as the interview continued for over three hours. Dry was questioned about every aspect of his relationship with Hart. As the interview was being concluded Limke said, "Well, Larry, do you want to help catch Gene Leroy Hart?"

Without a pause, Dry said in his best command voice, "Yes, but we must do it my way. I will say where we go and who we should talk to. I cannot be questioned about what we're doing or the methods used."

Cookerly watched Limke's face redden, knowing the young convict was about to receive his first lesson.

"Listen, stud," Limke began, his voice becoming cold as he pointed his finger across the desk a few inches from Dry's nose. "Let's get something straight. You're not leading anyone and you don't have a final say-so on any decision. If you get out of the joint to help us find Hart, you'll be directly under OSBI supervision and you will do exactly as you're told. We'll listen to your suggestions, but the final decisions will be ours. Now if you don't like this, we'll ship your ass back to the joint right now."

Cookerly was smiling as he watched Dry's demeanor change from cockiness to a quick understanding of the situation.

Limke was not finished. "And one other thing let's get straight. If at any time you don't follow orders, two things will happen. That big sucker sitting behind you will kick your ass all over greater Mayes County, and you'll be back in Granite before dark. Do we understand each other, Mr. Dry?"

"Yes," Dry said sheepishly.

"Do you want to help us then?" Limke asked, lowering his voice to a normal decibel.

"Yes, sir," Dry said softly.

Limke looked at the man sitting in front of him. Lord help us if we ever have to use this guy as a witness, he thought to himself. Dry's very mannerisms made him appear to be the stereotyped liar. By covering his mouth and refusing to look anyone in the eye, he appeared less than credible, to say the least. But at least part of the story had the ring of truthfulness in it. Limke knew that Dry was only telling the story in order to get out of prison. He knew that Dry realized that if he made a conscientious effort to find Hart, chances were good that he would be paroled. The possibility that Dry would escape seemed remote. Two things stood in his way: he only had a few months to serve and Sid Cookerly was watching him.

Limke walked back to the Deputy Director's office and told Dick Wilkerson to get Dry released to the OSBI. The Governor was contacted and a thirty-day furlough from Granite was arranged. Cookerly had some personal business to conclude in Las Vegas before the operation could be put in motion. But it appeared that Cookerly and Dry could be put together within a week. In the meantime Dry could take a bus to his home in Salina, Oklahoma, and stay there for a week without creating undue suspicion. To explain his presence he would simply tell the people that he got an earlier parole.

Within a week Dry was at home in Salina. He was to call Limke or Mike Wilkerson every day at 3:00 P.M. Failure to do so would mean that escape charges would be filed and a warrant issued for his arrest.

Dry had been in Mayes County for only a couple of days before he found trouble. There were two conflicting stories. Dry said that as he sat drinking beer in a local bar, two FBI agents came in and began to roust him. He claimed that they asked what he was doing out of prison. They offered to make him a paid informant and threatened him if he did not take the offer. The FBI's resident agent, however, when questioned by his supervisor, said that Dry had called him from the bar and told them to come to the bar to see him.

Already strained relations between the FBI and the OSBI were becoming more strained. Dick Wilkerson knew that one of two things had happened: either the FBI was trying to buy an OSBI informant, as they had a reputation for doing, or Dry was lying. Wilkerson chose to believe the latter. He reasoned that Dry had no money when he was released other than $20 given him by Limke. Dry may have figured that he could have the benefit of a state release from the penitentiary and federal money to spend. Wilkerson decided to have Dry returned to the reformatory at Granite.

Agents Larry Bowles and Roger Chrisco went to Dry's residence in Salina. Bowles told him what the FBI had said. Dry imitated righteous indignation and said, "Well, I see I can't work with you people. Why don't you just take me back and I'll do my time."

Immediately, he was handcuffed, searched, put in the car, and was en route to Granite. Dry knew that he had miscalculated and tried to engage the agents in idle conversation. Several times he said that he may have been hasty when he said he could not work with them.

The radio in the car crackled and a Highway Patrol dispatcher told Bowles to telephone OSBI Headquarters for Dick Wilkerson. Bowles stopped the car at a gas station and placed the telephone call. Wilkerson told him that the Governor had asked him to give Dry one more chance. Wilkerson asked Bowles what he thought and Bowles told him that Dry would love one more chance. In another half hour Dry was back at his residence.

Dry was given permission to start to work for a local contractor roofing houses. Some of the agents allowed themselves to believe that Dry would go straight this time, others were more pessimistic.

By April 6 the enthusiasm was dying. The task seemed almost impossible. Wilkerson met Bowles early that morning for coffee. Bowles had an idea. He said that he would ask his informant to call the Smiths' residence and tell Mrs. Smith he was a relative of Ella Mae's and was calling to warn her that several officers had just left Ella Mae's house in Locust Grove and were on their way to Sequoyah County to arrest Hart. The informant was then to tell her to go to the house where Hart was hiding and warn him to stay in the house to avoid detection. It was hoped that Eva Smith would have to make a snap decision without the aid of her husband who the informant said was working in Louisiana. Bowles suggested that an airplane be in the air enabling them to follow Mrs. Smith to Hart's hideout. The agents would have radio communication with the ground and they could move in at that time and make the arrest.

At 9:30 A.M. Don Sharp and Cary Thurman took off from the Tahlequah airport and a few minutes later were making a wide circle above the Smith residence. Ousley was on foot surveillance west of the Smith residence, and Agent Harvey Pratt was conducting vehicular surveillance east of the Smith residence. At 11:05 A.M. the informant called Eva Smith. He told her that he was a relative of Ella Mae Buckskin calling to warn her that several officers had left Locust Grove en route to Sequoyah County to arrest Gene Hart. He told Mrs. Smith to go to the residence where Hart was hiding and warn him. Mrs. Smith advised that Hart would be warned and not to mention any names or talk too long as someone might be listening on the party line.

Minutes passed—still no action. It was a long wait. An hour passed —still nothing. Two hours passed and still there was no movement at the Smith residence.

Mike Wilkerson called Oklahoma City at 1:00 A.M. to give them a status report. He told Limke and his brother that he thought Bowles and Pratt should go to the Smith residence, confront the woman with everything they knew about her and her husband, and generally bluff her into thinking that she was going to jail immediately. It was agreed that the time had come to bring the whole thing to a head. Mike Wilkerson hung up the phone, called Bowles, and told him of the plan.

CHAPTER 10

Larry Bowles walked slowly down the stairs of the OSBI Tahlequah office. This was it. All the eggs in one basket; all the work of the past several months could have been for nothing. He had just left Mike Wilkerson. At Wilkerson's insistence they had decided that it was time to move. He was to meet Harvey Pratt and they were going to confront the medicine man's wife with the information they had and hope she would give it up.

Bowles was scared. So much depended on his ability, his timing, his talent. As a young boy in eastern Oklahoma, he had had blind faith in the system. He had always believed that when a crime was committed that *they* would catch and punish the bad guy. *They* were some superhuman, almost sacred system that never made mistakes, that never blew it. Now *he* was in that position. What if the Smith woman clammed up? What if she said she didn't know what he was talking about? He would be helpless. Hart would know there was an informant and he would be no closer to catching him than he was the day of the homicides. He had always secretly hoped that the informant would call some night and say, "Hart is at so-and-so right now." No risk of missing him—no chance of a foul-up. He knew that the Smith woman was the best shot they had, but he was scared and he worried.

"Bureau 33—Bureau 54." Bowles monotoned into the microphone of his two-way radio.

"Bureau 54—Bureau 33, go ahead," came the response from the speaker on the floor of the Pontiac.

"I need to contact you, Roger. What's your 10-20?" Bowles said.

"I'm in the game refuge. I'll meet you at the gate," Agent Roger Chrisco's voice answered.

"Okay, in about ten minutes," Bowles said, and dropped the microphone onto the seat beside him. A few minutes later Bowles pulled to the side of the road at the main gate of the Cookson Hills Game Refuge. Chrisco was waiting for him in his personal pickup truck, an ancient yellow Chevrolet.

As Bowles heaved himself out of the car, Chrisco, in an old baseball cap and jeans, opened the door of the pickup and stepped to the ground. The only hint to his identity was the small walkie-talkie in his right hand. In his late twenties, a former juvenile officer and deputy sheriff, Chrisco still retained the boyish enthusiasm of a rookie. He had a round, cherubic face behind a perpetual smile, and showed a naiveté that made him the focal point of many good-natured barbs from the other agents.

"What's happening?" asked Chrisco.

"We're fixin' to take our best shot," Bowles answered wearily. After briefing Chrisco, the two agents traded vehicles in hopes that Bowles would be less conspicuous in the old pickup.

Bowles herded the old truck through the winding roads south of Tahlequah, trying to formulate some type of plan. How would he approach the Smith woman? What would he say? If he came on too strong she might clam up. If he didn't come on strong enough. . . . Oh, hell, Bowles thought, I'll play it by ear.

Marble City, what a joke, thought Bowles. A marble quarry in the middle of the Cookson Hills. Closest thing to a city was when some truck drivers met under one of those trees that's covered with marble dust to drink a beer.

A half-mile northwest of Marble City, Bowles met Harvey Pratt in the van. Pratt parked the van and slid in next to Bowles. Pratt asked Bowles if he thought this was the right time to approach the Smith woman. Bowles was tired of explaining—he had the same reservations as everyone else. "Oh, what the hell. It will be over one way or another today," replied Bowles. Either Hart would be caught, or they could go on about their business and wait for a break. At least the marathon would be over.

The two men rode the three miles to the Smith residence in silence. As they pulled in the driveway, Bowles was almost relieved. It appeared that no one was home. The two agents got out of their car and walked toward the fenced yard. They were greeted by two large dogs. Pratt's right hand instinctively slipped over his .357 revolver as Bowles talked quietly to the dogs while opening the gate.

"Anybody home?" Bowles shouted.

A figure, obscured by the screen door, appeared in the doorway. Bowles and Pratt produced their credentials and introduced themselves. A medium-sized woman in her late forties introduced herself as Mrs. William Smith as she opened the door and stepped out onto the porch. Bowles was surprised. This woman doesn't appear to be Indian at all, he thought. As the three sat down on the porch, Bowles began in a voice that could only be described as kind.

"Mrs. Smith, I'll get straight to the point with everything. I want to sit down and visit with you. Is Gene Hart at your house?"

"No, sir," she responded.

"Okay," Bowles continued. "Mrs. Smith, like I said, I'll get right to the point with you. I do know that you and your husband, William Lee, know where he is. I know that you got a telephone call this morning at 11:05. And, I know that Ella Mae Buckskin has been driven down here by her daughters to see you on several Saturday nights. This morning Hart's brother, Jimmy Buckskin, was indicted by the Federal Grand Jury and if you don't cooperate with me today, you and William could be next. I'm not interested in you, Mrs. Smith, or your husband. I don't want to interfere in your personal lives. I want you to keep living and stay happy the way you've been, but I want the man that killed those three little girls and you all are hiding him. We know all about you." Bowles's statements riddled her like a machine gun. "I know your maiden name is Pigeon. Your middle name is May. William Lee works in Louisiana for Kansas City Southern. He took two vacations last year. He's down there right now. He works ten-hour shifts, Tuesday through Friday."

Bowles paused, and with deliberate emphasis he said slowly, "And you did get a call this morning at 11:05 A.M."

"Yeah, somebody called me," Eva Smith said meekly.

"We want Gene Leroy Hart. If you and your husband can stand the embarrassment and the cost for attorneys, that's fine. I don't know where you would draw the line on helping someone. But I can't understand, you not being any relation or anything. Your only common denominator is that you're Indian. If I can get some cooperation out of you, you won't see me again. However, if you don't cooperate, the next time you see me it won't be in your best interest. I can assure you of that. We have been keeping a very close watch on you and our only interest in you is because you know where Gene

Hart is. We know you do. And if it's a game to you, I can assure you it has stopped being fun right now."

Not giving her an opportunity to respond, Bowles continued. "Let me tell you one more thing, that up to this point the three fathers of these little girls—they're pretty uptight. Even though it's been almost a year, they're still pretty uptight. One's a police officer, one's a doctor, and one's a businessman in Tulsa. They know that we know who the mediator is, or who Ella Mae's going through to send money and food to Gene. I can assure you if I leave here today without Gene Hart, by dark the parents will have your names. I know that a few weeks ago she brought some food items down on a Saturday night."

Bowles paused. He knew he was getting through. Mrs. Smith took a long draw from her cigarette and her chin trembled uncontrollably.

"I've got nothing to do with it myself," Eva Smith stammered.

She's breaking, Bowles thought. Just take it easy. Bowles's mind raced as she offered to let them search her home and as Pratt assured her Hart would eventually be caught anyway.

Bowles's attention was once again centered on the middle-aged woman as her voice grew husky. "Let me say, I don't . . . I mean, you know," she began. "I've got nothing to do with this. But, if you keep my name out of it, I could tell you where he's at."

Bowles suppressed a cheer. Oh, honey, I love you. I'd promise you anything, Bowles thought, his outward appearance still calm as he heard himself say quietly, almost casually, "Okay, I will keep your name out of it. As far as I'm concerned, William Lee won't even know anything about it. If he finds out, it will be because you tell him."

"It's not around here. He's close to Tahlequah somewheres," she sighed.

"Now you know exactly where. Where is he?" Bowles demanded.

"Yeah, but, like I said . . ." she began.

"Who's house is he in?" Bowles asked.

"It's an old man's house. The old man he stays with doesn't know who he is, I don't guess," she mused.

"Yeah, we're sure of that. He doesn't know." Bowles was impatient.

"The school kids will be home about a quarter to four. I'll write them a note and you just follow me over there. I'll drive real slow, and I'm just going to circle around, and I'm going to tell you where to go. Okay? I'll just motion. I'm pretty sure that's where he's still staying. That's where he was last time I heard."

Eva Smith explained that Hart had been staying with an old man named Sam Pigeon, who lived out in the sticks eight or nine miles south of Tahlequah.

With Pratt accompanying her, Mrs. Smith went inside to write her children a note while Bowles went to the pickup and contacted the airplane. "Advise all units we have the information desired. Meet six miles south of Tahlequah."

Bowles was excited. Excited and scared. Just a little luck now, with all the hard work. Just a little luck.

Bowles's thoughts were invaded by Agent Bud Ousley's voice emitting from the walkie-talkie in Bowles's hand. Ousley had been conducting surveillance from the woods across the road since that morning.

"Come on in, Bud," Bowles whispered into the radio. "Let's go get him."

Ousley emerged from the brush a few minutes later. An ex-Oakland, California, police officer with a master's degree, he had only recently returned to his native Oklahoma. He smiled as he tripped and almost fell in the brush. "The streets of San Francisco were never like this."

With Mrs. Smith driving her own pickup and Bowles, Pratt, and Ousley following, they began the trek back toward Tahlequah. Northwest of Marble City Bowles slowed his vehicle long enough for Ousley to jump out. He would retrieve the van and follow them to Ballew's store.

Mike Wilkerson stabbed the gas pedal as he entered a sharp curve on Highway 82 south of Tahlequah. Fifteen minutes before, he had been relayed the message, via the airplane, from Bowles. He knew that Bowles either knew where Hart was or already had him in custody. The eternity that had been spent on the case now seemed worthwhile. He tried to suppress his enthusiasm. Don't get too high and you won't have so far to come down, he told himself. As he approached Ballew's store at the intersection of Highway 82 and Marble City Road, he saw Bowles leaning against the yellow Chevy pickup. As he slid to a stop next to the pickup, Bowles was smiling and his face was flushed.

"The snitch was right on, Mike. I sent Harvey and Bud with the Smith woman to recon the place and make diagrams," Bowles blurted out as the dust from Wilkerson's sliding stop encircled him.

Wilkerson got out of his vehicle and the two agents stood in front of the old store as Bowles recounted Smith's revelations.

"We better call Oklahoma City," Wilkerson said as he started toward a phone booth next to the entrance to the store. His finger trembled as he dialed headquarters.

"It's Mike. He wants all of you on the phone," shouted Kathie Blackmon through the open door of the Director's office.

Dick Wilkerson and Ted Limke scrambled from their chairs, running to their respective offices a few feet away as Director Tom Kennedy spun around in his chair. As Dick Wilkerson passed the secretary's desk, Kathie excitedly asked, "Dick, can I stay on the line?"

"Yeah," Wilkerson answered, never breaking stride. The suspense in the headquarter's office of the OSBI had been terrific. The waiting, the anticipation, the curiosity, had been all but unbearable. For everyone, from the secretaries to the Director, it had been the same.

Mike Wilkerson heard several clicks as every telephone receiver in the front office was picked up. "Is everyone there?" he asked. A jumbled affirmative reply of familiar voices answered him. "Yeah." "Go ahead." "We're here."

Mike Wilkerson tried to control his voice. "We know where he is. What we need now is an administrative decision. Do you want us to take him down or do you want to wait until you can get the whole world down here?"

Again the jumbled voices, "Take him." "Hell, no." "Do it!"

Mike Wilkerson heard his brother say, "Mike, don't kill him unless you have to, but he can't get away."

"If he tries to run, blow him away," the Director added.

"Mike, you guys be careful," Limke interjected.

"Okay. I'll let you know as soon as I can," Mike said as he hung up the phone.

As Wilkerson and Bowles walked back toward their vehicles, Roger Chrisco slid Bowles's blue Pontiac next to them. Wilkerson tried to collect his thoughts. "How many guys have we got?" he asked.

"Five on the ground," Bowles answered.

"Roger, get that damn plane down. We need Sharp and Thurman," Wilkerson ordered.

"What's happening?" Chrisco asked, bewildered.

"We're going to get Hart. Have the plane land wherever it can," Wilkerson repeated.

As Chrisco lifted the microphone to his lips, Wilkerson and

Bowles turned back toward their vehicles. "Larry, it's your information. Set up the arrest any way you want," Wilkerson said.

"Let's get a Coke and talk about it," Bowles said as he started toward the store. He knew he had to come down from his adrenaline high before he could think straight.

Large sales volume, Bowles thought as he noticed a thick layer of dust on the sacks of potato chips and bread.

"Ma'am, could we park our cars here for a while?" Wilkerson asked.

The gray-haired middle-aged woman sitting behind the cash register smiled and said, "Sure," as Bowles opened a soft drink bottle with a beer opener secured to the counter by a thick, dirty string. "You boys goin' to take the bottles?" she asked.

Wilkerson smiled. They were about to leave $12,000 in automobiles as collateral for two pop bottles.

"We'll pay for them," Bowles laughed as he handed her a dollar bill. Directly over the woman's head was the largest rattlesnake skin Bowles had ever seen; over six feet long and one foot wide. "That must have been some snake," Bowles thought out loud.

"Oh, he was a big one," said the woman. "An Indian man down the road killed him with a hoe in his strawberry patch about fifteen years ago." The woman was a talker and wanted to visit. The two agents inched toward the door, trying to excuse themselves as she talked about the snake and the weather.

Wilkerson heard a car outside. "Must be our people. Nice talking to you, ma'am," he said as he and Bowles jammed in the doorway in an attempt to get away from their garrulous new friend.

Chrisco, Sharp, and Thurman leaped out of the car. Bowles relayed in detail what Smith had told him. "Get your stuff together so we'll be ready when they get back," Bowles suggested.

The five men collected their shotguns and bulletproof vests from the cars and reassembled. A tentative plan was drafted, subject to the information received from the reconnaissance. The five men waited anxiously. Don Sharp, an attorney and ex-FBI agent formerly stationed in New York, smiled at the thought of trying to explain to his New York friends about the Cookson Hills.

It was now close to 3:00 P.M. Cary Thurman saw the blue Dodge van approaching them from the north on Highway 82. "Here they come!" he shouted excitedly. As the van pulled to a stop the five men clustered around it. As Ousley began describing the layout, Wilkerson noticed the Smith woman walking toward her pickup. "Where's she going?" he asked.

"She's going home," Pratt answered. "She's got children coming home in a few minutes. She won't contact anyone. There's no phone where Hart is."

"Bullshit," said Wilkerson. "She's not going any place. We're not taking any chances. She's coming with us."

While Bowles broke the bad news to Mrs. Smith, the other agents squeezed into the rear of the van. Harvey Pratt, with a large drawing pad on which he had sketched a map of the area, began his briefing.

"The house—or it's really just a shack—sits on a hill. The main road going by the house has a turnoff that a car can get through," Pratt said as he indicated the spot on the map. "There is an old logging road rougher than hell that passes right in front of the house. You can't see the house from the main road at all."

It was decided that the van with five agents and Mrs. Smith would go to the back of the house while Chrisco, Wilkerson, and Agent Jack Lay—who was on his way to meet them—would cover the front. The house would be assaulted from both the front and rear with one agent covering either side. It was believed that since the house was surrounded by trees, if the agents moved quickly enough, Hart should not have time to get out of the house. Wilkerson told the agents what the Director had said and they nodded their approval.

"Let's get it on," Wilkerson said as he turned toward his car.

Bud Ousley turned the van north on 82 with Bowles sitting on the passenger side. Pratt, Thurman, and Sharp squatted behind them, with Mrs. Smith sitting sullenly to their rear. Mike Wilkerson, driving Bowles's beefed-up Pontiac, followed with Chrisco. They drove slowly, 40 to 45 mph, north on Highway 82 to the junction of Highway 100. Turning east on 100, they continued for a couple of miles. As Ousley slowed to approximately 15 mph to turn onto a blacktopped road, the shrill scream of tires broke the silence. As the screeching continued, the agents jockeyed for position in order to determine its origin. A cloud of dark blue smoke floated 50 feet in the air past Wilkerson's vehicle as he made the turn. From the thick smoke, a light blue Pontiac, sliding precariously sideways, emerged. Agent Jack Lay had arrived.

Wilkerson laughed nervously as Lay's voice drawled casually from the radio. "What have you got going?"

Lay had been told only to meet them south of Tahlequah as soon as possible.

"You know what we've been working on?" Bowles asked, trying to maintain some type of radio security.

"I think so," Lay answered. "What do you want me to do?"

"Stay with me," Wilkerson interjected. "Go in the front with me."

After traveling approximately three miles on the blacktopped road, Wilkerson keyed his microphone. "How much farther is it, Larry?"

"We're not even halfway," Bowles answered. "When we get close, I'll point at the driveway you're to take."

Just one shot, Wilkerson thought. That's all we get. What if the bastard is not there, maybe out hunting or something? Wilkerson worried. Should he call off the raid and take a chance on putting some agents on foot to watch the house until they saw Hart? What if they were spotted? The decision had been made, but what if they missed him? What if he got an agent killed because he hadn't taken more time? Why did he ever take this chickenshit Inspector's job anyway?

They were getting close now. Bowles leaned forward in his seat, cradling the .12-gauge riot gun between his knees and holding the radio microphone in his left hand. Ousley nudged the van faster. Bowles spoke into the microphone, "Mike, get ready. Your road is coming up."

The van shot past a small trail as Bowles thrust his right arm out the window. "There, Mike, there," Bowles's voice shouted over the radio.

Wilkerson accelerated the Pontiac and the glass-pack muffler roared as it shifted into a lower gear, tires spinning up the steep hill. Large rocks beat the bottom of the car and Wilkerson heard the muffler tear loose as it bounced and bumped up the hill. As he glanced in his rearview mirror, he could see Lay's car close behind. The van was going up a similar trail approximately 25 yards to his left. Out of nowhere, a small shack jumped into view. Wilkerson spun the wheel to the left and slid up to the side of the shack as Lay's car turned immediately in front. As they jumped out of their cars, they could see the agents running up toward the rear of the house. Wilkerson heard Bowles shout, "Halt or we'll shoot."

"Halt!" another agent screamed.

There was someone in the house. They knew that now. Lay was sprinting toward the front door as the other agents established a perimeter around the house. Without breaking stride, it seemed, Lay's kick splintered open the front door. "Freeze!" he shouted.

Wilkerson was in the door a split second later. Both shotguns were trained on a hefty Indian man who did not immediately come to a halt.

"Do you want to die today?" Lay growled, sighting down the barrel of the .12-gauge. "I said freeze!"

Chrisco was now at the front door.

"Put your hands on your head and turn around toward the wall," Lay commanded. The man did as he was told. As Lay slipped the first handcuff on his left wrist, the man began to struggle. Chrisco stepped over, put the shotgun to the man's head, and told him to stop. The handcuffing completed, Wilkerson ran out the front door and told the agents to move up to the back of the house, that they had someone in custody. As he returned to the front, Lay had led the man out and laid him on the ground in the front yard.

"Is there anybody else in the house?" Wilkerson heard an agent shout.

"Is there anybody else in the house?" he asked the man on the ground. There was no response. "We don't want to harm anyone, dammit, we want to know if anybody's in the house," he repeated.

"There's nobody in the house," the man answered.

Cary Thurman had entered through the back door along with Don Sharp and cleared the house. As he walked out the front door and saw the man prone on the ground, he asked, "Who's he?"

"Who's he? Where in the hell have you been?" Wilkerson laughed. "Who have we been looking for? That's Gene Leroy Hart."

Wilkerson bent down and addressed the young Indian on the ground. "Are you Gene Leroy Hart?" There was no response. "Are you Gene Leroy Hart?"

"I didn't kill those little girls," Hart answered.

"We'll see," Wilkerson said.

The agents were delirious—some on the point of tears. They shook hands, patted one another on the back.

Mike Wilkerson turned to Larry Bowles, his friend and partner for over five years. "One hell of a job, partner. One hell of a job.

"Somebody get a camera," Wilkerson yelled.

Bowles heaved Hart to his feet and stood him before the entourage of agents and the picture-taking began.

Wilkerson grinned. "This looks like the safari documenting its trophies."

There was something barbaric about it, something very unprofessional, but something very gratifying.

Hart was dressed in a tank top with cutoff shorts and hightopped shoes. He had gained thirty to forty pounds since he had last been seen, weighing in the neighborhood of two hundred thirty to two hundred forty pounds and did not seem to carry the weight well. The distracting thing, however, about his appearance was that he wore a pair of women's horn-rimmed glasses that tapered to a sharp point on either side.

Wilkerson took a quick walk through the house and noticed the barbells where Hart had apparently tried to keep himself in shape. There were no waffle-soled shoes.

As he walked out of the door the picture-taking was still going on.

"Let's get Hart out of here. Somebody in Oklahoma City will want to know about this," Wilkerson shouted.

The agents whooped and screamed at the thought of headquarters finding out what they had accomplished. Thurman and Chrisco were told to stay at the house and to arrest anyone who came there. Bowles, Sharp, Wilkerson, and Hart went in one car, with Wilkerson driving.

As Bowles ushered Hart toward the vehicle, Hart growled in a low voice, "You son-of-a-bitch. You or the OSBI will never pin those murders on me."

Bowles bristled. "Get your ass in the car while you've still got an ass," Bowles said through clenched teeth.

As the engine of the Pontiac came to life, Wilkerson began laughing. It sounded like a truck. Turning to Bowles, who was sitting in the back seat with Hart and Sharp, he said, "Well, Larry, I'm glad this is your car and not mine." Bowles laughed. He couldn't have cared less.

The twenty-minute drive back to Tahlequah was made for the most part in silence. Wilkerson asked Hart once if the handcuffs were cutting him. Hart acted indifferent, as if he didn't hear. On the outskirts of Tahlequah they stopped at a cafe and Wilkerson called Oklahoma City.

"Put the world on the phone," he said, trying to control his voice.

Dick Wilkerson, Tom Kennedy, and Ted Limke were on the phone. To the tune of "You've Got to Have Heart," Wilkerson sang, "We've got Gene Hart." There was a long pause. He heard someone in the background let out a cheer.

"Are you sure it's him?" Mike heard his brother ask.

"Hell, yes, it's him. He answers to his name like a dog. There's no doubt in my mind."

"Take one fingerprint. Let Harvey compare it to his card. We've got to be sure," Dick said. "Where'd you get him?"

"Somewhere over in Adair County," Mike answered. "I'll get the exact location when we get back to the office. I just stopped to call and let you know we have got him."

"Okay, but get the fingerprint," Mike heard his brother repeat.

Inspector Al Abernathy dialed the access code for the PA system for the entire OSBI office in Oklahoma City. "At 3:30 this afternoon, agents of the OSBI arrested Gene Leroy Hart."

It was the Fourth of July, New Year's Eve, the Mardi Gras—pandemonium reigned. Papers were flying, people were screaming, crying. It had been a long time coming. To be exact, the OSBI fugitive investigation had taken almost eleven months, with every agent at one time or another working on the case. Total uncompensated overtime for this period was in excess of 10,000 hours. It is estimated that well over two million dollars was expended by all agencies on Hart's capture.

CHAPTER II

"Dick," Mike Wilkerson said, "Pratt just took a fingerprint from the suspect and he is Gene Leroy Hart."

"Fantastic!" Dick exclaimed, his number-one worry laid to rest. "Has anyone called Pete Weaver?"

"Yeah, I called his office and talked to the under-sheriff. Pete's had a cow die and he's out at his ranch taking care of it. There's no phone so they sent a man out to give him the word. Al Boyer asked if we could wait a while before taking Hart back to the joint. I told him I'd wait. Is that all right?" asked Mike.

"No problem. Pete deserves to see him in custody." As an afterthought, Dick continued. "Ask him if he would like to help you all transport him back to McAlester."

"By the way," Mike began, "Boyer wanted to put Hart in the Mayes County Jail tonight. He thought there might be some legal problems about prompt arraignment."

"Bullshit. Don't worry about arraignment," Dick said. "The Governor has put a plane on standby to transport Hart back and forth from the penitentiary. He is an escaped convict and he'll be returned to the joint like any convict. By the way, where is Hart now?"

"He's in the next room talking to Ousley and Sharp about playing football and lifting weights. Oh yeah," Mike continued, "Hart told a Mayes County deputy a while ago that he didn't *think* he had killed those little girls but he thought he could find out who did. I believe this turkey is schizoid."

"Three Faces of Eve, huh?" Dick mused. In the background Dick could hear someone acknowledge Pete Weaver's arrival.

"Dick, Pete just got here. Tell the Director that Hart will be in the penitentiary in two hours," Mike said in his best official voice.

Turning around in his chair, he was greeted by the pale smiling face of Pete Weaver.

"Where's he at?" asked Weaver. Wilkerson pointed toward the door leading into the next room. Weaver opened the door, smiled, and quietly said, "Hello, Gene."

"Hi, Sheriff," Hart responded.

Really a lot of danger here, Wilkerson thought. If his family and the newspapers could have seen what had taken place today, they would know how ridiculous it was to think that these officers would shoot Hart on sight. Every agent had had an opportunity and a legal reason to kill Hart. When Hart tried to run out the back door, the agents could have legally shot him under Oklahoma's fleeing felon law. The agents who ordered Hart to freeze could have legally shot him for his refusal to immediately obey. And Pete Weaver is almost acting paternal toward him. So much for storm trooper tactics. Wilkerson's reflections broke off as Bowles walked into the room and said, "Mike, we're ready to go. Are you coming?"

"No," Wilkerson replied. "I think you've got enough help. I want you, Ousley, and Sharp with Hart. Shackle him hand and foot." Bowles turned toward the door.

"By the way, Larry," Mike said, smiling, "when you get to the prison, park in the parking lot just to the left of the guard gate and walk him to the entrance. Don't pull up in front. Those reporters won't have a chance to see their hero."

Bowles nodded his approval as he stepped through the door.

The OSBI in Oklahoma City had held a news conference and told of Hart's capture. All of the phone lines into the Tahlequah office began ringing almost simultaneously and on each line was a reporter wanting to know all about the capture. Wilkerson grew tired of talking and put all of the lines on hold as he heard someone running up the stairs. It was Chemist Dennis Reimer.

Out of breath and panting, Reimer said, "Mike, they said you caught Hart."

"That's right, partner," Wilkerson said, smiling proudly.

"Can I do anything to help?" Reimer asked.

"Matter of fact you can, Dennis. Why don't you go out to the Pigeon residence and help Chrisco search that place. He's going to try to get permission from Sam Pigeon. He's waiting there now. You know what is of forensic value and what we're looking for." Wilkerson quickly sketched a crude map with directions to the Pigeon residence and Reimer scrambled down the stairs.

In a few moments the old wood stairs again announced the arrival of visitors. Jack Lay and Cary Thurman had arrested Sam Pigeon and his brother Freeman Pigeon.

"Mike," Thurman began, "we were waiting there at the house like you told us and Freeman comes walking up. He says that he knew Hart was staying there. Sam says the same thing. So we've brought them both in."

"Good work. You take Sam in and question him, and Jack, you take Freeman and get a good statement from him. I'll decide what to do with them when you get through."

Sam Pigeon was a short, heavyset Cherokee who stood about five feet five inches and weighed approximately two hundred and five pounds. He was about fifty-five years old, but looked much older. He wore faded overalls and an old work cap. He was employed by a local plant nursery and was considered an excellent worker. Thurman knew that he would have to talk slowly and without aggressiveness or the old Cherokee would simply not talk at all.

The agent and the old man seated themselves at a desk in an adjoining office. After Thurman got the usual biographical information and gave Pigeon his Miranda warning, he asked, "Mr. Pigeon, who first approached you to take Gene into your home?"

"Smith," the old man replied without hesitation.

"Where did you first see Smith? Did he come to your home?"

Pigeon leaned forward, his elbows on his knees. "No, I met him at powwow ground near Smith's house in Marble City," Pigeon answered in a heavy Cherokee accent.

Thurman chose his words carefully. "What did he ask you?"

"Smith say to take care of Drum," the old man said flatly.

"Drum?" Thurman was confused. "Who is Drum?"

"Drum is Gene. Gene is Drum," explained Pigeon.

Thurman shrugged his shoulders and continued. "When did Gene come to your house and how did he get there, Mr. Pigeon?"

"Before the snow flew," the old man answered. "They come after sun go down in Smith's truck. Medicine man say to take care of Drum. He say that he will send money and food sometime."

Before the snow flew? Thurman thought. Late summer? Fall? Oh well. Thurman went on. "How long did Smith stay?"

Pigeon leaned back in his chair, looked thoughtfully toward the ceiling, and said, "About half-hour."

"Did Smith ever send money?"

"Yes. Him send fifty dollars about a week later."

"Did Hart say anything about the murders?"

Pigeon seemed bored as he nodded his head. "We were eating at the table one night and I ask why law wanted him. He say that laws say he kill three girls in Locust Grove and that he had to get out of there because everybody knows him. I ask if he killed girls, he say no."

"What did Hart do while he lived with you?"

"Him hunt, chop wood, clean house, make meals. Him good man."

"Now then, Mr. Pigeon, why did you hide this man when you knew it was against the law?"

The old man seemed surprised as he explained to Thurman as if he were a child, "Smith say to hide Drum. I hide Drum."

Thurman shook his head. Hiding Hart was not against the law to the old Cherokee. His medicine man had told him to hide the fugitive and that made it all right. There was white man's law and there was Indian's law.

Freeman Pigeon possessed the same almost childlike innocence as his brother. Freeman told Lay that Smith had come to his residence during the fall of 1977 to administer medicine to his wife, who had an inflamed knee. The medicine man told Freeman that he had brought Gene Hart to his brother's house to stay for a while. Freeman never questioned the medicine man about Hart nor asked whether he was guilty or innocent. From time to time Freeman would see Hart cutting wood or hunting squirrel behind the house. On one occasion he asked Hart if he had killed the Girl Scouts and Hart said that he had not. That was good enough for Freeman.

Lay stepped into Wilkerson's office and said, "Mike, these are simple men. They're not going anywhere. They've lived and worked in the same area all their lives. Let's not put them in jail. They've never been in jail in their lives. If we're going to arrest them, let's do it with a warrant." Lay stammered, searching for the words. "At least that will give them an opportunity to get lawyers so they can get bailed out right away."

Wilkerson nodded. "I don't think a damn thing can be served by putting 'em in jail tonight." Wilkerson stepped into the adjoining office and put his hand on Sam Pigeon's shoulder. "Mr. Pigeon, Agent Lay is going to take you and Freeman home now. Get a good night's sleep and we will talk to you tomorrow."

Sam Pigeon looked puzzled, then smiled. Freeman Pigeon nodded. "Thank you," he said.

Sam Pigeon's home was a three-room tar-paper shack. It looked to Roger Chrisco like a piece of true Americana. He had not believed that people still lived in shacks like the one he was walking through. He and Dennis Reimer had searched every inch of the shack and taken anything that looked like it might be of probative value. The house was littered with hundreds of items that could have been possible evidence. It was an awesome responsibility to choose what would be taken and Chrisco worried. They had stripped the beds for possible semen samples and hair follicles. They had taken several plastic bags, a hammer, items of clothing, and anything else that looked like it could have been taken from the Girl Scout camp.

The bedroom of the house had no dresser or chest for clothes, but rather an old icebox stood against the wall filled with old clothes, camping equipment, and dozens of other articles. On top of the icebox sat an old shaving kit that contained a rusty razor and blades, a small corncob pipe, and numerous other pieces of junk. Chrisco bagged and tagged the items that seemed to be of possible value. After a couple of hours the search had been completed, but Chrisco worried. Had he missed something?

Little of the evidence against Gene Hart had been released to the media. Since early in the investigation the OSBI had kept a tight lid on all of the evidence. The news media knew nothing about the similarities between the rapes of the women and the savage violation of the Girl Scouts. The OSBI never tried their cases in the news media. They were very cognizant that any unnecessary disclosures could result in undue prejudicial pretrial publicity, making it impossible for Hart to get a fair trial. There was speculation that there was no evidence at all against the young Indian. One Locust Grove resident said, "In a way, I'm glad he got caught. Now we'll find out if they've really got anything on him." Locust Grove was filled with reporters. Cameras were set up in pool halls and bars, and people were stopped on the street and asked their opinion of Hart. He was consistently referred to as a "full-blooded Cherokee," a "football star," and a "football hero." One newspaper headline screamed, "Townspeople Still Think Their Football Star Is Innocent. Locust Grove's Beliefs Unshaken."

"You know," Bowles once observed, "you'd think that out of the

1,500 residents in Locust Grove, a reporter would run across one person who'd say, 'Gene Hart is a punk,' or 'I believe he did it.' It's funny that they can't run across some of these people because I do every day."

If the media ever interviewed anyone with negative feelings toward Hart, it was never reported. Statements that seemed to depict Hart as an All-American celebrity were commonplace. The comments reported usually went no deeper than "Boy, poor ole Gene sure has put on weight," and "He sure could hit hard when we played football together," and "I think he was framed."

The Director of the OSBI denied that there had been an informant in the case. "There have been people who have given us information, but the reward will go unclaimed," he promised. Kennedy was unaware that Bowles had already promised his informant the reward.

To people outside of northeastern Oklahoma it might seem impossible that Hart could have stayed hidden for five years in an area of perhaps twenty-five square miles; but the natives were not surprised that he had remained in the area rather than go to another state. The Cookson Hills are a perfect hideout. The white people in the area are noted for their clannishness and the Indians rarely communicated with non-Indians. The terrain is rugged and beautiful. The crystal-clear lakes and streams are filled with fish and wild game abounds. Roads and trails are few, and even where there are roads they twist and turn and branch off into log and cattle trails.

Hart was a man of the woods. He relied little upon modern transportation. He was an accomplished hunter and fisherman. He had brothers, half-brothers, half-sisters, half-aunts, quarter-cousins, great half-uncles and aunts, and people who were just "kin." Incredibly, he had two hundred and fifty relatives living in a half-mile-square area. In short, he was the perfect fugitive for the area.

All of the Indians had migrated from Georgia and all of them seemed to be related. Most of the relatives were more than willing to hide Hart.

Before statehood, the hanging judge, Isaac Parker, drew most of his badmen fugitives from this area. Parker's court was only about sixty miles away at Fort Smith and was the only deterrent to lawbreakers for over twenty-one years. Of the 14,000 cases that Parker tried, the vast majority came out of this area. Outlaws such as Belle Starr, Rufus Buck, and Ned Christie were pursued into the Cookson Hills by great marshals such as Heck Thomas and Bill Tilghman.

During the earlier thirties, after the old West and the cowboy had died out, the Cookson Hills remained a hiding place for other colorful, more modern-day killers and robbers. It was the childhood home of Pretty Boy Floyd. Floyd remained at large for years in the area because friends and relatives were so tightlipped that he was able to walk around almost as freely as any other citizen. Floyd was looked upon as a hero, a modern-day Robin Hood who dared to fight the establishment. It was the era of the dust bowl, the depression, bank closings, and mortgage foreclosures; but to the Cookson Hills people, Floyd fought their frustrations. He robbed banks and legend has it that he paid off mortgages for some of the locals. Floyd was a killer but he never bothered anyone in the Cookson Hills. His brother served as Sheriff of Sequoyah County for over twenty years.

In the early 1930s approximately a thousand lawmen and national guardsmen surrounded the area and arrested twenty fugitives.

The land that had hidden Ned Christie, Pretty Boy Floyd, Rufus Buck, and Belle Starr had added another name to its infamous history—that of Gene Leroy Hart.

The day after the capture, Bowles consulted John Russell, District Attorney for Cherokee, Adair, Wagoner, and Sequoyah counties, about issuing an arrest warrant for Sam Pigeon on charges of Harboring a Fugitive.

Russell and the OSBI had a strained relationship. A couple of years before, Russell had been investigated by a Sallisaw Grand Jury for Soliciting a Bribe. OSBI Agent Jack Lay had conducted the initial investigation. The animosity that was created by the investigation resulted in an altercation between Russell and Lay outside of the Grand Jury Room which concluded with Assistant District Attorney John Butler firing a pistol into the ceiling of the courthouse.

Russell reluctantly issued the arrest warrant for Sam Pigeon. Bowles had decided to wait until he talked to William Smith before asking that a warrant be issued for him.

Hart was returned to Pryor the following day for arraignment. A court order was obtained for saliva, blood, and hair samples. Collected by chemists Janice Davis and Dennis Reimer at the local Pryor hospital, the evidence was transported to the lab in Oklahoma City. An analysis of Hart's blood confirmed that he had Type O. An examination of the saliva proved that Hart was indeed a secretor.

Ann Reed, OSBI forensic chemist specializing in hair comparison, said that hair taken from Hart's head matched exactly the hair found on the tape used to bind Doris Milner's hands. It was also her opinion that Hart's hair had the same characteristics as that found at Cave Number 2, where the canned goods were found.

As far as the Attorney General's Office, Sid Wise, and the OSBI could determine, there had never been a search warrant issued for sperm. Obtaining a seminal fluid sample was relatively easy. It required only a massage of the prostate gland. The only means, however, to obtain a sperm sample was to require the subject to masturbate and save the ejaculate, or to have him manually stimulated by another party, or for actual intercourse to take place. Various affidavits and search warrants were drafted and given to Wise in preparation for obtaining the consent to perform the masturbation. The OSBI located a urologist in Oklahoma City who said he would be willing to take the sample.

Meanwhile, Mike Wilkerson had contacted Bowles in Tahlequah and told him to go to a local store and buy several pairs of underwear. Wilkerson wanted to see that Hart got a clean pair of underwear every day. He felt that sooner or later Hart would either masturbate or have a nocturnal emission and a sperm sample could be procured.

Hart was transferred back to Mayes County Jail where he could more readily consult with his attorneys. The new underwear was taken, still in the plastic wrapper, to Pete Weaver at the Mayes County Jail. Weaver supplied new sheets for Hart's bed every day.

"Hello," Weaver said, shaking attorney Larry Oliver's hand. "How have you been?"

"Fine, Sheriff," Oliver answered. "I guess you know why I'm here. I've been asked by the family to defend Gene Hart." Oliver was a tall, ruggedly built Creek Indian. At forty-two years old he was a highly successful Tulsa attorney who had a flair for the spotlight and the success rate to keep him there. He was soft-spoken and friendly outside of the courtroom, but inside he was an aggressive street fighter. It was commonly known in the legal community that he could good-ole-boy you to death.

"He's back here, Larry. I'm sorry I missed you the last time," Weaver said, motioning for Oliver to follow him down the corridor to Hart's jail cell.

"Gene, I've got someone here to see you," Weaver said, stopping in front of the cell door and tapping the steel bars with his ring. Hart was lying on the old steel bed with his hands tucked behind his head.

He looked up at the two men for a moment, sat up on the side of the bed, and put his feet on the floor.

"He's all yours, Larry," Weaver said as he turned and walked back toward his office.

"Gene, I need to go over the case with you again," Oliver said as he thrust his hands between the bars. It was Oliver's second visit and he was impressed with his new client. Hart half stood and weakly shook the lawyer's hand and sat back on the bed. Oliver was a consummate people watcher. As a Tulsa police officer he had learned to ask probing, pointed questions and then watch for psychological symptoms of innocence or guilt. This talent had served him well as a policeman and had become even more important as a trial attorney.

During the next forty-five minutes the two men talked quietly about the case. Hart again calmly denied that he had committed the murders.

"Gene, there is something that you better be aware of—something that the press doesn't even know," Oliver cautioned, watching the young Indian's face. "They found a fingerprint inside of that red flashlight. That fingerprint isn't yours, is it, Gene?"

Hart was visibly shaken by the revelation. He looked up at the ceiling and took a long, shuddering breath. His gaze fell slowly downward as he ponderously bowed his head. A trembling right finger flicked at an invisible object on the floor. He did not answer.

"Gene, is that fingerprint yours?" Oliver repeated softly as he kneeled down until he was at eye level with his prospective client.

Hart continued to stare at the floor. "There couldn't be," he mumbled as if trying to recollect.

Oliver shook his head, stood up, turned, and walked up the corridor and out of the front door of the Sheriff's office. He had the answer he needed.

The next day Oliver announced that he had withdrawn from the case. He was replaced by two attorneys, Garvin Isaacs and Gary Pitchlynn from the Native American Center in Oklahoma City. The attorneys were relatively inexperienced, the chief counsel, Garvin Isaacs, having only four years of law practice behind him. Most of Hart's supporters were disappointed that he had chosen the young attorneys when it was rumored that he could have had any attorney in the United States.

On April 8 Hart pleaded innocent to seven felony charges stemming from his two Mayes County jailbreaks after 1973. He was accused of three Burglary counts, two counts of Injuring Public Property, and one count each of Possession of a Firearm and Escape.

Hart had been led, smiling and nodding to people around him, from the Sheriff's office, which was located directly across the street from the courthouse. All around him it was a circus. Hundreds of curious watchers ringed the courthouse to see Hart. The courtroom was packed and silent as District Attorney Sid Wise read the murder complaints, one by one, before Judge William Whistler. Wise first read the name of Doris Denise Milner, then Lori Farmer, and finally Michelle Guse.

During the proceedings Wise suggested that the prisoner be housed in the Tulsa County Jail for security reasons and because he had escaped from the Mayes County Jail on two different occasions. Judge Whistler denied the motion.

"Do you see anything wrong with the Mayes County Jail?" he asked Wise.

"No, sir, not at all," Wise answered.

"All right, we'll place him there at least temporarily," Whistler said.

It was announced that several defense fund-raising functions would take place. A special service was announced for Hart at the Snake Creek Baptist Church, east of Locust Grove.

Bowles had promised his informant that the reward would be paid to him if his information led to the arrest of Hart. Bowles felt that he deserved the money.

Tom Kennedy was against paying the money. He had already told the press that no reward would be paid. Bowles was adamant. He had given his word and he expected the reward to be paid regardless of what the press did with it. Kennedy and Bowles compromised and it was agreed that the informant would receive part of the reward.

With the preliminary hearing coming up, the investigation again intensified. Mike Wilkerson ordered that all of the agents in northeastern Oklahoma devote all of their time to the case. All of the counselors and Girl Scouts were to be interviewed again. Hair samples and major case prints, as well as saliva specimens, were to be taken from every male who was interviewed during the investigation. Five extra agents were assigned to the investigation.

The news accounts had renewed the public's interest in the case and had brought on a new rash of confessions and accusations that had to be checked out.

Linville and Pratt flew to Dallas; a man there had confessed to the murders. He readily admitted killing the three girls but could give no particulars of the incident. After a tough interrogation, he finally admitted he was confined to the U. S. Federal Reformatory in El Reno, Oklahoma, on June 13, and wasn't released until 10:00 A.M. A check with the reformatory confirmed that he had not been released until four hours after the bodies were discovered.

Information was received from the Delaware County Jail that one inmate had told another he had committed the murders. That inmate had since escaped but had been recaptured in California. Linville flew to Santa Clara, California. The suspect denied making the statement. His brother, who was also incarcerated with him and had escaped with him from the Delaware County Jail, said that he had no doubt that his brother had made the admission. He said his brother was a "braggart and liked to make up stories." There was nothing else to indicate that the suspect had committed the crime, but major case prints, blood, saliva, and hair samples were taken. The laboratory results later eliminated him as a suspect.

Bowles finally caught the medicine man, William Smith, at his residence. Smith asked Bowles into his home, appearing cooperative and frightened.

"Ella Mae Buckskin came out here last night with some friends," he began. "They accused me of turning Gene in. They told me that they were going to find out who did turn him in and when they did he wouldn't live long."

"Don't worry," assured Bowles. "They never heard it from us. I'll play straight with you as long as you play straight with me. All I want from you is the complete truth. Nothing more, nothing less. Okay?"

"Okay," replied Smith.

"Now, Mr. Smith, when and where did you first see Gene Hart?"

"It was about a week after the murders," Smith answered. "He just showed up at my house 'bout midnight. I just figured that kinfolks brought him here."

"What did he say to you?" asked Bowles.

"He asked if I'd take him back to Locust Grove and I said no. When I wouldn't do that, he asked me if I'd hide him. He said that he was wanted for them killin's and that the laws would kill him if they found him."

"What happened then?"

"Well," continued Smith, "I knew an old man named Sam Pigeon who lives near my wife's father whose name is also Sam Pigeon. I knew if I dropped Gene up by his house that ole Sam would take him in. So I told Gene to lay down in the back of the pickup and I'd drive him over there."

"Weren't you afraid someone would see him?" asked Bowles.

"No," replied Smith, "I had a shell camper on the truck and it was dark. These old roads down here are deserted at night. Anyway, I drove him over about a mile from Sam's house and let him out."

"How did he know where to go?" asked Bowles.

"Oh, well," Smith stammered, "I gave him directions to the house when he got out of the truck."

"Mr. Smith, I told you I would shoot straight if you would. Now do you expect me to believe that you took Hart up there and dumped him out without Sam Pigeon being contacted?" Bowles continued to probe.

"But, Mr. Bowles, I didn't go up there. I'm telling the truth," insisted Smith.

"When did you take Hart money and supplies, Mr. Smith?"

"Never," responded Smith, shaking his head. "I never took him money or supplies. I never saw him again till I went to treat Freeman Pigeon's wife for a bad leg."

"Mr. Smith," Bowles said accusingly, "you're giving me the information you know that I already have. But, you're leaving out the information I need. Now, I want some answers. Who brought Hart here?"

"I don't know," answered Smith. "I swear I don't know."

"What kind of shoes was he wearing, Mr. Smith?" questioned Bowles.

"I don't know. I didn't notice."

Bowles leaned forward in his chair. "Was he carrying any supplies?"

"I don't believe so," answered Smith meekly.

"Did he say anything about the murders?" Bowles said slowly.

"No, he did not," answered Smith with equal slowness and deliberation.

"Mr. Smith, I don't believe that you have been truthful with me. If you aren't truthful I have no other choice than to believe you have acted in bad faith. And, if I believe this, I have no other alternative than to get a warrant for Harboring a Fugitive."

"Larry," Smith said, trying to be friendly, "you are Indian. You know what is happening. You know what could happen to me and my family now."

"Are you sticking by your story, Mr. Smith?" Bowles asked coldly.

"I am," replied the medicine man.

"Then I suggest that you get yourself an attorney, because the next time you see me I'll have a warrant for your arrest." Bowles stood up and walked toward the door.

He drove back to Tahlequah and found Mike Wilkerson in his office.

"Mike, I don't believe Smith. He knows a hell of a lot more than he's telling."

"Well, let's arrest his butt," exclaimed Wilkerson. "We owe him and his wife nothing. They harbored Hart and bragged about it. Maybe an arrest will bring him back to reality."

"If that guy would just be truthful, he could help us a bunch," mused Bowles.

"Well, go get an arrest warrant and maybe the D.A. can talk to his attorney and a deal can be worked out."

The next day Bowles crossed the street to the old Cherokee County Courthouse and got the warrant. Smith was in Arkansas working and would not return for five days. Bowles believed that Smith would turn himself in when he heard about the warrant so he put out the word among the citizenry. A few days later William Smith, accompanied by Ross Swimmer, Chief of the Cherokees, turned himself in to the Cherokee County Sheriff.

Bowles called Nathan Young, the Assistant District Attorney for Cherokee County, and told him that he would like to make a deal with Smith if he would cooperate. Young said he would cooperate in any way he could.

Wilkerson decided to have Agent Fanning Young, a native of Tahlequah, contact Smith's attorney with the proposition. The red-headed agent went to the attorney's office and told him what the OSBI proposed. The lawyer was insulted. With a red face, he told Young, "You people bugged Smith's house and tapped his phone; you lied to him and now you want to make deals. You told him you wouldn't arrest him if he talked to you. I'll make no deals with you people. I'll see you in court."

Hart sat silently in his eleven by fourteen cell. No visitors other than attorneys were allowed in the Mayes County Jail. Guards rarely attempted to talk to Hart other than to ask him if he wanted his meals. Guards were posted both inside and outside of the jail; they were also periodically stationed on the roofs of both the courthouse and the jail. The sheriff was determined Hart would not escape again.

On Monday following Hart's capture, the lawyers filed motions with the Mayes County District Court asking that all law officers and prosecutors involved in the case refrain from commenting on Hart's prior criminal record. If the court approved the motions, authorities could be held in contempt if they mentioned Hart's convictions.

The court was also asked to order authorities to turn over all copies of interviews and statements obtained in the investigation. Another motion sought the names and addresses of the Girl Scouts and counselors who were at Camp Scott when the murders occurred.

The following day a circuslike atmosphere predominated. Approximately three hundred people were in the small town square as the five officers escorted the defendant from the jail to the courthouse across the street. At one point the sheriff had to push a cameraman back so the group of officers could proceed. Inside the courtroom it was standing room only with almost one hundred and fifty people present. In the crowd was a woman carrying a red and white sign reading, *Help justice, Leroy Hart and family.* She told the news people that she had received $150 in donations and that the money was now coming in from all over the United States, from people who had followed wire service and network news coverage of the story. She said she had attempted to set up a fund at the Locust Grove Bank but, "the damn place won't accept my money."

Inside the courtroom Hart pleaded innocent to all three charges of First Degree Murder. Under the laws of the State of Oklahoma, innocent pleas are automatically entered in such cases. By law, a person does not actually enter a plea until his preliminary hearing or until it is waived. The judge ordered that Hart be kept in the Mayes County Jail for at least another week until defense motions could be heard.

Judge Whistler granted a motion that allowed visits once a week from Hart's mother, sisters, and son. The visitors would be subject to a strip search before visiting Hart in his cell. Judge Whistler denied a defense motion that would have prohibited law enforcement officers and prosecutors from mentioning Hart's previous convictions.

Prosecutors again attempted to have Hart moved from the Mayes County Jail but were unsuccessful. They argued that the county jail had already reached its full capacity and the tight security measures at the old jail were creating a financial hardship. Other motions filed were general discovery motions in order to obtain any fingerprints taken from the bodies, plaster casts and molds of footprints at the death scene, tape gathered there, and any hair samples and slides of semen taken from the bodies. A third motion asked the court to dismiss the case on the alleged grounds that it lacked jurisdiction.

On April 15, as Mike Wilkerson was studying for a law examination at his home in Tulsa, he received a phone call from Pete Weaver. Weaver was excited and concerned. "Mike, I've got information from the FBI that AIM is going to break Hart out of here tonight. They told me that one of their informants said that a bunch of Indians are en route from Oklahoma City to bust him out. They are supposed to have automatic weapons. I think we had better move Hart but I'm under this damn court order."

"Bullshit, Pete! That court order doesn't mean a damn thing if there's a life-threatening danger. You can move Hart anytime you want to if his life is in danger. How good is your information?"

"Mike, it sounds like it's good. The special agent that told me says it's real good."

"Well, Pete, it sounds like a crock," Wilkerson said, "but let's not take any chances. I'll send some agents that way to pick up Hart and you contact the Highway Patrol and get a couple of units to follow. Can you contact the judge who issued the order so it can be rescinded?"

"No," responded Weaver. "He's gone somewhere."

"Well, don't worry about it. I'll call Limke and see if the Governor will issue an order for Hart's removal. But either way, Hart's leaving in an hour."

Limke contacted the Governor and the move was approved. At 8:30 P.M. Agents Bowles and Chrisco took Hart out of his cell. With two patrol cars escorting them, they transported him back to McAlester State Penitentiary.

Mayes County District Attorney Sid Wise was now deeply involved in his race for Attorney General. Even his campaign literature seemed to capitalize upon the murders. A brochure entitled *Make a Wise Decision* said:

> Sid Wise is one of those courageous people, who doesn't ask whose job it is, but whether it needs to be done.

During the early morning hours of June 13, 1977, a tragedy struck in Northeastern Oklahoma that was to be felt literally around the world.

Three little Girl Scouts, on the first night of summer camp, were brutally and savagely attacked and murdered at Camp Scott, near Locust Grove.

For three weeks, night and day, Sid lived at the campsite. He told one reporter, "Whenever one of those underpaid, overworked deputies, without sleep and covered with ticks and dirt, puts a footprint down, I'm going to stick a shoe in it."

It wasn't Sid's job, but he was needed and he was there . . . to coordinate the efforts of the more than 15 agencies working on the case, and an army of press people.

The list goes on, but the important thing is that for the first time, you will have a prosecutor, with a prosecutor's background in the highest legal office of this great state.

But Wise had bigger problems than his campaign brochure. The media finally got the goods on Wise and Grimsley. The following classified ad appeared in the Tulsa *World:*

INVESTORS for shares in book about Camp Scott murders by only reporter who covered the story continuously for 10 months from the inside. Shares $500 and up for percentage. Contact R.L. Grimsley 913-341-4600, 3 P.M. to 6 P.M. Wed. May 31st.

Vengeance was alive and well. Grimsley, the "news coordinator," and now Wise's campaign manager, had admitted in the ad what the media had suspected all along.

A news reporter dialed the number listed on the ad and a recorder answered, "This is Sid Wise speaking. You have reached my campaign headquarters for Attorney General at the Will Rogers Hotel in Claremore. There is no one here at this moment, but if you'll leave your name and number after the tone, we'll be glad to get back to you as soon as possible. Thank you very much for your help."

A reporter confronted Wise at a Tulsa hotel where he was serving as chairman for an Oklahoma District Attorneys Conference. The reporter asked Wise if he had any "financial investment in a book."

"No, I certainly wouldn't," a nervous Sid Wise responded. "No, no."

The news media again barraged the public with stories of bumbling officials racing to capitalize upon a tragedy. Newspapers and television stations carried a picture of a lawyer wearing a T-shirt on which was inscribed "Gene Hart for Attorney General." Profits from the sale of the shirts were to go to the Hart Defense Fund.

Grimsley was fired as Wise's campaign manager and disappeared for a while. But the people had not seen the last of the little chain-smoking reporter—not by a long shot.

CHAPTER 12

LIMKE, BOWLES, AND MIKE WILKERSON SAT IN THE TAHLEQUAH office drinking their first cup of morning coffee. They had discussed the various leads to be checked out prior to preliminary hearing and made small talk.

"Ted," Bowles began, "do you think that Sid has the ability to prosecute a case of this complexity?"

"I don't really think it's a question of ability," Limke responded. "I think it's a question of experience. Sid's an adequate attorney but in order to win a case against a living legend we're going to need the best. Ole Sid has got the news media so hacked at him, because of his favoritism toward that reporter from Pryor, that they're going to use every opportunity to take a shot at him. Sid picked one hell of a time to run for Attorney General. It looks like he's capitalizing on those kids' deaths. And that newspaper ad trying to sell stock in a book was unbelievable."

"That's no joke," agreed Bowles with a tone of disgust. "Have you seen Wise's campaign literature? It talks about the murders and how Sid took every step that the officers did. It's in bad taste and Sid is using piss-poor judgment. Ted, I don't think the people have the trust in Sid that is needed in this case, and that's where we're going to have to pick a jury."

"Me neither," said Wilkerson. "There are already accusations of a frame-up and planted evidence. All we need now to lose the case is a suspect prosecutor. Boy, would I like to have Buddy Fallis prosecuting this case, but I guess there's no way."

S. M. "Buddy" Fallis, Jr., Tulsa County District Attorney, was a five-foot-six, one-hundred-forty-pound dynamo. Virtually all his adult life had been spent prosecuting those he called the "scum who prey on innocent people." At age forty-five, he was recognized throughout the southwest as a top prosecuting attorney. His professional public reputation as a fearless and dedicated prosecutor was perhaps surpassed only by his reputation among the people who knew him best. As a trial lawyer, he had few, if any, peers. His ability to articulate his philosophy of law and order inspired all those with similar beliefs who all too often had been labeled gestapo or red-necks. A man constantly in motion, his entire life a cause, he infected all those who came in contact with him. No one had mild or indifferent feelings about Buddy Fallis. He was either worshipped or despised, depending on the perspective. Both sides agreed, however, that Fallis was dedicated, honest to a fault, and one of the most skilled prosecutors anywhere.

There was a twinkle in Limke's eye and a little-boy grin on his face that told the agents their friend and boss had been up to something. Tongue in cheek, Limke said, "Oh, there may be a way."

"Teddy, what the hell have you been up to?" Bowles asked, smiling broadly.

"Come on, Teddy. Spit it out," chided Wilkerson.

"Well, let me say this." Limke smiled. Leaning back in his chair, with his hands behind his head, he stared at the ceiling as if he were in deep thought. "The wheel has been greased. I have word from an informant who tells me that the families of the victims are going to contact Buddy and request his assistance as a special prosecutor."

"Can you do that?" Bowles asked excitedly. "I mean, can Fallis go into another county as a special prosecutor?"

"Damn right," Limke answered. "It's happened before."

"How's Sid going to take it? Is he going to buck up?" Wilkerson asked.

Limke smiled and said, "Sid is going to request that Fallis come in. Someone told me that if he didn't, the families would burn him to the ground over that damn campaign-manager's book. Pete asked Sid to request Buddy's help in the case. At first Sid said that he wouldn't and that he needed the publicity for his campaign. Well, ole Pete explained to him what the families were about to do and that 50 percent of the publicity was better than none. Wise said he would ask him."

"Ted, why the hell would Fallis consent to come into the case?" Wilkerson asked. "He has nothing to gain and everything to lose. If I was Fallis, I wouldn't take the case."

"Buddy will do it because it is the right thing to do," Limke answered. "It's that simple."

"Well, I don't want to throw any water on our fire, but you know what a great believer in history I am."

"Oh, God, here we go," Bowles kidded. "We are going to get another one of Wilkerson's little bits of trivia history."

"Yeah, that's exactly what you're going to get," Wilkerson said with his best Will Rogers accent. "This one is too good to pass by. Well, it seems that around the turn of the century in a little town called Fall River, Massachusetts, there was a young lady by the name of Elizabeth Borden who was accused of killing her mother and father. I don't know if you all have heard of the nursery rhyme, but it goes something like this. 'Lizzie Borden took an axe and gave her mother forty whacks. When the job was nicely done, she gave her father forty-one.'"

Bowles and Limke laughed. Even though they didn't want Wilkerson to know it, they enjoyed his stories.

"Well, anyway, now that I got the poetry over with, this lady was accused of killing her mom and dad and it was just almost an open and shut case. They had all but caught her with the axe in hand. Well, the prosecutor had the audacity to have this woman arrested. Boy, was there an outcry from the citizenry, because after all, no local person could have committed such a terrible crime. Hell, the ex-Governor of the state even defended her.

"Now, I want you to draw a correlation, boys, between this and the people in northeastern Oklahoma. Now, there's not a more clannish bunch of people in the world and I think you all agree with that. We are going to bring in the big slick Tulsa prosecutor. Now we, those foreigner OSBI agents, already caught the champion, football-playing Indian. I tell you what, boys—and I don't want to be negative—but I just wonder if there is a jury in this world that has got guts enough to convict this legend with the kind of peer pressure they are going to have. Linville calls it the Billy Jack syndrome.

"Oh, by the way, a postscript to the Elizabeth Borden affair. She was acquitted. Now, history tells us it wasn't because the jury didn't think she did it. They believed she did do it, but they figured they would show them outsiders regardless of the cost. I remember reading that some twenty-five years after the acquittal, a neighbor's little daughter asked to go over and play in Miss Borden's yard. The woman told her daughter, 'No, honey, don't go over and and play in Miss Borden's yard.' The little girl asked, 'Why?' and the woman said, 'Because she wasn't nice to her parents.'"

Limke faked a yawn and said, "Boooy, that's real interesting, Wilkerson. Don't you think so, Bowles?"

"Yes," Bowles replied. "I think I could have made it through the day without that much-needed piece of memorabilia."

Taking their fake mocking in stride, Wilkerson said, "Both of you go to hell."

A few days later Wise officially requested that Fallis assist with the prosecution.

On April 18 the forensic chemist from the Southwestern Institute of Forensic Sciences at Dallas came to the OSBI lab to assist in looking for semen and sperm.

On the same day, Larry Dry, who had been generally ignored for the past two weeks, was granted a parole by the Governor. He had, it appeared to the officers, tried in good faith to assist in the capture of Hart. He had taken agents directly to Cave Number 1 where the tape, newspaper, pictures, and glasses were found. He identified the cave as the area in which he and Hart had hidden after their escape. He was still unable to come up with the two threatening letters he was supposed to have received while in prison, but Dry would be a witness against Hart. He could identify the pictures found at Cave Number 1 as being in Hart's possession after he escaped from jail, and he could testify that Hart wrapped his flashlight lens in plastic to cut down the light beam.

If the motions hearing held on May 3 was any sign of what the preliminary hearing and trial were going to be like, the public was in for a show. Sid Wise and his assistant, Royce Hobbs, squared off against defense attorney Garvin Isaacs at the hearing.

The first motion to be heard was an order to issue subpoenas for the purpose of discovering whether the Mayes County Jail booking records—taken when Hart was booked in 1973—had listed the photographs and shoes. The photographs, of course, were the two photographs found at the first cave and later determined to have been processed by Hart. It is normal procedure in Mayes County, or any other county jail, that when a person is booked into jail, all of the personal items taken from him are inventoried and listed on a booking sheet.

Isaacs repeated several times during the hearing that he thought that the Sheriff's office was "trying to hide something" and that he had "reason to believe that these items were logged in 1973." He subpoenaed Deputy Sheriff A. D. David and told him to bring all of his records pertaining to the booking of Gene Leroy Hart. David had not been employed by the Sheriff's office until 1975 so he had no records.

Both Wise and Isaacs leveled verbal blasts at each other. At one point Isaacs said that Wise did not always tell the truth, which prompted Wise to spring to his feet. He had to be subdued by Hobbs, his assistant.

Isaacs again asked that Hart be moved from McAlester to Pryor. This motion was again denied.

While once again asking for a sixty-day delay in the preliminary hearing, Isaacs said, "It took you people ten months to screw this thing up and we have to try and unscrew it in two months."

Hobbs brought to the court's attention the fact that there were seven attorneys in the firm for which Isaacs worked and this was more than the number of deputies at Pete Weaver's disposal.

Associate District Judge Clanton, who would preside over the preliminary hearing, agreed to delay the hearing for one day and said that he would consider a motion for continuance after the prosecution rested its case at preliminary hearing.

On June 9 B. G. Jones, OSBI Inspector in Charge of the McAlester Office, received word from convict Jimmy Don Bunch that he had information about the murders of the three Girl Scouts. Bunch was known to the OSBI as a notorious liar. He had, however, testified against some of the top criminals in Oklahoma and occasionally his information was reliable.

Jones drove to the prison and had a guard bring Bunch from his cell on death row. He had been placed on death row because of death threats he had received due to his past activities as an informant.

At thirty years of age, Bunch had a long criminal record and had spent most of the last ten years in prison. He was a small-time thief who rarely ventured into violent crime. His one exception was an armed robbery in 1973 to which he had pleaded guilty and received ten years in McAlester State Penitentiary. When Bunch was returned to prison, several inmates stabbed him and left him for dead. He lived, however, and it was rumored that he had over two hundred stitches in his body. After the attack Bunch was transferred to the Hughes County Jail in Holdenville, Oklahoma, for protection. He promptly escaped from the jail and kidnapped a city councilman. Two days later he was arrested and charged with Escape and Kidnapping.

At Bunch's trial Garvin Isaacs, who had acted as his attorney in several cases, testified on his behalf. Bunch received five years after pleading guilty and was returned to prison in October of 1975. The following month he was placed on death row for his protection. He had remained there for the last three years.

Jones looked at the short, chubby, ruddy-faced convict sitting in front of him. He appeared scared—but he always appeared scared. It seemed Bunch always wanted to talk to police officers about something, so Jones had no illusions about the validity of the information he was about to receive.

"Jimmy Don," Jones said sternly. "Now let's cut the B.S. and get right to the point. What have you got?"

"Information," Bunch replied in a deep Oklahoma drawl. "Information y'all will be interested in. Information that Gene Hart told me."

"All right, Jimmy. From the top. Why would Gene Hart tell you anything? He's only been here a few days. What's he going to do, walk up to you and say, 'Jimmy Don, I killed those girls'?" Jones asked sarcastically.

"No, Mr. Jones," Bunch said politely. "I know Gene Hart well. You see, we were both in the Tulsa County Jail in 1969 together and we got to be real good friends. I got transferred to the prison in October and Gene was sent down a few days later. When he got down here, we got to be close friends. I got paroled in 1971 and Gene escaped from Mayes County."

"Had you seen Hart from that time until he was put back in here?" asked Jones, now feeling that Bunch's story had a spark of credibility.

"No, we kind of went our separate ways," Bunch responded. "I did see him again when you guys brought him in and put him on death row. A night or so later, Warden Hess brought Isaacs down there to talk to Hart. I could hear them talking about the case but could never hear what they were saying."

"When was the first time you talked to Hart after he was put on death row?" queried Jones.

"Well, after a week or so, the guards let Hart out of his cell to clean up the cell run," Bunch continued, noting that Jones was not quite so skeptical. "He stopped by my cell and struck up a conversation. 'Jimmy,' he says, 'how you doin'?' I said, 'I'm doin' okay.' I showed him a newspaper article that said that the convicts might try to kill him and he says, 'I don't know, but I think I still have some friends in here.'"

"Okay," Jones said, growing impatient. "What did he say about the murders?"

"Okay, okay," Bunch replied, sensing Jones's urgency. "Well, I asked Gene if he had killed those little girls and he looks at me and says, 'I don't know.' I then tell him, 'Well, Gene, if you were drunked up and really wiped out, you might be able to beat it.' Gene says, 'Well, all I can say is that I woke up in a cave with blood all over me. The thing seemed like a dream!' I then ask ole Gene if he remembered the girls and he says, 'In a way I do and in a way I don't. It was just like a dream. I was all drunked up.' Then I says, 'If you remember the girls and dreamed about the girls then you must have been there.' Gene says, 'That's what I know. I must have been there, but that don't sound like me.' Then I asked him, 'How tight do they have you?' and he says, 'They've got those fucking pictures.' I says, 'What pictures?' and he says, patting his pocket, 'I had some pictures and they got them. We're going to try to convince them that I left the pictures in jail when I escaped.'

"'Have they got anything else of yours?' I ask, and he says, 'They took a handkerchief out of the house where I was arrested. It had some pot in it.' Well, I tell Gene not to worry about a little ole pot. Gene says, 'I ain't worried about the pot, but the handkerchief has a design on it that can be identified.'" Bunch took a deep breath, fished a cigarette out of his pocket, and lit it with a match.

"All right, Jimmy, did Hart tell you anything about what he did with his clothes?" Jones asked as he dodged the stream of smoke blown from Bunch's cigarette.

"Yeah, as a matter of fact he did," Bunch replied as he tried to snub off a piece of the hot-box fire on his cigarette. "He said that he had gotten rid of his clothes. He laughed about them dogs trying to catch him because he said he could outrun them dogs."

"How long did you talk to Hart?" Jones asked.

"'Bout two hours," replied Bunch, "till they come to get me to go to the Chaplain's office. Boy, that's another thing. I talked to him for about an hour—you see, I've got religion—and then the guards took me back to my cell. After they put me in a cell, one of the guards brought me a kite [a note] in a magazine. The kite was from Gene and said something like, 'You know, Jimmy, what I talked to you about could get my ass burnt. You're the only partner I've got down here I can trust.' Well, the next day, me and Gene was talking again when Father Marx walked up and handed me a cassette tape through the bars. Well, Gene like to jump through his ass cause he thought I'd given the Father a statement on tape. Well, I say, 'Gene, it's a religious tape.' This seemed to make him unnervous and he said, 'You had me worried,' and I says, 'Why? We're partners.'"

"Where's the kite Hart sent to you?" Jones asked, expecting the note to be lost.

"Down in the cell," replied Bunch.

"Let's go get it," Jones said pointing toward the door and rising from his chair.

Bunch went to the cell with a guard and returned with a hand-printed, unsigned note.

Jones was very skeptical of the note. Convicts, he thought, seem to think they need a note or letter to verify their credibility. Usually they print the notes under the mistaken belief that a handwriting expert will be unable to analyze the handwriting.

"Jimmy," Jones said, "what do you want out of this?"

"Nothing," Bunch answered. "Just give me protection. I have three kids of my own."

"I'll talk to you later, Jimmy, after I have had someone look at the note," Jones said as he motioned for the guard.

Jones left the prison and drove back to his office and telephoned Limke. Limke laughed when Jones told him that Jimmy Don Bunch had given him a statement.

"B.G.," Limke said, "just to be safe why don't we make arrangements to have Bunch taken to the Tulsa County Jail until the note and his story can be checked out. We'll get Mike to polygraph him while he's up there."

After getting a handwriting sample from Bunch, Jones made arrangements for his transfer to Tulsa. The kite was sent to Oklahoma City for examination.

The OSBI had copies of several motions Hart had handwritten while an inmate in 1971. The motions were used as exemplars and were compared with the kite. Document Examiner Bruce Plank found no similarities between the motions and the kite. It was Plank's opinion that Bunch had written the kite and tried to disguise his handwriting by printing. The kite was then processed for fingerprints. Bunch's fingerprints were found all over the kite; Hart's fingerprints were not on the document.

Agent Joe Collins was given the task of checking out Bunch's story with the prison correctional officers. He was told by the officers that no inmate or guard ever went inside Hart's cell, nor was he ever allowed outside his cell while the cell run was being cleaned.

Almost every part of Bunch's story had been discredited. Both Fallis and Wise refused to consider using Bunch as a witness.

The preliminary hearing for Hart would make Oklahoma history for many reasons. The first involved the use of television in the courtroom. It was obvious that there would not be enough seats in the courtroom to handle the media, much less the throngs of spectators that were expected. KOTV, a Tulsa television station, asked the court's permission to set up a courthouse annex a short distance from the main courthouse. They proposed to put a TV camera into the courtroom so they could broadcast the proceedings to a Pryor auditorium where an additional two hundred and fifty or more people could watch the trial. Judge Clanton, after taking the motion under advisement for a few days, decided to allow the TV camera in the courtroom. There were a few stipulations, however. The camera would be operated by one technician. The camera had to remain stationary and take in the entire focus of the courtroom. The same formalities would be observed in the courtroom annex as in the main courtroom, including a search of everyone who entered.

This was the first time in Oklahoma history that a judge had allowed a television camera into a courtroom. Judge Clanton said he would make observations after the preliminary hearing and make recommendations as to the future use of cameras in Oklahoma courts.

The beginning of the preliminary hearing was like a Hollywood movie.

Hart was now some forty to forty-five pounds lighter and looked tired and drawn. He wore new glasses and a bright-colored sport shirt with slacks. A column of police officers led him from the Mayes County Sheriff's Office across the street. Cameras and reporters were everywhere.

As the small caravan moved through the crowd dodging cameras, shouts of "We love you, Gene," "Framed," "Sid Wise won't ride

Gene Hart into the Attorney General's office," and "Cover-up" rang out. Many of the people in front of the courthouse had been among the four hundred Locust Grove and Pryor residents who had attended a benefit chicken dinner, complete with live country music, held to raise money for the Gene Leroy Hart Defense Fund.

Inside the courtroom Hart's mother, Ella Mae Buckskin, sat in the front row, as did Mr. and Mrs. Guse and Mr. and Mrs. Farmer.

The preliminary hearing is a pretrial proceeding where it is determined whether there is probable cause to believe that the defendant committed the crime.

The first witness called was Dee Elder, who told of discovering the bodies.

Next Dr. Neil Hoffman, the State Medical Examiner from Tulsa, testified to his findings. Hoffman showed several gruesome pictures of the victims. Isaacs objected to admitting the pictures into evidence. He maintained that they were being offered in order to arouse the passions of the community. However, the photographs were admitted into evidence by Judge Clanton.

The families of the victims sat quietly during the testimony of Dr. Hoffman. Some of them appeared to be upset with Isaacs's continued objections to the admission of the autopsy photographs into evidence. One relative was heard whispering, "He wants people to forget what happened to the children."

A steady stream of prosecution witnesses testified about the crime scene, evidence collected, scientific tests, hair comparisons, pictures, and sperm.

Larry Dry tied Hart to Cave Number 1 by testifying that Hart had had the pictures with him when they escaped. But Dry was less than credible. He had been arrested a few days earlier for Armed Robbery and Burglary in Delaware County. The Tulsa *Tribune* added fuel to the fire of outrage by printing a front page story entitled "Governor Swapped Parole For Hart. Ex-Cellmate Freed for Helping Locate Slaying Suspect."

The article said that Governor Boren and OSBI agents had traded a parole to Dry in exchange for help in the manhunt and trial of Gene Hart. The Governor denied that he had traded the parole but said that he had given the convict a sixty-day leave. Dry was quoted as saying that the OSBI had told him that he would be given a parole if he was able to catch Hart. Deputy Director Dick Wilkerson denied Dry had been promised anything and produced the letter from Dry saying that he wanted to help the OSBI in the investigation and that he did not want anything in return. Governor Boren went on to say that he had handled the parole routinely and that he was not even aware that it was Dry's parole that he had signed. The Governor also stated that he would have paroled Dry anyway because he met all the requirements for parole. The article quoted one source close to the investigation as saying, "This is, to the best of my knowledge, the guy who gave the information that led to the capture of Gene Leroy Hart."

Now the public had their snitch; they had their informant. It seemed to make no difference that it wasn't the right person. It was enough that he was a convicted felon who had been given his freedom and a reward to inform on his best friend. The bureaucratic passing of the buck added more credibility to the story.

The prosecutors then called Ann G. Reed, an OSBI forensic chemist. She told of the hairs found on Doris Milner's body matching those of Hart. "The hairs were consistent in all microscopic comparisons," Ms. Reed said on the stand. She went on to say, "I cannot identify a person by hair comparison; however, these hairs came from Mr. Hart or from someone with exactly the same microscopic characteristics as Mr. Hart." She further testified that the foreign hairs found on the bodies and those taken from Hart at Grand Valley Hospital were very dark and bore basic Mongoloid characteristics with some Caucasian characteristics.

The prosecution rested its case on June 13, one year to the day after the murders.

Defense Attorney Garvin Isaacs had promised during the hearing that he would make smoke when the defense's turn came to present its case. He had also promised news reporters that he would have a bomb when it came time to present Hart's case. There was great speculation that Isaacs had a surprise witness that would blow the State's case wide open. The OSBI learned that the bomb Isaacs was going to make smoke with was none other than Jimmy Don Bunch.

Ted Limke learned that Isaacs had gone to the Tulsa County Jail the night before and talked to Bunch. Agent Roger Chrisco interviewed Bunch. According to Bunch, Isaacs, accompanied by Pitchlynn and an Oklahoma City newsman, had visited him at 10:30 P.M. the previous night. Isaacs smuggled a small tape recorder into the cell in his coat pocket which he used to tape the conversation between himself and Bunch. According to Bunch, the reporter, referring to him being transferred from the State Penitentiary to Tulsa, said, "We're going to stop this mess that is going on. They aren't going to be hiding any more witnesses. We have coverage now and it is taken care of." Bunch said Isaacs started the conversation with, "I've done you some favors before."

According to Bunch, Isaacs wanted him to say that OSBI agents had gone through a guard on death row at McAlester and had asked Bunch to testify against Hart. He was to say the guard asked him to testify that Hart confessed to him. Bunch told Chrisco that Isaacs had visited with him approximately three hours, most of that time spent rehearsing the story until he had it down pat. Isaacs then recorded a fifteen-minute statement. He said Isaacs was fully aware that the story he was giving was a lie.

Chrisco found Bunch very elusive when he tried to pin down fine points regarding his relationship with Isaacs and the conversation that had transpired. Bunch said that he had left Isaacs with the impression that he would testify for Hart.

Chrisco didn't believe Bunch's story. "Jimmy, will you take a polygraph test?" he asked.

"Sure," Bunch said confidently.

"Okay. I'll go tell the Sheriff and we'll be there in ten minutes," Chrisco responded, moving to the door.

"But, but, wait. I don't know whether Fallis wants me to take one," Bunch stammered.

Chrisco studied Bunch's demeanor. In five seconds the man had fallen apart. His hands shook as he took long draws from his cigarette and his voice shook as he talked.

"Jimmy, I'll be back to get you in a minute."

Chrisco walked over and lifted the telephone to call Mike Wilkerson.

"Mike, this guy's stinkin' up the place," Chrisco said. "There's no way to tell which side this guy's on. One thing for sure, he turned to crap when I mentioned the polygraph."

"Come on back to the office," Mike ordered. "I don't think Isaacs would put a person like Bunch on the stand."

Later that day deputies transferred Bunch to the Mayes County Jail so he could be readily available to the defense.

The stuffy courtroom was packed and there was a feeling of excitement and anticipation as Garvin Isaacs called his first witness.

"We call Jimmy Don Bunch," Isaacs said smugly.

Bunch was escorted into the court by police officers. He was dressed in a brown three-piece suit, wearing dark glasses, with his hair combed straight back. He took the oath to tell the complete truth, took his seat in the witness chair, and waited for the first question.

Bunch told of his previous association with Isaacs and about his prior felony convictions.

Isaacs then inquired, "In April of 1978, did you talk to Gene Hart?"

"Yes, sir," responded Bunch.

"What did you talk about?"

"Oh, about this case."

"Did he ever tell you at that time anything pertaining to the matters before this court?"

"I don't understand your question, Garvin."

"All right, Jimmy, in April of 1978, when they brought Gene Hart to the penitentiary, did he say anything to you about the case?"

"Just briefly."

"And what was that?"

"Oh, well, we discussed it several different times. What do you want? Do you want me to explain what we discussed or . . ."

Isaacs interrupted Bunch before he could finish, sensing something was wrong. "Did anybody ever come to you and want you to testify that Gene Leroy Hart confessed to you about killing those little girls?"

"No, sir," responded Bunch.

Isaacs stared at Bunch incredulously for a moment, seeming to sense a sinking ship. He finally asked, "Did Mr. Mike Pulchny [prison guard] ever come to you and talk to you about testifying for the State of Oklahoma?"

"No, sir, he didn't," Bunch repeated.

Isaacs now knew there was something wrong but attempted to salvage some of his defense. "Did he ever ask you about Gene Hart?"

"Just—did I know him, you know."

"Did he ask you anything else about Gene Hart?"

"He asked me if he thought Gene was guilty—if I thought Gene was guilty."

"Did you tell him?"

"I told him, yeah, I did."

Isaacs was losing his composure. He shook his head and his hand shook as he fumbled with some papers on the counsel table. He glared at the prosecution table for a split second. Shaffer, the D.A.'s assistant, and Thurman had their heads down; Thurman, to hide his embarrassment for the green attorney and Shaffer, trying to suppress his laughter.

Finally Isaacs said, "Your Honor, at this time, I'd like to be permitted to cross-examine the witness. I've been surprised by his testimony and I have a sworn statement that I took from him in the Tulsa County Jail."

Fallis objected. "If it please the Court, at this point I would say there's been no showing of surprise. He's answered the questions asked of him, I believe, Your Honor."

"How do you show surprise?" Isaacs asked. "Faint in the courtroom? Ask somebody to revive you?"

Under the rules of evidence, if an opposing counsel can show surprise to his witness's testimony, he may cross-examine the witness, that is, ask the witness leading questions.

Judge Clanton allowed Isaacs to cross-examine the witness.

"Why doesn't he leave well enough alone," whispered Thurman under his breath.

In an effort to impeach Bunch, Isaacs read from the statement Bunch had signed for him in the penitentiary. "Were you telling me the truth down there, Jimmy?" Isaacs demanded.

"No, sir, I wasn't."

"And why did you not tell me the truth at the state penitentiary?"

"Well, I made a deal with Gene Leroy Hart to come up here and lie on the stand."

There were gasps from the audience and the reporters were writing feverishly. As one reporter observed, Isaacs was indeed making smoke with his first witness and there was the faint smell of a burning fuse.

"Garvin, I admit the statement I gave you," Bunch responded to Isaacs's attempt at impeachment by reading his prior statement. "I'll save you a lot of trouble reading it. I submit that I gave you that statement, but I am saying that the statement is completely false and you know it is."

Isaacs pointed his finger at his chest. "I know it is?"

"Yes," replied Bunch. Snickers could be heard throughout the courtroom.

"And how do I know that?" Isaacs asked, as if he wanted to be embarrassed. Co-counsel Gary Pitchlynn looked at the floor and shook his head.

"Well, Garvin," replied Bunch, never taking his eyes off Isaacs, "me and you discussed the case several times."

The two continued bantering back and forth like two men arguing on the street. Finally Isaacs asked, "Did you sign this statement under oath?"

"I signed them statements under threat," Bunch said, pointing at the statements.

"Threat from who?" Isaacs shouted.

"You," Bunch shouted back.

"What did I threaten you with?" Isaacs again asking a question to which he did not know the answer.

Bunch replied, "You told me a Tulsa law officer would kill me, and you said if I didn't sign this statement, then I was subject to get a bullet between my eyes."

At one point during the cross-examination Isaacs seemed to be pleading with Bunch as he said, "Jimmy, I can't believe you're doing this to me."

At another point Bunch exclaimed, "I'll take a polygraph test."

Isaacs, ruffled and shaken, said, "Boy, Judge, I've heard some lying in my life . . ."

Fallis objected, saying, "I think there is a possible two-way street here."

Bunch went on to say that the prosecution had not promised him anything to testify but he said Isaacs told him that he would appear before the parole board with him and that he was a friend of Charles Chesnut, Chairman of the Parole Board.

On cross-examination by Fallis, Bunch related the same story he had given the OSBI. He said that Hart told him he woke up in a cave with blood on his clothes.

On redirect examination Isaacs asked Bunch, "Jimmy, why did you get up here and lie like that?"

Fallis objected, saying, "If it please the Court, I am going to object to the comment of counsel. He called this man as his witness. He's making comments . . ."

Isaacs interrupted, saying, "He sure surprised me."

Fallis retorted, "Well, I'm sure it is surprising to be exposed."

The final insult to Isaacs came when his witness put his hand in his coat pocket and produced a picture of his three children and blurted out, "Mr. Isaacs, here's why I came to Court to testify, because there was three little girls murdered. I've got three children myself."

Looking tired, drawn, and embarrassed, Isaacs asked and was granted a ten-day continuance. As the judge adjourned, there was a mad dash by reporters to find free telephones. A reporter asked Pete

Weaver what he thought of Bunch's testimony. Weaver said wryly, "I hope all of his witnesses are like this one."

As one observer said, "I can't believe that he kept questioning Bunch after he knew something was wrong. I have never heard of a lawyer being so embarrassed by a witness. There is a cardinal rule in the legal profession that you do not ask a question of a witness when you do not know the answer. He not only asked questions he did not know the answers to, but kept on asking them. It was like trying to drown out a fire by pouring gasoline on it."

Ron Shaffer grinned. "I've never seen anything like this in my life. Never!"

Isaacs probably best summed up the experience when he said, "My bomb just blew up in my face!"

The hearing dragged on for days after the continuance. Isaacs seemed to be disorganized and frustrated as he recalled all of the State's witnesses. He was using the hearing as a discovery device to ascertain what other evidence the State had against Hart. He questioned the agents who arrested Hart as if he thought they had not listed all of the evidence that was seized. He asked several agents if they had seized a smoking pipe. When Mike Wilkerson took the stand, Isaacs brought the inventory sheets of items that had been taken during the search. He asked Wilkerson to go through them item by item and swear that he was holding back no other evidence.

As Thurman listened to the questioning, he realized that something had been missed at the Pigeon residence, something that had the defense scared. It had to be some item Hart had told Isaacs about, something that could tie Hart to the crime scene. Thurman knew then that there would have to be another search.

Because of the lack of news coming from the courtroom, the press interviewed unusual people outside the courtroom. One such person was a fifty-one-year-old man named Tex Baker who wore an off-white wool suit that he had been given by the Pryor Rescue Mission. Tex stood five feet nine inches and weighed one hundred and thirty pounds. He said he was a private investigator and that he patterned himself after TV's McCloud. Tex had hitchhiked into Pryor from Texas to help Gene Leroy Hart. He offered his help to both the defense and prosecution but neither accepted.

The next day Tex was arrested on the first floor of the Mayes County Courthouse and charged with Carnal Brutality to a seven-year-old in Franklin County, Arkansas. The Sheriff of Franklin

County had learned of his whereabouts when he read an article about him in the Sunday Tulsa *World*. As he was led handcuffed out of the courthouse, he screamed, "False arrest, false arrest. Someone help me."

Across the street at the Sheriff's Office, he was photographed, fingerprinted, and read his constitutional rights. When asked whether he understood those rights, he replied smugly, "Certainly, all of you know that I have read them many, many times to other people. I do not need them read to me, thanks!"

When told he could make a phone call, he called the Governor of Arkansas collect. The Governor's aide who accepted the call was familiar with Tex and told him he should get a lawyer, then hung up.

A couple of weeks later Tex was sent to Eastern State Hospital in Vinita, Oklahoma, for observation. The doctors ruled that he could not tell right from wrong and was unable to defend himself.

The preliminary hearing was winding to a close as Jack Shroff took the stand. He looked nervous and strained as he bitterly recalled his experience. A hospital identification band dangled from a trembling right hand.

The last day of Hart's hearing was just as exciting and unpredictable as the entire case had been. At 10:13 A.M. on the last day, Tom Kennedy, the Director of the Oklahoma State Bureau of Investigation, was on the stand. Judge Clanton looked over his shoulder and saw someone motioning him from his chambers. "We'll take a short five-minute recess," Clanton said as he quickly left the bench. In a moment he returned to the courtroom. "This court requests that spectators in Courtroom A get up and quickly leave the courthouse by way of the stairway."

Almost two hundred people rushed from the building. There had been a bomb threat. Someone had called the Court Clerk's office and said that a bomb would go off in the courthouse at approximately 10:30 A.M. After Oklahoma Highway Patrolmen, deputies, and OSBI agents searched the building, the preliminary hearing resumed.

Sheriff Pete Weaver had a good idea who made the bomb threat and promised that he would put a little sunshine in his life.

It was a fitting end to the longest preliminary hearing in Oklahoma history. After seventy-five witnesses had been called, the defense rested its case. Without arguments, Gene Hart was bound over on three charges of First Degree Murder.

CHAPTER 13

On July 25 Glen Eberle, an investigator for the District Attorney's office in Tulsa, contacted Mike Wilkerson and told him that they had received a letter from an inmate named Sidney Thomas Brown in McAlester State Penitentiary. The convict said that he had information about Hart and the murders. Hart had allegedly made some damaging admissions to him and he wanted to share this information with an officer.

Wilkerson contacted the OSBI Regional Office in McAlester and told Inspector B. G. Jones about the letter from Brown. Agent Joe Collins was sent to the penitentiary to interview the inmate.

Brown had been incarcerated at the penitentiary since September 14, 1976. He had been convicted of Armed Robbery in Pottawatomie County and sentenced to twenty-five years. He had borrowed money from some of the prison's loan sharks, which he could not pay back. They sent word that they were going to kill him and he asked to be placed in the maximum security area of death row.

Approximately two weeks earlier Hart had come to Brown's cell and asked him to testify for him at his trial. He wanted Brown to say that he had seen letters written by Tulsa D. A. Buddy Fallis and Corrections Director Ned Benton to Jimmy Don Bunch. The letters offered help in obtaining a parole if Bunch would help by testifying against Hart. In return for this testimony, Hart said he would buy the Indian bead work that Brown made in the prison industry program for twice the money that Brown had been receiving. When Brown asked Hart where he was to get the money, Hart told him that his lawyer was smuggling in $100. When Brown appeared to be receptive to Hart's proposition, Hart added some more details to his plan. He told Brown that he also wanted him to testify that while the preliminary hearing for Hart was taking place in Pryor, he, Brown, had sent a letter to Hart and his lawyers in care of the Mayes County Jail, telling them about the letter to Jimmy Don Bunch. After Brown testified, Hart said that his attorneys would show great surprise and say that they had never received the letters. Because tampering with the mails is a federal offense, Hart's attorneys would ask that the FBI come to the prison and investigate why Hart did not receive his letters. This would help to show that there was a conspiracy by law enforcement against a poor Indian from Locust Grove.

Hart promised Brown that his lawyers would see he was transferred to another prison and that Benton and Fallis would not be in a position to seek revenge.

Three or four days after this alleged conversation, Brown said, Hart came to his cell again. Hart said that he wanted to add something to the story. He wanted Brown to testify that he had received a threatening letter saying that if he testified for Hart he would be killed. Other inmates on death row were also to testify that they had received letters threatening them if they testified. The letters were to have been dropped in the inmates' cells between 9:00 and 10:00 P.M., when only correctional officers are allowed outside the cells. Hart's attorneys would contend that the correctional officers were passing the letters.

Hart then allegedly produced three letters that threatened the inmates. The letters were written by an inmate, but Brown never met the letter writer. On the night of June 21 Brown said that he did, however, overhear a convict on the next level above death row yell down to Hart, "I've only got a couple of minutes to talk to you, Gene. I'll tell you this real fast. I've got the notes ready and I'll get them down to you as soon as possible."

Hart's attorneys would supposedly come down and take Brown's statement, have it typed, and have him sign it under oath. Another inmate named Boone, who was also under protection on death row, had agreed to lie for Hart. Both of the inmates were allegedly told by Hart that if they backed up on their statements as Bunch had done, they would be charged with perjury.

Collins asked whether Hart had ever discussed the Girl Scout murders with him. Hart supposedly told Brown, "The law doesn't have enough evidence to point to me. That handwriting on the wall can't be tied to me. I am an artist and can change my handwriting style anytime I want to." Brown said Hart told him that he had been around the Locust Grove area and the caves ever since his escape from the Mayes County Jail and commented that he knew that the police could not get "his prints off the death tent because he had taken precautions."

Collins asked Brown if he would submit to a polygraph examination to verify his truthfulness. The convict said that he would gladly take the test. He said he would also testify to all of his statements, but only if he were transferred to another penitentiary where he was not known as a snitch.

Collins believed Brown was telling the truth, but he felt he should be polygraphed to make sure. The OSBI arranged with the Department of Corrections to have Brown transferred out of the maximum security facility at McAlester to the Oklahoma State Reformatory at Granite. This would be accomplished through normal procedure and would take about a week. Brown would be polygraphed within the next couple of days.

Two days later the Tulsa District Attorney's office again received a letter from two inmates, Larry Boone and Andrew L. Hendricks. The letter said that Hart had told Boone that he (Hart) committed the Girl Scout murders, and Hendricks had overheard the statements. It went on to say that Hart's attorneys were due to visit them later in the week to see if the convict would testify for Hart.

The District Attorney's office again contacted Mike Wilkerson. Agents were sent to McAlester to interview the two men.

Cary Thurman drove to McAlester where he met Joe Collins at the penitentiary. Hendricks was interviewed first. He had been convicted of Second Degree Burglary and had been in the penitentiary since February of 1976. He had been placed on death row to protect him from the other convicts because he was a snitch for the prison's security chief. He had helped find illegal drugs and weapons among the inmate population.

Collins produced the letter and asked the convict if he had written it. Hendricks admitted that he had written the letter, but most of the information had been supplied by Boone.

He said that Hart had never personally approached him and asked him to testify, but he had approached Boone. Hendricks's cell was next to Hart's and every night he could hear Hart praying. There was a small hole in the wall through which Hendricks could peek. Hendricks said that Hart would kneel and ask God to forgive him for killing those three little girls. Hart talked in his sleep and several times he was awakened by Hart cussing Jimmy Don Bunch. He said that one night Hart woke him up babbling and thrashing around. When he looked through the hole, Hart was choking his pillow and saying, "You sorry son-of-a-bitch."

Although Hart had never asked him to testify, Hendricks had overheard him ask Boone to testify. Hart supposedly asked Boone to testify that he had gotten to know Hart and did not believe that he was capable of killing the three Girl Scouts. In return for his testimony, Boone was to receive $500. Hart told Boone if he pulled a Jimmy Don Bunch, his wife and children would be killed.

Boone asked Hart, "Did you kill those little girls?" Hart, who was standing outside of Boone's cell, glanced into Hendricks's cell. Hendricks acted as if he were asleep. Hart said that he had killed the girls and said he was "sorry for it, but it's because of what my wife done to me while I was in the penitentiary. After I did it, I spent the night in the cave."

After listening to the long, rambling story, Collins asked the convict if he would take a polygraph examination. He said that he would. He volunteered to testify but only if he were transferred to another prison where he would not be in danger.

After Hendricks was returned to his cell, Larry R. Boone was brought to the prison interview room. He had received a four-year sentence on a charge of Obtaining Money Under False Pretenses. Boone was scheduled for parole at Christmas. Boone seemed extremely nervous. Before the two agents could introduce themselves, he told them that he had to have protection because Hart already knew that they were talking to him. Thurman told him that he would check into the matter but would not promise him anything.

He said that he first met Hart two and a half months before when Hart was captured. Boone was already on death row because of death threats from other inmates. After about a month Hart approached him as he lay in his cell and asked him if he would help him in court. "I need you to testify for me," Hart said.

Boone laughed and asked, "How the hell can me, a con, help you by testifying?"

Hart told him that he wanted him to tell Hart's attorneys that he had received a letter from Buddy Fallis asking him to testify against Hart. Hart said that his attorneys could handle Sid Wise but were too afraid and intimidated by Fallis. He wanted Boone to say that he had seen another letter to Bunch from the Department of Corrections saying that Bunch was to get a quick parole and protection if he testified against Hart.

Boone asked Hart if he had killed the Girl Scouts. Hart said he had killed the children "because I was drinking and then smoked some marijuana." Boone asked what he did when he went into the tent. "I looked around, thought they were grown women in the tent. There were three people in the tent and they were in sleeping bags. I had to kill two of the girls in the tent and while I was doing that, the third girl woke up and started to scream so I put my hand over her mouth and then dragged her into the woods and then fucked her and then killed her," Boone quoted Hart. Hart claimed he stayed in the woods for three or four days after the murders.

Boone claimed that Hart's attorneys were watching a man in Oklahoma City who knew Hart had committed the crime. Hart offered Boone $5,000 if he would kill the man after he was paroled.

Boone rambled on about Hart and the more he talked, the more the agents disbelieved him. On one occasion Hart supposedly told Boone that while he was raping "the last girl, she pulled my hair out."

As the interview drew to a close, the agents asked Boone if he would submit to a polygraph. Boone became extremely nervous but reluctantly agreed.

At about 5:30 that afternoon a very nervous Larry Boone was escorted to the OSBI Regional Office by correctional officers. He was polygraphed on various aspects of the alleged statement that Hart had given to him. After approximately three hours Bill Sparks, an OSBI polygraphist, contacted Wilkerson in Tulsa and told him that the tests were officially going to be called inconclusive, but he had very grave doubts about the convict's story. Sparks said that he would contact Agent Sam Sparks (no relation) in Poteau the following day and ask him to assist in polygraphing the two subjects. Sam Sparks had over fifteen years of experience as a polygraph examiner, and on a case of this magnitude Bill thought it was better to have a second opinion.

The following day Sam and Bill Sparks met at the McAlester office and formulated their tests for the polygraph of the two inmates. Boone was the first to be polygraphed. His polygraph charts of responses to all relevant questions dealing with every part of his conversation were indicative of deception. In the examiner's opinion Boone's story was a lie from beginning to end. With this information in hand they confronted Boone, who denied that he had lied and steadfastly maintained that Hart had made the statements.

A few minutes later Andrew Hendricks was given a polygraph test. His responses were also sufficient to indicate that his story was a lie. After the test Hendricks admitted that he, Boone, and Brown had fabricated their stories and that Hart had never talked about the case to any of them. He went on to say that they had made up the story so that they could be transferred to a minimum security prison. When they took the stand to testify for the State, they were going to do what Jimmy Don Bunch had done to Garvin Isaacs. Hendricks said that he really wasn't going to lie for Hart. He still had a couple of years to do and just wanted to get an early parole or be sent to a minimum security institution. He said he would lie on the stand against Hart in order to get what he wanted.

Boone was again brought in and again steadfastly denied that he had lied. Nervously, he demanded the statement he had originally given the agents. The agents laughed as Boone said that he would go to federal court in order to get his statement back. Bill Sparks told him to do just that. Shortly thereafter the convicts were returned to the penitentiary. Brown's transfer to Granite Reformatory was cancelled.

CHAPTER 14

THREE DAYS AFTER THE PRELIMINARY HEARING, SAM PIGEON, through his attorney, John Ghostbear, agreed to allow the OSBI to search his home again.

The men got out of Eberle's van and gathered around Mike Wilkerson in the front yard. "Roger, I want you and Reimer to search the house," Wilkerson said as he pointed toward the shack. "Glen, why don't you search the south side. Larry, you take the back and I'll take the north side."

The men dispersed and moved to their respective search assignments.

"Mike," Chrisco shouted from inside the shack, "could you come here a minute?"

Wilkerson had a stick in his hand poking around in a trash pile in a clump of bushes. "I'll be right there," Wilkerson answered, walking toward the house through waist-high weeds.

"They've cleaned the place up, Mike," Chrisco said as Wilkerson stepped into the front room.

"Damn," Wilkerson said, surveying the interior. Most of the furnishings had been removed, new fiberboard placed on the floor, and the walls had been painted. There was a kind of sterile atmosphere in the house.

"All of Hart's belongings have been removed," said Chrisco, pointing toward the bedroom. "You can't tell the man has ever been here."

"Well, go ahead and give this place an inch by inch search. Keep your eyes out for a pipe," Wilkerson said, feeling that the search effort was in vain. He turned and walked out the front door. As he stepped from the porch, he heard Chrisco shout, "Mike, here's a corncob pipe." Wilkerson burst back through the door, almost running over Chrisco, who was holding a small, souvenir corncob pipe.

"Mike, the pipe was up there in that shaving kit," Chrisco said, pointing to a small shaving kit sitting on the old refrigerator that Pigeon used for clothes storage. Wilkerson looked at the small pipe skeptically as Chrisco continued, "It was there when I searched the place the first time. I just didn't think it was of any value."

"I don't think it's of any value now," Wilkerson said as he pitched the pipe back to Chrisco and started toward the door.

"Do you want me to take it?" Chrisco asked, feeling better that his boss had said he wouldn't have taken the pipe in the first search either.

"Yeah," Wilkerson said, stopping in the doorway. "Bag and tag it."

"What about this mirror?" Chrisco asked, displaying a small, blue, dust-covered mirror.

"Where'd you find it?" Wilkerson inquired, taking the mirror from the agent's hand, being careful not to destroy any fingerprints.

"In the same shaving kit," Chrisco responded.

"Yeah, go ahead and bag and tag it," Wilkerson said indifferently as he handed the mirror back to Chrisco.

After approximately two hours the men met on the front porch and surveyed what their search had yielded—a corncob pipe, a yellow scarf, a small blue mirror, several newspaper clippings showing women in short skirts, cheerleaders, buxomy women from X-rated movie ads, a felt-tipped pen, a small quantity of tobacco, and a small aluminum key ring.

"Damn," Wilkerson said, looking at the small pile on the porch. "It wasn't worth the effort. Whatever Isaacs was afraid of is gone now. The family probably has it and doesn't even know about it." He reached down, ran his hand into the brown paper bag, and pulled out a fist full of long-leafed tobacco. Medicine tobacco, he thought to himself. It seems like you just can't get away from medicine in this case.

He threw the tobacco back into the sack, dusted his hands against his trouser legs, and said, "Let's get out of here."

They locked the door on the old shack and got into Eberle's van. As they drove down the rocky trail and neared Freeman Pigeon's residence, Bowles said, "let's stop here a minute." Eberle pulled the van in front of the house; Bowles got out, opened the gate, and walked to the porch where a young Indian boy was sitting. After a few minutes of conversation with the boy, Bowles returned to the truck. "Hart's relatives came and got his belongings about three weeks ago. Whatever we overlooked is gone now," Bowles said as he mounted the vehicle.

The men drove in depressed silence for several miles. "Well, regardless of how worthless these things look," Wilkerson broke the silence as he pointed to the collected evidence on the floor, "we're going to check them out. Larry, the scarf and the mirror look like the only items that could belong to a little girl so show them to the victims' parents. Roger, show the other stuff to Pigeon and see what he says about 'em. You can describe the scarf and the mirror to him." Neither Bowles nor Chrisco answered; both knew that it was a waste of time.

The victims' parents could not identify the scarf or the mirror. Pigeon told Chrisco that the felt-tipped pen and key ring belonged to him. He said that the other items "must be Gene's." During the next few weeks all of the counselors and scouts were contacted and asked if they owned the pipe, mirror, or scarf. Boredom had now taken over the investigation. Contacting the scouts for the third time was a tiresome, monotonous job that none of the agents enjoyed. The children were now literally scattered all over the United States. Some were under psychiatric care and could not be talked to by the agents, while the parents of others were becoming irritable and believed that their children should be left alone. But the job no one liked continued without a spark of hope that it would yield anything.

On July 31 Jack Shroff filed a million-dollar lawsuit against reporter Don Hayden and the Tulsa *Tribune* for defamation in the article published about his polygraph test.

On August 22 the primary elections for state offices were held. Sid Wise finished a distant fifth in the Democratic Primary in a five-man race. He received 6.8 percent of the vote.

On August 27, at 8:30 A.M., Sheriff Pete Weaver suffered a massive heart attack. According to a medicine man the heart attack was looked upon by some of the Cherokee people as a sign of Weaver's bad faith in persecuting Gene Hart.

On September 20 Jimmy Don Bunch requested an early parole to pursue a career in the ministry. When Warden Norman Hess was asked whether he believed Bunch was sincere, he said, "Bunch is an opportunist who will say whatever will help him the most. Do I believe him? Of course not. I don't believe him because I've heard so many lies of his." The parole board unanimously denied the parole request.

On October 16 the Chief of the Cherokee Nation, Ross Swimmer, announced that the Tribe was contributing $12,500 to the Hart Defense Fund for expert testimony and transcripts. They said that in no way did they "want the money to reflect that Hart is either guilty or innocent. We just want to make sure he gets a fair trial."

Mike Wilkerson sat in his office.

The buzzing of the telephone broke the monotony of going through the paper mountain on his desk.

"Yes," Wilkerson answered, still looking at a report.

"Harvey Pratt on line two," the secretary answered.

Wilkerson flipped the lighted button and greeted his friend. "How's it goin', hoss?"

"Fine, Mike. I just called to ask if you were still interested in talking to someone about the Indian ways and, in particular, our friend Gene Hart?" Pratt said in his usual silken tone.

"Damn right," Wilkerson responded enthusiastically, jumping at the chance to get away from his paperwork. "Who and where?"

"He's in your part of the state, in the boonies. It's hard to find so listen closely to the directions," Pratt warned. As he described how to get to the person's house, Wilkerson copied his instructions on a note pad. It was indeed in the boonies, and the last mile had to be traversed on foot.

"Damn, son. This old boy doesn't want to be found, does he?"

"Very few people ever see him. He is very respected and very powerful. He must be treated with respect."

"Don't sweat it, Harv. I would love to talk to him. When should I go?"

"You may go any time after dark. I have talked to him and he will be expecting you. I told him you were Cherokee."

"I'll try to get down there in the next few nights," Wilkerson said. Then he and Pratt exchanged good-byes.

Tulsa's television stations filed a motion with the Oklahoma Supreme Court asking that the trial be televised. In a landmark decision the Court said that the trial could be televised if certain conditions were met. Chief Justice Ralph Hodges released recommendations that a specially appointed committee of judges and lawyers be set up, calling for the Court to approve limited and restricted coverage by television, still cameras, and tape recorders. Hodges said that the Court would rule upon the recommendations some time in October. Hodges went on to say that before television could be allowed in the courtroom, the defendant, his attorney, the District Attorney, and the judge would have to consent.

The initial reaction from the District Attorney's offices in both Tulsa and Mayes counties was less than enthusiastic. Sid Wise said, "I'll have to study the decision long and hard before approving or disapproving." Privately, however, he said that he would be opposed to cameras in the courtroom. Both he and Fallis feared that witnesses might consider themselves prima donnas or actors, thus reacting differently from the way they would normally. Wise said that he was concerned about the power of the media to edit these types of proceedings. "It very well could influence the overall perspective of the trial if excerpts were taken out of context." They did not, however, want to be whipping boys for the media. Both prosecutors were all but certain that Hart and his attorneys didn't want the trial televised either. Another Jimmy Don Bunch embarrassment before a TV audience could destroy a budding law career.

When first asked about the possibilities, Isaacs said that he wouldn't make a comment until he had studied the Court's decision. "I don't do anything unless it's in the best interest of my client. We'll want to study this and proceed with caution," he said.

The initial reaction of Judge Whistler, who would preside over the trial, was, "We ought to give this thing a try. If they [the Supreme Court Justices] say we're going to go with the whole bit, that's fine with me as long as it doesn't disrupt the proceedings."

On October 20 Isaacs filed fifty-nine motions in the Pryor District Court. One of the motions requested that television cameras not be allowed in the courtroom during the trial. Judge Whistler granted the request. Discouraged and disgusted, KOTV announced that it would not provide closed-circuit television to the courtroom annex.

Since there would be no television coverage of the trial, Judge Whistler was forced to lay down certain rules. He said that there would be two pews in the ninety-seat courtroom allotted to the news media—approximately twenty seats. Press passes would be written by the Court Clerk, signed by Whistler, and have a court seal placed on them. One pass would be issued per major newspaper, television, and radio station. News organizations would, if they wished a pass, write a letter naming the specific employee who would cover the trial. The media, Hart's family, and the families of the slain girls would be allowed to enter the courtroom prior to the general public. The remainder of the seats would be filled by the public at 8:45 A.M. Each day's testimony would begin promptly at 9:00 A.M. After all seats were filled, anyone else would be cleared from the courtroom and the halls of the third floor of the Mayes County Courthouse. A security station would be established on the stairwell between the second and third floors. Those wishing to attend the proceedings would, in all likelihood, be searched with a metal detector before entering the courtroom. Members of the news media would be allowed to leave the courtroom during the trial and return to their seats. One reporter from the group would be selected by the media to attend hearings in Judge Whistler's chambers and report back to the other media representatives.

The rough gravel road abruptly ended as expected. The headlights of Wilkerson's car lighted the first row of the thick forest that awaited him. He flipped on the interior light and read the instructions he had copied from his conversation with Pratt, then backed up the car slightly and turned to the right. The headlights fell upon a time-obscured trail. His left hand reached to the glove compartment to retrieve his flashlight.

"Shit," he muttered when he discovered the flashlight was gone. Well, it's a moonlit night, he thought, looking into the star-bright sky. He turned off the dome light, killed the engine, and turned off the car lights. Then he sat and stared at the dark woods until his eyes got accustomed to the darkness.

In a few minutes Wilkerson stepped from the car, locked it, and walked toward the scarlike trail. Only the sound of his breathing and his feet falling upon the rocky surface of the trail could be heard. No crickets, frogs, or creatures of the night had made their presence known. As he walked, his eyes adjusted to the darkness until he could easily navigate the rough terrain. He occasionally walked into spiderwebs that stretched across the trail, quickly wiping the silken strands from his face and hoping that a deadly black widow or fiddleback spider would not find its home in his shirt. Ten minutes dragged by when the trail opened into a small clearing a hundred yards in diameter. Located in the center of it was a tiny shack.

This couldn't be the place, he thought as he walked up the front of the archaic structure. The little shack appeared to have only one room with a small porch sheltering a closed doorway.

Wilkerson cautiously walked around the little hut looking for some appearance of habitation. The windows located on the other three sides were covered with curtains made from burlap. There was no electricity or plumbing. He again arrived at the door and was startled to find it standing open. He lay his foot softly upon the wooden porch, which creaked as if it was in agony. His eyes tried to pierce the darkness of the open door but he could see nothing. He was fighting himself to keep from drawing his gun. He lay his hand upon the rough doorfacing and stepped inside the shack. The faint smell of tobacco and bacon fat permeated the thick air in the room.

The room was dark, totally dark except for a shaft of moonlight that spat from a hole in the wood-shingled roof. The dull ray of light came to rest upon an old, wrinkled hand. Wilkerson's eyes strained to make out the shadowy figure to whom the hand belonged. His feet squeaked out one more step on the old wooden floor and a figure seemed to materialize from the darkness. It was an elderly Indian man sitting cross-legged, Indian fashion, on the floor. His long hair hung from his bowed head and lay upon his stooped shoulders. Wilkerson thought him to be very old.

"Sir," the agent whispered, feeling his voice crack the silence like a whip. "My name is Wilkerson. I'm told that you may be able to help me. Harvey Pratt says that you will talk with me about medicine and Gene Hart."

The head of the old man slowly raised until he looked the large white man in the eye. "Pratt says that you are one who can be trusted," the old man grunted in a heavy Indian accent. "You are of Cherokee blood?"

"Yes, sir. My great-grandmother was Nancy Ellen Lucas. She was a Cherokee but I have mostly white blood," Wilkerson said, searching the man's face for a sign of disdain. There was none.

The man smiled. Even in the darkness Wilkerson's light Irish complexion belied any hint of Indian blood. "Yes, I can see that you are white, but you have Cherokee blood." The old man lifted his right hand and held it out in a gesture for the white man to sit before him. Wilkerson sat his two hundred pounds awkwardly before the old Indian. When he was seated in Indian fashion, the man said, "My name is Crying Wolf. How may I help you?"

"First of all, Crying Wolf, are you a medicine man?" Wilkerson shyly asked.

The old man nodded and said, "All Cherokees use medicine. I am a member of the Katowa or Nighthawk Society. It is a religious society or medicine clan of the Cherokee people."

"Isn't Gene Hart a member of the Nighthawk Society?"

"No, no. I don't believe so," the old man hastened to answer. "His mother, Ella Mae Buckskin, maiden name was Ella Mae Sullatuskee. She is a member of the United Katowa Band. This is not to be confused with the Nighthawk Society. I believe the United Katowa Band was organized sometime in the 1930s. It's an organization of Cherokee people, but is not a clan unto itself. Again, the Nighthawk Society is one of the original seven clans of the Cherokee."

"Now let me get this straight," Wilkerson said, somewhat confused. "Is Hart a Nighthawk or in the Katowa Band?"

"As near as I can determine, he is not a Nighthawk, nor is he in the Katowa Band. He is simply a Cherokee Indian who receives the benefits of the clan, the medicine and the knowledge of their ways, because his mother is a member of the Band. And because she is a member of the Band, he becomes a natural member."

"What do you mean when you say he receives medicine and knowledge from the Katowas?"

"Just what I said," the old man began slowly. "From different people within the Band, he learned Cherokee medicine. That is, how to use tobacco."

"You mean he learned different medicine from different people?"

"Yes. For instance, he would learn a secret from one medicine person, and then he would go to another medicine person and learn his secrets. And then he would go to another, and to another, and to another, until he knew much medicine."

"Forgive my ignorance, sir, but is the medicine the tobacco or is it the smoke?"

"Both," the old man replied. "But in the very true sense, it is the tobacco. The way the tobacco is remade is the main ingredient in the medicine."

"What do you mean remade?" Wilkerson asked.

The old man reached over to his side and produced a small brown paper sack. He untwisted the top, reached his hand in, and pulled out a fist of what appeared to be raw tobacco. "Have you touched a dead person in the past four days?"

"No, sir, I haven't," Wilkerson responded, somewhat startled.

"Are you sure?" Crying Wolf repeated with great seriousness. "If you have touched a dead person in the last four days you will ruin the medicine in this tobacco."

"No, sir, I have touched no dead person in the last four days," Wilkerson vowed.

"In answer to your question, remaking is a ceremonial process whereby tobacco is washed and sprinkled with water," the old man explained as he ran his index finger through the tobacco that rested in his left hand. "And when it is washed and when it is sprinkled, it is prayed over. These messages or prayers are in Cherokee and are designed to serve certain functions which I will not discuss with you. Each tobacco is remade for a special medicine purpose. It must be remade in certain places, at certain times, with certain types of water. Running spring water is ideal for remaking tobacco."

"May I see some of your tobacco?" Wilkerson asked, reaching toward the old man's hand.

Crying Wolf nodded and Wilkerson took a couple of short sticks of tobacco from the Indian's hand. "Does it make any difference what kind of tobacco? I mean, whether it's store-bought or raw tobacco?" Wilkerson inquired as he smelled the sticks.

"It would have seemed to have made a difference long, long ago," the old man replied, "because the only tobacco that was used in medicine was tobacco that was grown for a particular purpose. However, I know for a fact that some practitioners in this area used tobacco of the chewing or smoking variety, usually Cotton Boll twist. I have also seen some people remake tobacco from Pall Mall, Camel, or Winston cigarettes."

"When filter cigarettes are used, are the filters usually thrown away?"

"Most of the time. It depends upon the tribe. For instance, I saw a Cheyenne woman use a Winston cigarette as medicine. She did not remove the filter. I cannot recall ever seeing a Cherokee smoke tobacco without removing the filter."

"Is this tobacco store-bought?" Wilkerson asked, pointing to the tobacco in his hand.

"No, it is not," replied Crying Wolf proudly.

"What is this tobacco for?" Wilkerson pressed.

The old man shook his head and said, "That is not for you to know."

"Well, is there a different type of tobacco that contains different power?"

"Yes, there is, but there is also power in knowing how to use the tobacco. I cannot discuss how to use the tobacco with you. However, I will share this with you. I have in my possession the most powerful medicine tobacco that there is. It is called the Ancient One, or the Old One. It is grown in the shade of a tree. While it is growing, it is never seen by human eyes."

"You say it is called the Ancient One or the Old One? How old is the tobacco?"

"I can only give you a relationship. There is one tribe of Indians that most other tribes refer to as Grandpas. They are referred to as Grandpas, because they are very, very old. The Delaware Tribe is the Grandpas. If I meet a Delaware Indian under any circumstances, I will call the person grandmother or grandfather or grandpa regardless of their age. It is a means of showing respect. They have a very ancient heritage and these people are entitled to the respect because they are looked on as being the heart of the universe. Anything that was on this earth before man is called grandpa by the Cherokee people. In some ceremonies we refer to rocks as Grandpas. In certain ceremonies where medicine is used, we refer to that medicine, if it was here before man, as Grandpa. There are grandpa fires—fires that were here before man. And then there is the Ancient One. This tobacco takes its proper place as Grandpa and is cared for and respected as much as fire because it is as important as fire. It is Grandpa."

"Could Gene Hart use this medicine for bad purposes and get it to work?"

"Yes, he could," the man said, "but of course he would condemn his soul forever. He would be daring God to strike him dead. But unless Hart knows much medicine, which he may, he should be recognized by the medicine men as being deceitful."

"Is there no way he could hide this deceit and still get medicine men to help him?" Wilkerson asked, not really believing that he was asking the question.

"Let me put it this way. Now, I can only put myself in Hart's place and tell you how I would escape. Assuming that he did these crimes—and I am assuming only for the moment that he did—he committed something that was against the very nature of all Indian people—he violated little children. This is too horrible to think that a Cherokee would do, and all the Cherokee people being kin would not accept him. Because of this kinship, the Cherokees around him would not believe that he committed such an act, because if they did, they are admitting that a relative is a child molester and killer. So consequently, living a life of deception, which Hart is certainly accustomed to, is nothing new. He is accustomed to having his people and family rally around him and assist him in his escapes and help him do whatever he wants to do. He is almost like a pampered child. I think you can see it in his nickname Sonny. I don't think anyone who helped him could admit that he would commit such an act because it would make them partly responsible for the things that he had done. So, if I had committed these atrocities, I would want to maintain my status within the community, my society, and my family. One of the first acts I would do would be to cleanse myself and cloak myself with protection: a shield of medicine that would prevent any medicine person from looking into me and reading me for what I am. This medicine, which Hart is most capable of using, would work almost like deflecting a bullet. If someone was attempting to physically read me, the attempt would ricochet off in another direction to another race of people. By ricocheting into another race, the Cherokees would rally behind me. That's what I would do and then I would go to the medicine person who I knew could benefit me through his medicine. This medicine might be the ability to hide and it doesn't necessarily mean that this is the ability to vanish into thin air. It can be merely just a good knowledge of the land and the Cherokees living on the land. You will find that the Cherokees are notorious about keeping their mouths shut."

"Yes, I know," Wilkerson answered, smiling. "What exactly is reading?"

"It can be compared with what white men call ESP. All powerful medicine men have the ability to read a person."

"Are you telling me that all of these people who are helping Hart believe he is innocent?"

"No, I am not telling you that they believe he is innocent. I am telling you that they can't believe he is guilty. I believe that the medicine men believe he is innocent. If, in fact, he is guilty and is deceiving the medicine men and using his medicine for evil purposes, his soul was in fact damned at the first moment that he used the medicine."

He pondered his next question for a moment and asked, "By the way, Crying Wolf. Do you know what a Stageny is?"

"No," the old man snapped, obviously not telling the truth. Wilkerson knew that he had hit upon a sensitive point and was afraid that he had spoiled the rapport that he had built in the last few minutes.

"Well, let me tell you what I know about the Stageny. I have heard that it is the great medicine owl which sleeps under the cedar tree. I have also heard that Gene Hart has the ability to change himself into the Stageny. Personally, I believe this is ridiculous, but I would just like to get your thoughts on it."

"First of all, I will not discuss the Stageny with you, because this is something of which you should not know. But, I will answer you like this. The Cherokee believe that there is kinship with every part of nature, with every animal, with every rock, and with every blade of grass. We are kin to the earth and anything that grows from the earth. There is a direct correlation in this kinship creed and the Indian people. Some people believe that through mystic arts and big medicine, men can actually transform themselves into other animals or substances. It is not a metamorphosis in its literal sense, but it is merely diffusion of matter and reclamation into other matter."

Wilkerson's eyebrows raised as he heard the list of six-syllable words come from a man he had thought ill-educated. It was becoming more and more obvious that the old man before him was not only well-read, but in fact well-educated and extremely intelligent.

"The belief in this transformation is quite prevalent," Crying Wolf continued. "A great number of Cherokee people believe that a person can transform himself into another being whether they want to hide under a leaf or to go into a rock, or whether they want to literally become an owl or any other animal."

Wilkerson smiled wryly and asked, "Do you believe Gene Hart could do this?"

"No, no," the old man grunted. "I don't believe that he could. He may, however, use these legends to his own benefit. He is not the quality of person who could perform these deeds. But he could enhance his image by using the terms and knowledge of the old Cherokee ways so that he may give the appearance that he is performing these deeds. Opportunities to use these tricks would simply enhance his image."

"You're not going to talk to me about the Stageny, are you, Crying Wolf?" Wilkerson chided.

"No, I am not," the old man responded as hard as granite. "Again, these are things that you should not know."

"Is there any way that you as a medicine person can determine whether or not Gene Hart is guilty?"

"If Hart is in fact guilty and is disguising himself with a veil of deceit, he probably is beating the medicine man's reading. If this be the case, his fate has been decided. His soul is damned. I have no power to alter God's justice. I can, however, use the Old One to cause the ultimate test to be made."

"The ultimate test?" Wilkerson questioned.

"Yes, life and death, that is the ultimate test. By smoking the Old One and performing certain rites, and depositing the grandpa tobacco at certain places, God can determine whose heart is true. The Cherokee people believe that Gene's heart is true. They believe that Pete Weaver's heart is bad. In other words, we can determine the truth. If either man has misused his God-given ability and talents, he has in fact said, 'God, strike me dead if I am lying.' "

"Do you ever foresee using your medicine to cause the final test of truth?"

The old Indian man paused for a moment pondering his answer. "Mr. Wilkerson, you might find this hard to believe, but I was a law enforcement officer most of my life. I believe in the law. I believe in the white law and I believe in the Indian law. I am not under any illusion that justice is always done in the courtroom. In my long lifetime, I have seen men go to jail who didn't deserve it and I saw men acquitted who were guilty. But one thing I am sure of—God decides the ultimate truth. I have enforced justice with my medicine and the will of God. In answer to your question, yes. I would use the Old One if it became necessary."

"What would be the final outcome if you used the Old One?" Wilkerson asked, making sure that he understood clearly.

"What do you mean, the final outcome?"

"I mean, what would happen to a person if he were not telling the truth?" Wilkerson inquired, pinpointing the remedy.

"Considering the seriousness of the crime and assuming that the punishment would fit the crime, the guilty party would, of course, die," Crying Wolf replied with no indication of indecisiveness.

Wilkerson shook his head skeptically and said, "Sir, I am sorry, I am a modern man and I cannot believe that a person's fate can be determined in this way. I don't say this to insult you, but I tell you this truthfully and with great respect."

"I don't expect you to have faith in my medicine. By your own admission you are white. You know little of medicine. Perhaps if you knew more of what medicine can do and has done you would not be quite so skeptical. We are at a standstill because some of the things of which I talk can only be talked of in Cherokee, to a Cherokee."

There was no hint of ridicule or outrage in the old man's voice. "I will do what must be done," the old man continued. "I still love the law in my heart. I will still see justice done and I know God will see justice done."

The old man slowly bowed his head as if he were praying. Wilkerson knew that the discussion was at an end. He put his hand on the floor and boosted himself to his feet. "Thank you, sir," he said.

Crying Wolf did not look up or acknowledge him. Wilkerson turned and walked out of the door toward the trail that led him back to his car and the twentieth century.

On October 31 Thurman came to the OSBI officer in Tulsa to try to contact the remaining twenty-eight Girl Scouts and counselors left on his list. He poured himself a cup of coffee, made small talk with Wilkerson, then walked slowly into his office, sat down, and flipped to the list of names. With a long, deep breath he dialed the number of Karen Mitchell in Stillwater, Oklahoma. She had been a counselor-in-training in the Choctaw Unit at Camp Scott.

"Hello, Karen, this is Agent Cary Thurman with the Oklahoma State Bureau of Investigation," he began as he had done on three or four hundred other occasions. "I've got four or five items here I would like to describe to you on the phone and see if you have ever had any of these items in your possession while you were at Camp Scott."

Thurman had talked to so many scouts that he had a pat spiel that could be compared to a sales pitch.

"Uh-huh, yes, okay, these are the items." Wilkerson could hear Thurman talking in the next office. "I have a little blue mirror. . . . What?" Thurman gasped. "Now, wait. Let me describe it to you," he said again.

Wilkerson stopped his paperwork and listened intently.

"Okay, it's a blue mirror with flowers on the back. . . . It's yours! It is yours!"

Wilkerson jumped up from his chair and ran to the doorway of Thurman's office. Thurman's hand had begun to shake.

"Now I have some other items here. I have a yellow head scarf. Okay, that's not yours. And I have a small corncob pipe—that's yours, too?"

Wilkerson looked down at Thurman and mouthed the words in almost a whisper, "We're going that way. Tell her there'll be somebody there in a few minutes to show her the articles personally."

Thurman thanked her and told her there would be someone there within two hours. As he hung up the phone, Roger Chrisco walked through the door.

Thurman was visibly shaken. "Mike, if this is righteous, we've got that son-of-a-bitch. We've got that son-of-a-bitch," Thurman said with the emotions of a man who had lived with a case probably too long—a case that had been too big a part of his life.

"Cary," Wilkerson said, "I want you to stay here. Roger, I want you to go to Stillwater and talk to this little girl. Get a good, full interview. Show her the mirror and the corncob pipe and see if there's any way she can identify them. To me, this sounds too good to be true."

"What the hell is going on?" Chrisco asked.

Thurman and Wilkerson laughed; in their excitement they hadn't explained anything to Chrisco.

"We think this little girl can identify these items—the corncob pipe and the mirror that you took from the Pigeon residence, Roger," Mike Wilkerson explained.

"You're kidding!"

"Yeah, that's the reason I want you to jump in the car right now because you're already in the chain of custody on the pipe and the mirror and I won't have to get Cary in the chain on it."

"Okay, I'm gone," Chrisco said as he started toward the door.

"Don't you think it would be a good idea if you got the girl's name and address?" Wilkerson laughed.

"Yeah," Chrisco said sheepishly. "That would be a good idea."

Pale-faced, Cary Thurman wrote down the name and address and handed it to Chrisco.

"You call me from her house," Wilkerson told Chrisco. "You call me from the house as soon as she either does or doesn't identify them."

•

It took Chrisco just over an hour to drive the seventy miles between Tulsa and Stillwater. He found himself in a nice residential neighborhood as he located the house indicated by the address he held in his hand. A pretty, young, black girl about eighteen years of age answered the door. "Ma'am, I'm Roger Chrisco, an agent with the State Bureau of Investigation," he said, showing his identification. "May I come in?"

"Yeah, sure."

They walked into the living room and sat down, and Karen introduced Chrisco to her mother. As Chrisco sat down, he opened a large, brown envelope and produced the blue mirror.

"That's mine," the young girl squealed. "That's the mirror I took to Camp Scott."

"Is there any doubt in your mind, ma'am?"

"No doubt in my mind whatsoever," she said. "This is my mirror."

"Is there any way you can identify the mirror other than by the fact that it looks like your mirror?" Chrisco hoped.

"It is just my mirror," the young woman answered. "That is all there is to it."

Chrisco tried to suppress his excitement as he produced the corncob pipe.

"That's mine—that's mine, too," she said. "I had it on a straw hat. I took both of them to Camp Scott."

"There's no doubt in your mind?"

"There's no doubt in my mind," she said as she took the pipe from Chrisco's hand. "See these teeth marks? These are my teeth marks and there should be some teeth marks around the top of the bowl where I bit it there. Yes, there they are. See?" she said, pointing to the teeth marks on the bowl. "I had an old hat—an old hillbilly hat—that we bought at some park someplace and this was sewn on it."

"Why did you take these items to Camp Scott?" Chrisco asked.

"Well, we had what we called a brown bag skit," she said. "It's kind of an improvisational entertainment and all we do is produce one of these items and do a small skit on it."

"Let's see, now, Karen, you were a counselor-in-training?"

"Yes."

"And you were assigned to Choctaw Unit?"

"Yes, that's right."

"When is the last time you saw these items?"

"Oh, it seems like it was Sunday night. The little girls got there about five in the afternoon. I took a towel out of my footlocker and it seems like I saw them then. However, I can't be certain but I know that they were there from June 5th on because, you see, we got there a week early to get everything set up and they were there then."

"Did you miss these items?"

"Yes, I missed them but there wasn't any big deal," she replied. "I thought maybe that I had just left them on the ground or something."

"You say the last time you saw them was Sunday night?"

"Yes, after we got back from eating supper, it was raining, you remember? I tried to get into the footlocker to get a towel and the lock was jammed on it and I had a hard time opening it. I thought at the time somebody must have been messing with it. When we got the footlocker back to Stillwater after all of that happened, we had to take it to a locksmith to get it open because it was really jammed then."

"Did you bring the footlocker back yourself?"

"No, I left it there and it didn't get here until about two weeks later."

"Ma'am, can I use your phone?" Chrisco asked Mrs. Mitchell.

"Yes, of course."

As Chrisco dialed the phone and waited for the answer, he asked, "Mrs. Mitchell, what do you do?"

"I'm a bailiff for a district judge here in Stillwater."

"And Mr. Mitchell?"

"He is a doctor and a professor of biochemistry out at Oklahoma State University."

Wilkerson answered the phone. "She identified it, Mike."

"Oh, you're kidding!"

"Yes, yes, she did. She identified it."

Thurman was on the other line. "We've made that son-of-a-bitch! We've made him!"

"Thanks for calling, Roger," Wilkerson said. "I'll talk to you when you get back."

Chrisco knew that the chain of custody would have to be established on the footlocker. He would have to get the name of every person who had handled the footlocker from the time Karen had last seen it at the Girl Scout camp to the time that it had been returned to her. It had already been established at the preliminary hearing that Hart's defense would be that the State of Oklahoma needed a scapegoat. If the chain of custody could not be established, it would only add fuel to the fire that evidence was being planted in the case.

Chrisco continued his interview with Karen, writing down the names of everyone who had seen the pipe and mirror while they were in her possession. He got the name of the locksmith who had opened the locker. After the interview he drove to the campus of Oklahoma State University, where he interviewed Dr. Mitchell. When Chrisco asked whether the doctor had ever seen the mirror, the doctor explained, "There's no doubt in my mind that that's Karen's mirror. I bought it for my daughter about six or seven years ago."

Thurman telephoned District Attorney Buddy Fallis and his First Assistant, Ron Shaffer, and told them what they had found. Both realized that it was probably the biggest break in the case to date. Arrangements were made for Shaffer and Thurman to go to Stillwater the following day and talk with the girl.

Thurman called the District Attorney's office in Pryor and told District Attorney's Investigator Beverly Hough what had been found. "I took that locker to the police department a couple of days after the murders," Hough exclaimed.

"What police department?" Thurman asked.

"The Locust Grove Police Department—I took it there and stored it. The little girl had run off and left it and no one had taken it to Tulsa."

Thurman called the Locust Grove Police Department and talked to Eddie Moody, the dispatcher there. He remembered a girl bringing a footlocker in and leaving it a few days after the homicide. He said that the police department had held it for eight or nine days and then it disappeared.

Thurman then talked to a patrolman on duty when the trunk was brought in. He said that he had seen the trunk sitting in the police station, but didn't know who brought it in. One night when there wasn't anything to do, he decided that he would pick the lock on the trunk and see what was inside. He picked the lock and a small part of the lock fell out. He tried to replace it inside, but it was obvious that the lock was broken.

Damn, Thurman thought. The worst that could happen had happened. The locker had been contaminated by a law enforcement officer who had no reason to pick the lock other than boredom and curiosity. Of course, in the officer's defense, he had no idea that it could turn out to be one of the most important pieces of evidence in a triple murder. The officer went on to say that a girl and her parents came by and claimed the trunk a few days later. He didn't remember what the people looked like, however. The officer contended that he did not take anything out of the locker and didn't remember a mirror or corncob pipe.

The same day that the mirror and pipe were identified, the OSBI identified the last print in the death tent. It was the right palm print of Agent Aupy Linville who had been away for three months attending the FBI National Academy. The agents laughed as the usually stone-faced Linville confessed that he had touched one of the cots in the death tent.

On November 1 Roger Chrisco, Cary Thurman, Buddy Fallis, and Ron Shaffer met with Mr. and Mrs. Mitchell and Karen at the courthouse in Stillwater, Oklahoma. She told basically the same story she had related to Chrisco except that now, after some reflection, the last time she could remember having the mirror was the Wednesday prior to the homicides and she could not remember specifically having them after that. But she remained strong in her statements and said there would be no problem with her testifying. Dr. Mitchell was equally strong on his identification of the mirror and said that he would be glad to testify.

OSBI chemist Janice Davis took Hart's sperm samples and the samples from the victims to Dr. John MacLeod at New York Hospital. MacLeod was recognized as America's foremost authority on male infertility and the study of sperm. He had made it his life work and believed that individual sperm could someday be matched to a particular individual.

On October 29 Buddy Fallis and Ron Shaffer went to New York Hospital to talk to the doctor. They wanted to ascertain what his final report would say and what kind of a witness he was going to be. Dr. MacLeod said his final report would state that all of the spermatozoa that were examined from Hart's underwear came from the testes and the ejaculate of the same individual. He went on to say that it would not be unreasonable to come to the conclusion that the spermatozoa found in the bodies of the three victims could have had the same source as specimens taken from Hart's underwear. He also said that, conversely, there was no evidence detected in the morphology of the spermatozoa found in the bodies of the three victims to exclude the accused as a source of the spermatozoa.

Working closely together, Dr. MacLeod and Janice Davis conducted a probability study. When all known variables were taken into consideration (non-white male, 6.4 percent of the population; blood-type O, 45 percent of the population; secretor, 80 percent of the population; elongated type sperm, 4.4 percent of the population; and acute tapering form sperm, 2 percent of the population), the number of people in the United States that could statistically meet all these criteria would represent approximately .0020 percent of the population.

CHAPTER 15

ON NOVEMBER 16 AT 11:00 A.M. THE PHONE RANG AT THE OSBI Regional Office in Tulsa. "Mike," the gravel voice of the Director said, "Isaacs is coming by your office with a subpoena for all of our reports."

"What the hell for?" Wilkerson snapped. "We've been through this before. Is the judge such a pea brain that he would sign another subpoena for the papers?"

"There may be something more to this than meets the eye," Kennedy said, as if he knew more than he was telling.

"What do you mean, Tom?" asked Wilkerson.

"Janice Davis says she talked to Pete Weaver who says Wise gave some of our investigative reports to that newspaperman, Ron Grimsley."

"Shit!" Wilkerson said. "Wise wouldn't do that." Wilkerson paused for a moment and pondered his statement. "Well, surely Sid is not that flaky?"

"Well, I just wanted to call you and let you know that Isaacs will be there in a minute," Kennedy repeated. "The subpoena is for tomorrow."

"Tom, transfer me to the lab. I want to talk to Janice," Wilkerson said, and bid the Director good-bye. Davis confirmed that Weaver had told her that Wise had given Grimsley OSBI reports. Weaver had gone on to say that Isaacs was going to try to show that because Wise had given the reports to an unprivileged third party, the reports were no longer confidential. Thus, the defense was entitled to them.

Wilkerson had Davis transfer him to the OSBI Legal Advisor, Miles Zimmerman. "Miles," Wilkerson began, "I'm going to get a subpoena from Isaacs in a little while, ordering me to produce the OSBI reports tomorrow at a hearing."

"Hell, Mike, we've been through this before. Isaacs can't get our reports with a subpoena. Who signed it, anyway?" Zimmerman asked, as if he were bored.

"Kennedy says it was Whistler," Wilkerson responded.

"Oh, that's a different story," Zimmerman said with a newly discovered interest. "Why would he subpoena our records? He knows better than that."

"That's what I want you to find out, Miles. There's no telling what the hell's going on. Janice said Pete told her Wise had given OSBI reports to that squirrely newspaperman."

"Oh, God!" Miles said. Miles thought out loud, "I had better call Whistler. I'll call you back."

About ten minutes later Zimmerman telephoned Wilkerson. "Mike," Miles began, sounding puzzled, "there is something up. I just talked to Judge Whistler and he says he doesn't know anything about the subpoena or why it's being served. He says our work product is not discoverable. There's something strange going on here. A District Judge would not lie to me. Have they served the subpoena yet?"

"No," Wilkerson answered.

"Well, when they do serve it, call me and let me know who it's signed by," Zimmerman asked.

About 4:00 P.M. Isaacs served the subpoena on Wilkerson. Wilkerson immediately telephoned Zimmerman. "Miles," Wilkerson began, "the subpoena is signed by Judge Whistler—Judge William Whistler."

"Well, I'll be damned," Miles said slowly. "He lied to me, but why?"

"Well, I just wanted to renew your faith in our system of justice. I'm going to Fallis's office and see if he's heard anything," Wilkerson said as he hung up the phone.

Wilkerson drove to the Tulsa District Attorney's office in rush-hour traffic; he hoped that Fallis would still be there.

As he walked into the reception area, he noticed that Fallis's door was closed and that there was a gathering of men in Ron Shaffer's office. As Wilkerson stepped through the door, he was greeted by the sober faces of Shaffer and Investigator Eberle.

"What's happening?" Wilkerson inquired.

"You know what's happening," Shaffer said, smiling wryly.

"Bullshit," Wilkerson said. "All I know is Isaacs slapped a Subpoena Duces Tecum [an order to produce documents or papers] on me, and some friends say that Wise is giving our confidential reports out."

"Well, that's just exactly what's happening," Shaffer said. "Isaacs is going to allege that Wise gave the reports to Grimsley in order to write a book."

"You're shitting!" Wilkerson responded. "He gave our reports to that flake to write a book?"

"Well," Shaffer said with some skepticism, "Sid says he did not give them to Grimsley."

The door that joined Shaffer and Fallis's offices opened and Fallis appeared, smiling at Wilkerson. "Come on in, Mike."

Wise sat solemnly in front of Fallis's desk, his hair ruffled, wearing a cardigan sweater. Wise rose and shook Wilkerson's hand. "Boy, Mike, them SOB's are really trying to get us."

"What do you mean, trying to get us?" Wilkerson asked curtly.

Wise said that he had signed an agreement with Grimsley in the fall of 1977 to write a book about the murders. "I thought it was harmless," he said, flailing his arms. "Well, to make a long story short, Grimsley went with me to Vinita to copy some of the OSBI reports. He may have taken some of them."

"Come on, now, Sid," Wilkerson said, looking at the ceiling, *"may* have taken some of them?"

"Well," Wise continued as if he had not heard Wilkerson, "as you know, Grimsley was my campaign manager and I really trusted him, as did you and the others."

"I've never seen the man in my life," Wilkerson interjected to set the record straight.

"Well, a lot of people trusted him," Wise continued, his long arm emphasizing every word. "He was my campaign manager and I had to fire him over that book ad that he ran. Well, it looks like him, Isaacs, and Whistler have got together to embarrass me."

"Well, let's not worry about being embarrassed. Let's worry about the defense getting our work product," Wilkerson said as he handed the subpoena to Fallis.

"This is what the *ex parte* [secret] meeting between Isaacs and Whistler was about," Fallis said, handing the piece of paper to Wise.

Wise took the subpoena, read it, and nodded.

"Mike, do you know what Sid says those sons-a-guns did?" Fallis continued. "Whistler and Isaacs had an *ex parte* meeting behind closed doors about this thing. That's a violation of the Judicial Code of Ethics."

"Well," Wilkerson said, "it looks like Whistler lied to Zimmerman. He told him at one o'clock he didn't know anything about a subpoena and three hours later I get a subpoena signed by him."

"Well, maybe Judge Whistler signed it after he talked to Zimmerman," Fallis suggested.

"No way," Wilkerson responded. "Isaacs had the same subpoena at our office in Oklahoma City three hours before that."

"Is that right?" Fallis asked.

"Do you know what that damn Whistler did?" Wise asked rhetorically. "He told a lawyer friend of mine this afternoon not to miss the motion hearing. He told him to come and see the fireworks. Whistler hates my guts, but not as bad as I hate him."

"This crap makes me sick," Wilkerson mumbled, seeing himself on an emotional merry-go-round.

The following day Wilkerson took the OSBI investigative files to Pryor, Oklahoma, where the hearing on the reports was to be held. Apparently every member of the media in the state had been alerted to the upcoming fireworks.

Isaacs called Sid Wise to the stand. He inquired as to the disposition of an Embezzlement charge against Jolene Grimsley, Ron Grimsley's wife. Mrs. Grimsley had allegedly embezzled almost $5,000 from her former employer, the Sentinel Bonding Company of Enid, Oklahoma. Wise admitted that he had deferred prosecution of Jolene because she and the bonding company had agreed that she would pay the money back in installments. Mrs. Grimsley had failed to make the payments, but Wise had not pursued the case.

Isaacs produced a partnership contract between Wise and Grimsley dated October 20, 1977. The agreement said that Wise and Grimsley would coauthor a book about the Girl Scout murders. Wise was to receive 75 percent of the profit and Grimsley 25 percent. The contract went on to say that in case of Grimsley's death, Wise would receive 90 percent of the profit and Grimsley's heirs 10 percent. Wise was embarrassed and angry as he admitted signing the contract. He denied that his failure to prosecute Grimsley's wife had anything to do with the one-sided terms of the contract.

Isaacs then called Barry Cousins, a Lawton attorney who acted as his investigator, to the stand. Cousins said that Grimsley had come to Isaacs's home in Oklahoma City on June 17, eleven days after Hart was bound over for trial. Cousins said that Grimsley was paid almost $700 for twenty-six pages of OSBI reports. Grimsley was to act as an investigator and retrieve more of the reports which he supposedly had at his home in Kansas City. According to Cousins, Grimsley signed an affidavit stating that Wise had given him twenty-six pages of the OSBI report so that he could write the book. According to the affidavit, after Hart's arrest Wise and Grimsley drove to the Craig County Courthouse in Vinita, Oklahoma, where two copies were made of the report. Wise gave Grimsley a copy and he retained the other.

Isaacs argued that the affidavit should be admitted into evidence under the Exception to the Hearsay Rule known as Admission Against Penal Interest.

Judge Whistler did not accept Isaacs's argument and ruled that the affidavit was inadmissible as hearsay.

Isaacs then asked the judge to issue a bench warrant for Grimsley's arrest because he had failed to honor a subpoena to appear at the hearing. The attorney intimated that the State was hiding Grimsley so that he could not testify.

The judge issued a warrant for Grimsley's arrest and continued the hearing until Grimsley could be found.

The reporters had another field day with Wise. Grimsley and the prosecutor were writing a book. Wise was reminded by a reporter that on a previous occasion he had denied any financial interest in a book. Wise had grinned and said, "No, I told Grimsley that at the appropriate time, if it ever came, I would give him the first opportunity."

Wise now had to admit that he had signed the contract with Grimsley. He had been caught in a lie and he chose to attempt to talk his way out of it before the hostile reporters. Wise attributed his denial of the existence of a contract with Grimsley to semantics.

The reputation of the State of Oklahoma was on the line. The media had depicted Wise as a bungling, money-hungry ogre and his statements to the press had done little to dispel the image. He was seen as a state official capitalizing upon the deaths of three children.

Grimsley was referred to as a "Bogus Check" writer who had "mysteriously disappeared."

Another paper chided:

> ... almost immediately after the Girl Scouts' bodies were found Grimsley became a press agent of sorts for the District Attorney's office and several law enforcement agencies involved in the case. Several newspapermen questioned Grimsley's new role, because it gave him access to areas where regular reporters were barred. At the same time Grimsley continued writing about the case in the Pryor *Daily Times.*
>
> Grimsley and Wise who at one time appeared to be good friends had a falling out ...

Wise also drew criticism from Oklahoma County District Attorney Andrew Coats, who questioned whether Wise's conduct was a violation of the ethics standards of the Oklahoma Bar Association.

Publicly the OSBI, the Tulsa District Attorney, and the Mayes County Sheriff's Office made no comments to the press about Wise and Grimsley; privately they were incensed. Larry Bowles summed up the feelings of OSBI's agents when he said, "I wish I could just go take a shower and wipe this dirt off me. I don't care a thing about helping him [Wise] clean up his skirts. Everything we do from now on will make us look like we're defending Wise and Grimsley."

Fallis asked that the OSBI use all available manpower to find Grimsley. Sheriff Weaver told Wilkerson that he believed he could find Grimsley. All that he needed was an agent to accompany him into Missouri. Bowles was assigned to assist Weaver.

The following Saturday evening Wilkerson received a phone call from Fallis. "Mike," Fallis began, "I've just got a call from Sid. He says that Grimsley called him at his house. He supposedly told Wise that he read about what happened in the paper and said that Wise was being bad-rapped. Grimsley is supposed to meet Sid at the Tulsa Bus Station at 6:00 P.M."

"Oh, hell, Buddy! That's all we need to lose all credibility in this case—for Sid to meet with Grimsley!" Wilkerson exclaimed disgustedly.

"I know, Mike," Fallis assured. "I told Sid if he met Grimsley, they would have a field day with him and us."

"You know Sid's not thinking straight. All he wants to do is clean up his act. I don't think he knows that this thing is rubbing off on all of us," Wilkerson said.

"Yeah, I know," Fallis responded. "We're losing ourselves in these damn collateral issues that have nothing to do with the case, but that's what Isaacs wants. It's a delaying tactic designed to make the State look like the villain and with Sid's help, it's working."

"Boy, the Director is ready to let Sid have it in the media," Wilkerson added. "He feels that if we don't make a statement against Wise, it will appear that we're condoning what he did."

"Tell Kennedy to hold up on that kind of release," Fallis said with a sense of urgency, "until we can see whether Sid gave those reports to Grimsley. He swears to me that he didn't and Grimsley will prove it."

"Well, I wish I shared your belief in Sid at this stage," Wilkerson volunteered.

"Mike, Sid is supposed to call me back and I'm going to meet with Grimsley. I just wanted to alert you. I'll call you back and let you know what happens," Fallis said as he hung up the phone.

The next day Fallis telephoned Wilkerson and told him that he had talked to Wise. Grimsley had not been on the 6:00 P.M. bus.

On November 20 Bowles met Pete Weaver at his office. Weaver said that he believed that Grimsley was somewhere in Independence, Missouri, because Jolene Grimsley was known to be in that area. Although the judge had issued a bench warrant, Grimsley was out of the Court's jurisdiction and he would have to voluntarily come back to Oklahoma. Weaver suggested that Pryor *Daily Times* publisher Larry Williams accompany them. Williams was a close friend of Grimsley's and felt that he could convince him to return to Oklahoma. Weaver had run Grimsley's name through the National Crime Information Center and found that he was wanted in Kansas for Bogus Checks. He would have him arrested if he had to.

At approximately 5:30 P.M. the three men left for Independence, Missouri. They arrived around 11:15 that evening and drove to the Smile Awhile Motel, where Jolene Grimsley was rumored to be working. Weaver stepped out of the car, walked into the motel, and found Mrs. Grimsley working as a clerk. She smiled as she recognized the leather-skinned sheriff. The tall, slender, thirtyish woman stood up, walked over, and hugged him. "How are you, Pete?" She told Weaver that her husband was scared that Isaacs and Pitchlynn would kill him. He never came home during the daylight hours and before he would return late at night, he would drive by the apartment several times to make sure no one was there.

"Jolene," Pete began kindly, "I want Ron to come back with me. Do you mind if we wait for him at your apartment?"

"I don't mind at all, Pete," she responded, lighting a cigarette, "but you had better hide your car someplace or he'll never come in."

The three men, accompanied by Mrs. Grimsley, drove to the decaying apartment complex. They walked up the five creaking steps and Mrs. Grimsley opened the door, which led into an austere living room furnished with a chair, divan, and one lamp. There were no pictures decorating the plain, drab walls. The officers and newspaperman seated themselves and waited.

"Is Ron working on a book about the murders?" asked Bowles, breaking the silence.

"I don't know," Mrs. Grimsley answered. "He's working on something because I can hear him typing all hours of the morning."

"Where does he work?" asked Bowles as he stood up.

"In there," Mrs. Grimsley replied, pointing to one of the darkened bedrooms.

Bowles took a step toward the door.

"My mother is asleep in there," Mrs. Grimsley said.

He glanced into the darkened room, walked back, and sat down. Bowles looked at his watch; it was 12:44 A.M. The sound of footsteps climbing the stairs of the apartment caused Bowles to move to the side of the door. The door opened and a short, slightly built man stepped into the apartment. He was shocked to see strangers in the apartment and looked for a moment as if he wanted to run but Bowles blocked his way. As he recognized Weaver, the tension seemed to disappear.

"Oh, it's you, Pete. I thought Isaacs had found me." Grimsley agreed to return to Oklahoma, but only if Weaver guaranteed his safety from Isaacs and Pitchlynn. The officers loaded Mr. and Mrs. Grimsley into the car and began the long drive back to Pryor. As they drove, Grimsley, chain-smoking with a hacking cough, told the officers about his relationship with Sid Wise. He said that he had first met Sid Wise while he was newspaper reporter for the Pryor *Daily Times*. A few days after the murders Wise came to him and asked him if he would make all news releases. Grimsley and Wise had signed a coauthorship agreement. From the time he entered the case as press coordinator, he was privy to every part of the investigation. He was allowed to attend meetings with officers and discuss the case with them as if he were part of the team. While he was at Camp Scott, he made notes on everything that took place. Grimsley went on to say that Wise borrowed the OSBI file from Cary Thurman one afternoon, telling Thurman he needed it to "review the case." Later that evening, Wise telephoned Grimsley, saying he was going to make some copies of the report. To keep from being disturbed, they traveled to Vinita, Oklahoma, to use the copying machine. As they copied, both he and Wise scanned the pages. Grimsley said that when he saw something that interested him, he made two copies, one for him and one for Wise. After six hours of copying, they left and returned to Pryor.

After Wise fired him, Grimsley went to work for a newspaper in Drumright, Oklahoma. He could not stay out of trouble and was arrested for writing a bogus check and put in the Creek County Jail in Sapulpa. He retained the services of Jack Sellers, a local attorney. Fallis and Sellers were long-time enemies, stemming from Fallis's vigorous prosecution of Sellers's clients. While Grimsley was telling Sellers what assets he had to pay the legal fees, he mentioned several OSBI reports and the coauthorship contract he had in his possession. According to Grimsley, Sellers laughed, made a comment about Fallis, and telephoned Garvin Isaacs.

Isaacs and Pitchlynn drove to Sapulpa and took Grimsley back to Oklahoma City where they made copies of the confidential reports and the coauthorship agreement. Isaacs paid Grimsley $685 for the reports from the Gene Hart Defense Fund and Grimsley promised that he could get more reports, which he had stored. In return for these reports Isaacs told Grimsley that he would give him an exclusive interview with Hart and take care of the bogus check charges. Grimsley was named as an investigator for Isaacs.

With Grimsley designated as an investigator, the communications between him and the lawyers came within the attorney-client privilege and could not be communicated to another party without permission. Isaacs was very aware of another case, "People versus Juan Corona," where Corona's attorney had a monetary interest in the outcome of the case. The California Appellate Court had reversed Corona's conviction and reprimanded the lawyer for his conduct. According to Grimsley, he spent a good part of the evening being threatened by Isaacs and Pitchlynn. When it was time to retire for the night, one of the attorneys pitched a sleeping bag by the door and Grimsley watched as he put a pistol under the pillow. After leaving Isaacs, he never contacted him again.

"What did you do with your book and the rest of the reports?" Bowles asked.

"I burned all of them when this thing happened," Grimsley answered, wiping his perspiring bald head.

I'll bet, Bowles thought to himself.

The following day a moody Mike Wilkerson again loaded the OSBI records into the trunk of his car. He drove to the Tulsa District Attorney's Office where he picked up Fallis. They drove toward Pryor for almost an hour in total silence when Wilkerson slapped the steering wheel with his right hand and blurted out, "Buddy, when the hell is somebody going to stand up for us in this thing!"

"What do you mean?" Fallis asked, somewhat bewildered by the spontaneous outburst.

"I mean, we're going through all of this mess and everyone has forgotten why we're here to begin with. You know, I don't think the people give a damn anymore."

"Oh, I don't think that's the truth, Mike," Fallis interjected.

"Damn right, it's the truth. You know the public is bombarded from all sides by the news media which described the most heinous crimes in the world. They brought Vietnam into our homes. Day after day we saw broken bodies, dead men, women, and children, and unspeakable horror. They are saturated with violence day in and day out. There is so much crime about us that we have lost our sense of outrage. When they read about three children being savagely raped and murdered over their morning cereal they simply say, 'Well, I'll be damned, Harriet. Three kids were killed. Well, isn't that a shame.' They don't stay pissed-off. They're no longer outraged. They no longer want to get the killer. And here you and I are taking a load of papers to a meaningless motion hearing in Pryor, Oklahoma. It's not to decide the guilt or innocence of a man. We're simply putting on a sideshow. Buddy, let me tell you the people have forgotten about those kids."

"Oh, no, they haven't, Mike. No, no, they haven't," Fallis said. "They . . ."

"Damn right they have," Wilkerson interrupted, releasing the emotions and frustrations he had kept inside for so long. "You know, most murders and kidnappings are named after the victim. The Lindbergh kidnapping case, the Mullendore murder, and the Hearst kidnapping. Hell, in this case they can't even remember the victims' names. I run a little private survey all the time just to show people how they've forgotten about what happened. I ask them if they can name the defendant in this case. 'Of course. Gene Leroy

Hart,' pops out immediately. I even asked if they can name the prosecutor and Sid Wise's name jumps out. And then I ask them to name even one of the three victims. Usually they can't. More people know the names of the defense attorneys than know the names of the victims. That's got to tell you something."

"Yeah, it does tell you something, Mike. But somebody's got to fight them and that's the reason why we're here," Fallis said with no sign of corniness.

"Well, I'll tell you what, Buddy," Wilkerson continued. "I've said it before. I don't know why you came in on this case. You had absolutely nothing to gain."

"The name of the game is not gaining," Fallis said firmly. "The name of the game is doing what's right."

"Well, Buddy, I'm not like you. I have to be told every now and then that I am doing a good job. There has to be some appreciation for laying my butt on the line. I have to be told every now and then that people still give a damn. I'm so tired and sick of this crap from the press and the judicial system. It's all a goddamn game and we're just little pawns. Sometime, somewhere, somebody is going to have to stand up and say, 'What's going on here is wrong.'"

"That will never happen," Fallis said. "If you hold your breath waiting for that to happen you will suffocate."

Wilkerson gave a left-turn signal and parked his car in front of the Mayes County Courthouse. He watched in silent contempt as hordes of reporters milled around the courtyard.

"Blood-suckers," he mumbled. "Parasites." He didn't like this part of his personality. It was a dark side that rarely surfaced. But lately that darkness was spreading, consuming the goodness that had made him a good cop. He had seen the cynicism in cops who had been around a long time. They rarely smiled unless they'd heard a dirty joke. They proudly showed homicide crime-scene pictures as if they were baby pictures. They hit people with little provocation. They bitched about the job and were apathetic toward victims. Wilkerson had vowed when he took the job that he would not let the darkness consume him.

Wilkerson had been with the OSBI since 1973. He thrived on pressure and competition, and was immediately recognized as a "comer" of the future. He was a tenacious manhunter who always got his man. In his six years with the OSBI he had never been assigned a case where a violation of the law had not been cleared by arrest. Diplomatic and well-liked among the agents, he was admired for his competence, but sometimes viewed as a threat by those senior to him. He was recognized as an outstanding polygraph examiner whose record of success was unmatched. Wilkerson was totally honest, and would not tolerate being associated with dishonesty, impropriety, or poor judgment. When he first read a jaded article about the search for Hart in the *Oklahoma Monthly* entitled, "Killer or Scapegoat?" he tore the magazine in half and threw it against the wall. He later went for a walk and cried in frustration. He knew that he was not alone in his feelings. The other agents felt the same way but they could not speak for themselves. Any public statement they made would be in violation of OSBI policy. The agency was expected to take its lumps silently.

Wilkerson weighed his options. He lacked one semester of law school, and knew that he could make much more money as a polygraph examiner. Law enforcement was everything to him; he owed the OSBI and the men of the OSBI for the most fulfilling six years of his life. If he quit the OSBI now, at the apex of his career, he would maintain his credibility and reputation, thus being a more viable advocate. He made up his mind at that moment; he was getting out of the business. Some way, somehow, the public had to know the real story.

Later that morning Isaacs called Grimsley to the stand, saying, "Judge, I think what we're going to see here is 'Jimmy Don' Grimsley."

A shaking Ron Grimsley denied that Wise had ever given him the OSBI reports. He told of the deal he and Isaacs had made and recanted the affidavit, saying that he had been threatened by Isaacs and Pitchlynn.

Judge Whistler denied the motion to discover the OSBI reports and chided both Isaacs and Wise for their conduct.

Wise was again questioned by hostile reporters as he walked toward his office. The reporters would not be his biggest problem, however. Waiting for him in his office were Dr. and Mrs. Farmer. After approximately fifteen minutes, the parents of Lori-Lee Farmer emerged from Wise's office. Wise stood at the door with tears in his eyes, shaking his head.

On Thursday, November 23, Wise announced that he was withdrawing from the case, saying that he had suffered an emotional, physical, and mental drain. On the same day T. Jack Graves, the newly elected District Attorney, said that he was going to ask Buddy

Fallis and his staff to assist in the prosecution of the case. The trial that was to begin on Monday now seemed hopelessly lost for the year even though the names of nine hundred prospective jurors had been drawn in October. Under the laws of the State of Oklahoma, a new jury would have to be drawn if the case was to be tried after January. Wise told the press that he had expected the trial to be held within a year of Hart's capture. He said, "I did not anticipate the seemingly ridiculous collateral issues which the defense attorneys would come forth with in an attempt, I believe, to further cloud and confuse the real issue which, as we all know, is the guilt or innocence of Gene Leroy Hart."

On November 28, Judge Whistler ordered that the trial be postponed until March 5, 1979. He said this was an agreement between him, the prosecution, and the defense attorneys. Isaacs had asked that the case be dismissed on grounds that Wise had filed the charges against Hart in bad faith because he had a financial interest in the outcome of the case. The judge denied the request, saying the point was moot since Wise had withdrawn from the case.

Three days after Christmas, Agent Tom Puckett, Chief Polygraph Examiner, received word from an attorney in Bartlesville that a woman had come to him with information about the Girl Scout murders. Puckett and Larry Bowles drove to Bartlesville on icy roads and met with the attorney and his client, Joyce Ellen Payne.

Payne told the agents that a few days before the murders she had loaned her red and white flashlight to an acquaintance named Bill Stevens.

The day after the murders Payne and her common-law husband, Duane Peters, were sitting on the porch of their home in Okmulgee, Oklahoma, located approximately thirty-five miles south of Tulsa. They were talking about the murders when Stevens drove up and parked his car in the yard. Stevens walked up to the porch very slowly, appearing to be exhausted.

He told them that he had gone to visit his daughter in Eastern State Hospital at Vinita, but he had taken a wrong turn and his car had broken down in Locust Grove. Unable to fix his car, he had slept at the side of the road.

Payne noticed some dark spots on Stevens's boots. When she inquired about the spots he told her it was barn paint. Stevens asked if he could try to wash the paint off in her house. She gave him permission and he tried to wash out the spots but was unsuccessful. Later that day he drove into town and purchased a new pair of black boots.

In November of 1977 Peters and Stevens were arrested in Garden City, Kansas, and charged with Rape and Kidnapping. When Joyce Payne visited Peters at the county jail, he told her that Stevens had said he had killed the Girl Scouts.

Joyce Payne contacted Isaacs and told him of her revelations. She met the attorney at the OSBI Headquarters in Oklahoma City. She identified the flashlight as being the one that she had loaned Stevens. Approximately one week later her son, Owen, identified the light as his. According to Payne, Isaacs was ecstatic. He vowed to "change the trial into a circus with this new testimony."

Payne told the agents that she felt Isaacs was going to treat her "as a sideshow to get Hart off without any effort to catch the real killer." She was also very concerned that Isaacs was taking no precautions to protect her husband. Defense attorneys had gone to the Kansas State Industrial Prison and interviewed Peters.

The agents didn't believe a word of Payne's story, but they both knew that if her statement wasn't discredited it would make the trial a sideshow.

A couple of days later Bowles, Puckett, and forensic chemist Janice Davis returned to the Industrial Prison in Hutchinson, Kansas. They first interviewed Peters.

His story was virtually the same as that told by Joyce Payne except he maintained that the flashlight loaned to Stevens was a standard three-cell type rather than a 12-volt lantern type. He said that Stevens had told him he had worked with his father in the Locust Grove area prior to the murders and had gotten to know the Camp Scott area. He said that Stevens did not give details of the actual killing. Stevens did allegedly tell him that he had covered the front of the flashlight lens with tape and then scratched a hole in the tape so that only a small amount of light was emitted. Peters said that at first he did not believe the story, but later thought that the story was plausible.

After Peters's interview was concluded, the agents talked with Stevens. He vehemently denied that he had anything to do with the murders. He said that he did not know anyone in Locust Grove, had never worked in the area, and had never borrowed a flashlight from Payne.

Before leaving the prison Davis obtained blood, major case prints, pubic hair, scalp hair, saliva, and seminal specimens from both inmates.

Scientific tests eliminated both men as suspects but the agents knew that scientific tests alone would not suffice at trial.

On January 1, 1979, Mike Wilkerson resigned as Inspector-in-charge of the Northeastern Oklahoma Regional Office to enter private business. Larry Bowles was promoted to the vacated position.

CHAPTER 16

ON MARCH 1 THE OKLAHOMA COURT OF CRIMINAL APPEALS refused to give Hart's attorneys the OSBI reports. The Court also refused to postpone the trial.

The following day Isaacs walked into the offices of U. S. District Court Judge H. Dale Cook and filed a million-dollar lawsuit against Sid Wise, Sheriff Pete Weaver, and former newspaperman Ron Grimsley. The suit claimed that the men had conspired to violate Hart's civil rights and that Hart suffered "irreparable injury to his civil rights that could not be eliminated by trial." The suit asked that the Court hand over all OSBI reports and that a temporary injunction be issued delaying the start of the trial so the attorneys could study the reports. The strategy observers in the federal courthouse theorized that defense attorneys filed the suit late in the day so that Hart's trial would have to be continued the following Monday since Judge Cook would not have a chance to hear the motions. But the wiley judge stayed at the courthouse until 6:30 P.M. and denied the injunction. He said, "It is settled that the federal courts cannot enjoin a state prosecution."

It appeared that the task of selecting twelve jurors from the nine hundred people who had been summoned for duty would proceed as scheduled.

Attorneys for Hart had engaged the services of psychologist Kathy Bennett to help in jury selection. She told the press that she would attempt to get some insight into the prospective jurors' backgrounds and use this background, as well as body language, to pick the best jury for Hart. She said that all she was concerned with was "a fair shake for the jurors," as well as for Gene Leroy Hart.

Bennett said that juries favored the prosecution side of trials "simply because a person is accused of a crime." She went on to say that the odds were "stacked against defendants in a court of law." She voiced criticism that First Degree Murder can carry the death penalty. She voiced concern that only people who would vote for the death penalty could sit as jurors. Finally she said flatly, "It's basically unfair. We want him to be judged in the courtroom and not in the media. We are looking for jurors who can do that."

March 5, 1979, had finally arrived. The old Mayes County Courthouse at Pryor was again filled to capacity as well-wishers, curiosity-seekers, newsmen, and police watched Hart make his way from the Mayes County Jail across the street to the courthouse.

Outside the courtroom it was pandemonium. There were approximately sixty available seats in the courtroom left after the twenty-six representatives of the news media and members of the victims' families were seated. On each day of the trial there would be a waiting line outside the courthouse. Fistfights and cursing bouts would become daily occurrences.

At the defense table with Hart were Garvin Isaacs and Gary Pitchlynn, codefense counsels, and psychologist Kathy Bennett. At the prosecution table were Chief Prosecutor Buddy Fallis, his First Assistant Ron Shaffer, OSBI agent Cary Thurman, and Mayes County District Attorney T. Jack Graves.

Two minutes after the court was called to order, Isaacs stood and told the court, "I want to announce at this time that the defense is not ready," and asked for a continuance. Judge Whistler denied the motion and ordered the jury selection to begin.

After the first day of jury selection, five jurors were tentatively seated.

Outside, a spokesman for the Pryor Chamber of Commerce caused an uproar when he allegedly told two newspaper reporters that the murder trial would pump one million dollars into the Pryor economy. The statements were quickly criticized by law enforcement officials, local businessmen, and the general public. A spokesman for the Chamber of Commerce denied the allegation, saying that he was "misquoted." The two reporters said they had not misquoted him.

Mayes County Sheriff Pete Weaver was livid. "You can't measure lives in dollars and cents," he said. "The reputation of Pryor is more important than the economy." A local businessman observed, "The Chamber is gloating over money at the expense of three Girl Scouts."

During the second day Judge Whistler warned the young psychologist that she would become a spectator if she granted any more interviews. The dressing-down came after Fallis had criticized remarks by the psychologist quoted in a newspaper interview. The judge told Isaacs in chambers, "I am going to admonish you and Miss Bennett not to comment on this case. If she does not care to abide by that, she'll become a spectator at that point."

Tempers again flared between the defense and the prosecution. As Isaacs was questioning a prospective juror, he suddenly wheeled and accused Shaffer of trying to elicit answers from a juror while he was questioning her. "If you've got something to say, would you stand up and say it," he screamed.

Shaffer coolly stood and addressed the judge. "Your Honor, would you please tell Mr. Isaacs to address the Court."

Whistler called both to the bench and told Isaacs, "There's only one God in heaven and only one judge in this courtroom and I'm it. Are you prepared to conduct yourself accordingly?"

"Yes, sir," Isaacs said meekly. "I apologize to the Court. I'm trying to represent my client as competently as I can."

Shaffer walked slowly back to the prosecution table. As he sat down he whispered to Thurman, "That sorry son-of-a-bitch."

During the questioning of the prospective jurors, Isaacs said several times that Hart faced three hundred and five years in prison for Rape, Kidnapping, and Burglary convictions that dated back to 1966. He repeatedly asked the jurors if they could make their decision based on the evidence of the case alone.

He also asked the jurors, "Do you know why an elected law enforcement officer would try to fabricate evidence?—Do you know Pete Weaver?"

As the tedious jury selection wore on, several Indians were excused by peremptory challenges by District Attorney Fallis. Each side in the case was allowed six peremptory challenges which enabled them to eliminate a prospective juror without giving any reason. Isaacs accused the prosecution of systematically eliminating Indians from the jury. He accused Judge Whistler, who was part Indian, of "bending over backwards to show that he is not prejudiced for an Indian on trial for his life." One juror tentatively seated realized that she was a distant cousin of Hart's and was excused for cause by Judge Whistler. This brought an uproar from the crowd outside the courtroom accusing her of being coerced by lawmen into her revelation. She told reporters that no one had coerced her. She merely felt that she would not be a good juror if she had not told the truth.

As the jury selection progressed, defense attorneys announced that, with Judge Whistler's permission, Gene Hart would hold a news conference. Judge Whistler had no objections and the news conference was tentatively scheduled for the noon recess of the first day of trial. Isaacs made it plain that all questions would be submitted by reporters several days in advance, and that Hart would answer only the questions he chose. No questions would be answered about the murders, his capture, or what he did after he escaped from the county jail. In all, twenty-nine questions were submitted by the news media.

Bowles was contacted by his informant and told that the press conference for Hart was going to be for the entertainment of the media. The informant said that Gene Hart had been rehearsing his answers for several days but was having trouble memorizing his lines and was becoming frustrated. His attorneys had been working diligently with him and were confident that he would be ready for the press conference. Hart was to be depicted as articulate, intelligent, and gentlemanly. He would show his creativeness by showing two of his drawings. It was then hoped that the media would continue to depict him in a favorable light so that if there were a second trial public opinion would be more in his favor. The informant said that Hart considered the media gullible and sheeplike and felt he could lead them wherever he wished.

Hart was to answer "no comment" to any question that had not been rehearsed, if he forgot his lines, or if any question required an extemporaneous response.

Although two years had passed, Michelle Guse's room remained the same as it had been the day three strangers knocked on the Guses' door and told them Michelle was dead. The room was decorated in white, lavender, and deep purple. A three-tiered shelf holding small dolls from all over the world was set upon a bureau in the corner. Dick Guse walked to the window and smiled as he gently touched the purple petals of the African violets that sat upon the windowsill. Violets were Michelle's favorite flower and Mrs. Guse kept them blooming the year around. On the wall was a picture of the Powder Puff soccer team, with Michelle smiling proudly, holding a soccer ball. To the left of the picture hung a 1977 calendar. On June 6 Michelle had written in little girl penmanship, "Beginning of Day Camp." On June 15 she had written, "Mom and Dad's Anniversary." The Guses no longer celebrated anniversaries because June 15 was the date Michelle's body had been released to them by the medical examiner.

Mike Guse was a smallish eighth-grader when his sister was murdered. He now stood six feet four inches and weighed over one hundred and ninety pounds. Mr. Guse remembered the day that Michelle's clothing was packed away and removed from the house. Mike tearfully asked, "We're not just going to forget her, are we?" They held their son and assured him that Michelle would be with them always. Mr. Guse remembered the heartbreak when Mike asked his mother in a department store if she ever wished he would have died instead of his sister.

Mr. Guse had tried to find some consolation for his grief. Although he had joined various groups and written an article in support of scouting, he could find nothing constructive in his daughter's death.

Dick Guse dreaded walking into the courtroom and feeling the stares of contempt and hatred from the gallery. He had little doubt that he was now the enemy.

Crying Wolf's legs ached as he climbed the flights of stairs to the courtroom. There was an elevator available, but a man of his stature did not take the white man's elevator. As his line of sight became level with the floor that led into the courtroom he smelled tobacco, not white man's tobacco, but Indian tobacco. He stopped for a moment, laid his hand on the rail, and rested. Although his body was old, his eyes and mind remained sharp. He surveyed the entire floor slowly. In a small corridor to the right he saw an Indian man whom he recognized immediately. He was one of the most powerful medicine men in northeastern Oklahoma. The smoke was billowing from his pipe and Crying Wolf could tell that he was praying. As Crying Wolf took the final three steps to the floor, the medicine man turned suddenly and looked at him. He also knew Crying Wolf and what Crying Wolf represented. With a look of disdain the medicine man turned away and continued to smoke and pray in silence. Crying

Wolf walked over to one of the old court benches that had been set in the corridor for potential witnesses to sit on. In a few minutes the medicine man stepped out of the corridor, gave Crying Wolf a disapproving, if not fearful look, and hastily walked to another corridor located on the other side of the room.

Crying Wolf knew what the medicine man was doing. He was smoking at the four corners of the courtroom. His smoke was meant to confuse the judge, prosecutors, and law enforcement officers. The medicine man's medicine was not meant to confuse the jury; this would come later. Crying Wolf stared at the floor for a moment and then stared back at the medicine man who was again puffing away and praying. I cannot let this happen, he thought. I cannot let confusion reign over these representatives of the law. In his pocket was a small sack that contained the Ancient One. Taking out his pipe, he walked to where he had first seen the medicine man. He stuffed his pipe with the Ancient One, lit it, and prayed. He knew that his medicine was stronger. When he was through he looked for the medicine man. He was gone. He knew that if the medicine man hadn't been to the other corners of the courthouse, he was now making his rounds. Crying Wolf walked over to where the medicine man had been and again smoked. He then went to the other two corners of the court building and smoked. He did not feel good about what he was doing and he knew that he was probably doing more than he should. The medicine man should be shown respect, not competed with.

He walked back to the door that led to the courtroom and peered through the small window. There was color division in the courtroom. The Indians sat on the right side behind the defense table. Most of the whites sat on the left side except for two Indian men whom Crying Wolf recognized. One was the medicine man who had been in the lobby and the other was another great medicine man from northeastern Oklahoma. Crying Wolf smiled as he thought, they are on the left side because they are closer to the jury. If he could think of a violation of white man's law that the medicine men were committing it would be jury tampering. Crying Wolf pushed open the swinging door and stepped into the courtroom; he was recognized immediately by the Indians. One young Indian man stood and respectfully offered his seat to the old man. Crying Wolf nodded his thanks to the man and sat down in the seat where he would remain throughout the trial.

·

During the noon recess he watched as one of the medicine men stationed himself near the door closest to the jury. As the jury returned from lunch he watched the wiley old man light his pipe. The medicine man had gauged the drift of the air currents perfectly. As the prospective jurors seated themselves the smoke flowed over each one of them. He would repeat the process for the next four days. Crying Wolf knew that he could interfere, but the man who was using the medicine was a man who was shown much respect by the Cherokee people. He decided to simply watch and wait. Hart and his family had much power and energy working for them.

The Mayes County courtyard was perfectly landscaped with deep spring grass running up to the trunks of the ancient trees that peppered the courtyard. The World War I cannon that stood in the southwest corner of the courtyard sparkled brightly in the crisp morning air as Gene Hart and his entourage of cowboy-hatted deputies and highway patrolmen again trekked from the Sheriff's office across the street, onto the courthouse sidewalk, and passed the plaque commemorating the war dead from 1776 to 1976. They brushed quickly past the milling crowd and through the glass doors of the three-story orange brick and cut gray stone courthouse. The men's heels clicked loudly against the hard marble floors, the sound echoing off the rock-hard walls. They entered the elevator, and a deputy pushed a black button on the control panel. The door slowly closed and the elevator ascended with a loud groan. It stuttered to a stop on the third floor.

After ten days and the questioning of one hundred thirteen people, six men and six women had been seated as jurors. There was expectation in the air. Everyone seemed to realize that all the cards were now on the table. The game was ready to be played out to the end.

A wavelike murmur swept across the packed courtroom as the gallery and court officers acknowledged Hart's arrival. Both the prosecutors and defense attorneys were dressed in dark suits and were seated at the dark wooden tables set parallel in front of the dark, thronelike judge's bench. Directly behind the bench, hanging on the dark wooden walls, was the Great Seal of the State of Oklahoma flanked on each side by flags. The Court Reporter sat quietly in front of the judge's bench, the Court Clerk sat at the left of the bench, and the Bailiff was positioned next to her. The witness chair to the right of the bench was slightly elevated. All of the participants in the drama were grim-faced, and there was a heavy air of reverence in the room. Hart shook his two attorneys' hands, nodded to the female psychologist, and sat down. He turned to the audience and nodded and smiled to his mother and two sisters, who sat on the first bench directly behind him. It was then he first saw Crying Wolf. Hart forced a smile; Crying Wolf did not smile back. Sitting on the first bench directly behind the prosecutors were the victims' families; Mr. and Mrs. Guse, Mrs. Milner, and Mrs. Farmer. Behind the first row reporters sat impatiently while making notes and doodling on their writing pads. They raised their heads only momentarily as the jury quietly filed in and seated themselves in the orange-backed swivel chairs that comprised the jury box, located to the judge's right.

Both sides seemed to be satisfied with the jury. They included an airline mechanic, an antique-store owner, an electrician, a fourth-grade teacher, a basketball coach, three housewives, a Pryor city employee, a grocery store checker, a plant foreman, a department store worker, a grocery store employee, and a welder. Many of the jurors had sons and daughters and relatives who were active in scouting. They admitted that they had followed newspaper accounts and had talked about the case with friends and neighbors. There were no Indians on the jury. After they were seated the jurors quietly chatted to each other, with occasional glimpses at the defendant, who stared sadly at them.

Sheriff Weaver seated himself in a chair by the swinging doors.

"All rise," the Bailiff barked. Everyone in the room sprang to their feet. "The District Court of Mayes County is now in session, the honorable Judge William Whistler presiding." A black-robed Judge Whistler walked swiftly from his chamber door to the right of the bench and seated himself on the bench.

"Be seated," he said.

Bowles had received word from his informant that Hart was going to make an opening statement and make a bid to act as his own attorney.

The informant was right again. Isaacs asked that Hart be allowed to make an opening statement to the jury. Isaacs had earlier told the judge that he had reviewed Hart's outline and notes for the opening statement and that he had critiqued the Indian on courtroom etiquette and procedure. Fallis vigorously objected, stating that Hart did not know the rules of evidence. Judge Whistler denied the request, saying "the situation is fraught with too much possibility of error." The lawyers then made their opening statements to the jury.

Fallis described in detail what had happened on the first day of camp and the discovery of the bodies. He told about the flashlight, the tape, the pictures, the hair, the newspaper, the cave, the assault on the children, and the women's sunglasses. He concluded by saying that the items taken from the cabin where Hart was arrested would satisfy Hart's guilt beyond a reasonable doubt. "I am satisfied," he said, "at the conclusion of the testimony you will have no difficulty carrying out your duties."

Isaacs told the jury through clenched teeth to "follow the evidence, pay attention to who had the photographs, and how they came to the cellar area." He told them to "watch the pictures, they will tell you a lot. They will tell you that Mr. Hart is an innocent man." He intimated that the evidence in the case had been fabricated. He cautioned the jurors to fasten dates and times to each one of the forensic tests that were performed, insisting that this was the key. Isaacs added that the evidence would show "that many people had access to the house [where Hart was arrested] and had opportunities to put things in that house after all of Hart's personal belongings were gone." He promised that members of the Hart family would take the stand and put their freedom on the line because of their love for him. He said that Hart had left the Camp Scott area approximately ten days before the girls were murdered and had returned to his home some four days after the murders. "I don't know whether we are going to produce some of the people who were with him," Isaacs added.

After the opening arguments the State called the camp counselors to the stand. They again testified to the horror of finding the bodies and the episodes that had taken place the previous night and the following day. Dr. Neil Hoffman, forensic pathologist and State Medical Examiner, coldly testified about the sexual assaults and the causes of death. The prosecutors set up a screen in front of the jury, the lights were dimmed, and grizzly slides of the victims were shown to the jury. In a monotone, Hoffman pointed out details as the colored slides flicked across the screen. Some of the gallery craned their necks in attempts to see the colored pictures, but they were unsuccessful because the screen was opaque at the back. The parents of the victims sat stoically with only an occasional bobbing of the head or a stare at the floor. They had long since become hardened to what had happened to their children. Isaacs objected to the showing of the slides and maintained that the only reason they were being shown was to "arouse the passion of the jury." Judge Whistler overruled the objection. Recess.

The small cramped room of the court library was jammed to capacity with reporters from all over the nation as Gene Hart entered the room dressed in a dark blue, three-piece suit and flanked by his attorneys. As one reporter observed, "All that is lacking is 'Hail to the Chief.'" Radio and TV reporters' voices intermingled as they told their live audiences of the arrival of the star of the show.

America was finally going to hear from the enigma. They were going to hear from the full-blooded Cherokee, the football hero, the woodsman, the escape artist, the convicted rapist, burglar, and kidnapper, and the accused triple slayer.

Gene Hart sat down behind a desk jammed with microphones and tape recorders. The bright, hot TV lights showed a ruggedly handsome, classic Cherokee face with high cheekbones, and trimly cut jet-black hair. The face wore a stoic expression.

Richard Dowdell, Tulsa radio reporter, was the person Hart had chosen to ask the twenty-nine questions.

In a reverent and overly dramatic tone Dowdell began, "I am speaking to you from the Mayes County Courthouse in Pryor inside the law library of that courthouse. Just a few feet from me is a door that leads into the courtroom. In that courtroom the trial of Gene Hart is being held. Today's session is presently in noon recess. Gene Leroy Hart, the man charged with the deaths of Lori-Lee Farmer, Michelle Guse, and Doris Denise Milner, has agreed to be interviewed now—not about the case, but nevertheless, we may get to know this man just a little bit better." Then, directing his comments to Hart, Dowdell said, "Gene, let me first thank you for giving us this time. The first question, Gene: If you were a free man right now, what would you do with your life?"

"I would enjoy my freedom and probably get some type of formal education," Hart answered.

Dowdell asked Hart about his likes and dislikes, what he did in his spare time, what books he read, and his favorite authors. One reporter described the event as a "sad day for news reporting."

Just as the informant had said, Hart seemed to have his answers memorized. When Dowdell or other reporters asked a question that seemed to demand a spontaneous answer, he replied, "No comment."

Hart told Dowdell that he considered the number one institution in his life to be his family, and that religion was very important in his life, both Indian and contemporary religion.

When asked what authors he liked, Hart responded, "James A. Michener, Hemingway, Graham Greene, Louis L'Amour westerns, and I reserve judgment on Sidney P. Wise and Ron Grimsley." What was obviously intended for a large laugh drew only an uncomfortable polite chuckle from Dowdell.

Dowdell then displayed two crude drawings that Hart had copied from originals. These drawings were held up before the whirring cameras for the world to see.

Then Dowdell asked, "Have you had any kind of experience in your life that makes you feel that Native Americans are discriminated against?"

Hart appeared to be a first-grader struggling with lines in a school play as he answered, "Prejudice isn't always open and obvious. Sometimes it takes the form of subconscious attitudes and thoughts— the motivation for the way some people relate to other people. You can look all around you. This is Indian country. It's obvious who owns the land. We have nothing left but our freedom and our dignity."

When a reporter asked Hart if he was a symbol, he replied, "It would have to be symbolic. I am not a hero. I have no desire to be a hero."

The final movement to the orchestration took place when Hart took a final slap at Wise and Grimsley by saying, "There have been many requests [for a news conference] and we decided instead of showing favoritism to one individual, that we would include all of the press."

The interview concluded with Dowdell saying, "Gene, I think that takes up all of the questions the reporters seem to have. Thank you very much for your time. We just concluded an interview that may have given us some insight into this man who is the defendant in one of Oklahoma's most publicized murder cases. It was not meant to determine if Gene Hart is guilty or not guilty of the murders of three little girls. That's not the duty of the news media. That awesome task is placed in the hands of twelve citizens of Mayes County. I'm Richard Dowdell, KRMG News."

The following day one newspaper headlined, "Hart Says That He Is No Hero." Other media reporters described Hart as "handsome," "articulate," "intelligent," "extremely brilliant," "high I.Q." Another paper questioned, "Could this man kill three little girls?" An Oklahoma City radio reporter said, "No one will ever believe that this man we saw and heard today could ever do such an act."

It was obvious to most of the people associated with the trial that the "news conference" had been a bad play, but the media gave it the credibility it lacked. Not a single reporter had attempted to ask a newsworthy question. Gene Hart had been shown the respect and awe usually generated by an elder statesman. It had been a bloodless coup with the media acting as insurgents.

Some of the news media admitted they had been used. After the news conference Dowdell apologized to Sherri Farmer for his role. The apology was not accepted.

The next day a Tulsa *Tribune* editorial stated:

The Hart Interview

> The Oklahoma news media has rarely looked worse than it did in the television interview of Gene Leroy Hart. For 30 minutes Hart was bombarded with a series of marshmallow questions—was he supported by his family, did he believe in God, etc. The image was that of a politician running for Good Guy of the year.
>
> From Hart's point of view it was a public relations coup. He is articulate and intelligent. The obvious question is planted in the minds of the TV audience: Could this man be guilty of three heinous murders? The image obviously defied the question. . . .
>
> But the media should never have accepted the stipulation that no questions about the crime or the trial would be answered. That made the whole interview a sheer matter of media manipulation, complete with inane questions and fawning responses to Hart's answers. . . .
>
> Gene Leroy Hart is either guilty or not guilty, of the murders of three Girl Scouts. That is all the whole proceedings at Pryor is about. Until that question is resolved we might do better to forget about the side shows.

Back in the courtroom Arthur Linville described the crime scene and the collection of evidence; the meticulous bagging and tagging, vacuuming, cutting up the floor of the tent, and dusting for fingerprints. Testimony was received about the finding of the pictures, the subsequent identification of the pictures, and then linking the pictures to Hart. Other testimony described the finding of the glasses and the newspaper at the cave, and the matching of the tape and newspaper found in the flashlight at the death scene to the newspaper and tape found in the cave. Ann Reed, forensic chemist, took the stand and said that Hart's hair and the hair taken off the tape that had tied

Denise Milner's hands were Mongoloid and were consistent in all characteristics.

Chrisco testified about finding the pipe and the mirror. He went on to say that he had seen the pipe in the same shaving kit on top of the old refrigerator at the time of Hart's capture.

Dr. John MacLeod, Ph.D. and Professor Emeritus in Anatomy at the Cornell University Medical Center in New York, testified that the sperm taken from the victims and the samples taken from Hart's underwear had "an unusually large number of elongated and tapered forms. It would not be unreasonable," he continued, "to infer that sperm found in the bodies of the three victims could have been from the defendant. There was no evidence to exclude the defendant as the source of the spermatozoa." In cross-examination, Isaacs pressed the elderly professor, "You're not telling us that Gene Leroy Hart is the one who killed those little girls, are you?" Isaacs asked.

"No sir, I am not," was the answer.

"You're merely saying that there are some similarities," Isaacs insisted.

"Some very definite ones," MacLeod responded.

"And there are other people with the same similiarities, are there not?" Isaacs queried.

"I would consider it rather remarkable to find the same pattern—based upon all my studies of semen smears over the many years," MacLeod responded. He admitted that he had been paid $6,000 by the Oklahoma State Bureau of Investigation to perform the tests.

Convict Larry Dry testified that he had frequented the area of the caves and cellar with Gene Hart. He also identified the photographs that were taken from the cave as being the ones that were in his and Hart's possession when they were escapees together.

The prosecution rested after Karen Mitchell dramatically testified that the pipe and mirror found at the Pigeon residence belonged to her.

After the prosecution had rested its case, Fallis was asked by reporters in the lobby if he was satisfied with the case. Fallis said, "I am very satisfied with how the evidence was presented and received." Another reporter facetiously asked Fallis if he thought the prosecution "had gone out with a whimper or a bang?"

"Such questions do not merit an answer," Fallis sharply replied.

It didn't matter, however, whether Fallis answered or not; the reporter's question was quoted in more media publications and broadcasts than Fallis's observations. The news media also emphasized the fact that the pipe and mirror were found three months after Hart's capture. One newspaper article stated that the items were "obvious pieces of evidence" that anyone would have taken in the original search.

Dick Guse was in court every day. He read his newspapers every morning and evening, and watched the news on TV. He compared the reported stories to his firsthand knowledge. "It's like two different trials," he observed. "The one I'm watching and the one that the media is reporting on. What's happening at the trial is not what is being reported."

The prosecution had concluded after six full days of testimony. It was now the defense's turn. Isaacs and Pitchlynn experienced embarrassing witness problems from the start. One witness testified about a cellar and cave area with which he was familiar. It was not exactly clear what Isaacs was trying to determine with this witness, but it became apparent to everyone that the witness was describing a different cave and cellar area from the one in question. After several minutes the embarrassed attorney told the jury that the witness was testifying about the wrong cave. The defense next called Hubert Maxey, a forensic chemist, who testified that the hair comparisons made by Ann Reed were certainly similar, but that was all. He drew the analogy that "My two thumbs look alike, but they aren't." He also testified that the slides used to compare the sperm that Dr. MacLeod had examined had been handled too many times, kept under unusual and different temperatures, and had been stained several times. "Any time you restain it," he said, "you change the chemistry."

Hart's cousin was sworn in and identified the glasses that Hart was wearing at the time he was captured. The cousin was then asked if she had given the glasses to Hart in 1973. She was advised by her attorney not to answer the question and to stand upon her Fifth Amendment rights against self-incrimination.

In an attempt to impeach Ann Reed's testimony, Dr. John Moore, an anthropologist and Professor at the University of Oklahoma, testified that, "Nearly everybody is expected to exhibit mixed Mongoloid and Caucasian characteristics." He then went into a lengthy dissertation about the history of the European races and how they had intermarried with Asians, thus producing Mongoloid characteristics. When cross-examined by Fallis, the professor admitted that he was not a hair expert, but noted that many people exhibit Mongoloid characteristics even when they do not have a Mongoloid ancestry. He said that the actor who played Charlie Chan in the old movies was in fact a Swedish actor rather than a Chinese. He also said that actor Charles Bronson had portrayed an Indian in movies and was in fact Polish. Fallis pressed the professor by asking him if he did not sometimes rely on visual characteristics to determine a person's lineage. "You can't tell ancestry by looking at the person," the professor responded.

Fallis then asked Dr. Moore if he "could not look at entertainer Sammy Davis Jr. and determine that he was of Negroid ancestry?"

The professor responded by saying that he could find a Lebanese who looked like Davis.

"So Sammy Davis Jr. may be Swedish," Fallis said, shaking his head as he sat down again at the counsel's table.

Pete Weaver was then called to the stand and asked by Isaacs if anyone had ever told him to put articles in the cave areas in question. Weaver answered negatively. Weaver's deputy, A.D. David, was next queried as to whether he had ever been in the Locust Grove police station where Karen Mitchell's trunk had been stored. David responded that he had been in the station on at least two occasions and did recall the trunk being there but could not describe it.

As expected, Isaacs called Joyce Payne and her son to the stand. They told essentially the same story about Bill Stevens that they had told the OSBI.

Kimberly Lewis, a young scout who was at Camp Scott during the murders, also took the stand. She testified that she saw a man who resembled Bill Stevens at Camp Scott. She said that she had lifted up the back of her tent and shone a flashlight outside and saw the man. She believed that three other girls who were in the tent with her had seen the man too.

Thurman was flabbergasted. Why had the little girl not shared her colorful revelations with law enforcement?

Allen Little, an ex-jailer, whom Pete Weaver had fired in 1973, testified that he remembered seeing the photographs found in Cave Number 1 in Weaver's desk in the Sheriff's office. The ex-jailer went on to say that he had seen the pictures as he glanced into Weaver's desk with Deputy John Ross after Hart had escaped the second time.

The last witness for the defense was a waitress at a truck stop in Chouteau, Oklahoma. She nervously took the stand and said that she recognized Bill Stevens's picture while watching the news the previous night. She said he looked like the man who had come into the cafe in which she worked on the morning of the murders. She said that the man kept "looking down at his boots."

The defense concluded its case with Gene Hart conspicuously not taking the stand.

The State called its rebuttal witnesses.

Weaver testified that he had never seen the photographs prior to their discovery at the cave. He produced jail records that showed that Hart had only a belt and a pair of nail clippers when he was booked into jail in April 1973. Weaver said Hart had no property at all the second time he was booked.

The children who had been in the tent with Kimberly Lewis said that they hadn't seen anyone in the camp on the night of the murders. They went on to say that Kim had not told them that she had seen anyone. Chemists testified that the hair and semen taken from Stevens at the penitentiary excluded him as a suspect. Deputy John Ross testified that he had never seen the photos in question. He said the photos were not included in the group that he and Little had looked at in September of 1973.

The following day the defense reopened its case by calling Sam Pigeon to the stand. The old Indian who had harbored Hart said that he had never seen the corncob pipe or blue mirror that were taken from his house.

Fallis cross-examined, "You speak English, don't you?"

Pigeon addressed his interpreter in Cherokee, who answered, "Two or three words." Fallis quizzed him about his conversation with the OSBI, but the old man said he didn't understand the agents.

"And do you remember telling them [OSBI Agents] they weren't yours [the mirror and pipe]; they must be Gene's." Through the interpreter Pigeon replied that he hadn't said that. He told them he had never seen them.

After a recess the court officers returned to the courtroom to find the flip-type blackboard turned toward the jury. Written in large letters for the jury to see was the word "FRAMED." Obviously a member of the audience had written it on the blackboard during the recess.

Crying Wolf was troubled. He felt that the testimony certainly had linked Gene Leroy Hart to the murders of the three young girls, but this was not what troubled him. The jury was confused. The medicine men had done their jobs. He knew that the ultimate test of truth would not occur in the courtroom. The trial had produced the truth as far as testimony and evidence were concerned, but it had not produced the ultimate truth—of life and death. If Hart had killed the children, he was standing upon their blood and swearing to God that he had not committed these acts. In the Cherokee religion where God is supreme and reigns over all men, truth is the medium which is found in the Cherokee tobacco. This is the very thing that God provided for the Cherokee people to depend upon. If it is misused to the point that a life or death is involved, then that person who caused its misuse shall ultimately stand upon his decision. Crying Wolf had prayed for an answer for many nights and now knew what must be done; he would use the Old One—one more time. He would use this medicine in a way to insure that the "cards are going to lay face up." It seemed to Crying Wolf that there were two men who were at opposite ends of the poles in the controversy; Pete Weaver and Gene Leroy Hart. He would use the Old One as a vehicle to determine who was telling the truth. Crying Wolf knew that the final determination would be exacting. He knew that either Pete Weaver or Gene Leroy Hart would die. He also knew that he could not do it by himself. He was old and needed the legs, the understanding, and the faith of another good man.

It was 5:00 P.M. and Mike Wilkerson knew that he had a law school class in less than thirty minutes. He had listened to the radio off and on all day and knew that the jury had retired. Since resigning from the OSBI, he had kept up with the case through the newspaper. He decided to telephone Cary Thurman from his office before he went to class.

As he dialed the number of the District Attorney's office in Pryor he thought of the insignificance of his 5:30 Criminal Procedure class compared to what was happening now. When the secretary answered, Wilkerson asked for Thurman and contemplated skipping his class. Thurman's voice brought Wilkerson from his fleeting thoughts.

"This is Agent Thurman."

"Cary, this is Mike. How is it looking down there?"

"Mike, it's looking real good. I think they will convict the sorry bastard," Thurman said.

"Do you really, Cary?" Wilkerson responded with cautious hopefulness.

"Mike," Thurman said excitedly, "Fallis and Shaffer were fantastic! They said all the things we've been wanting to say for two years. Boy, have they given Isaacs a lesson in lawyering. Damn right, we've got it. We've got that sucker."

Wilkerson loved Thurman's enthusiasm and he felt better. But at the same time he was the eternal pessimist. He believed that Hart would be found not guilty and wanted to prepare Thurman for the worst. Most of all, he made the telephone call to tell everyone how he felt.

"Cary," Wilkerson began as he stumbled for words to express his feelings, "I just called to say thanks. Thanks for giving a damn. Thanks for working your butt off and doing everything that I asked you to do on this case." Wilkerson's voice began to quiver as he paused to regain his composure. After a deep breath he continued. "What I'm trying to say, Cary, is that I, as a private citizen, am glad that there are people like you and Fallis and the rest out there. No matter how this damn thing turns out, I want to be on record as saying thanks."

"Mike, I appreciate that. Now get your butt down here and have a drink with us and wait on the verdict. That is, if you're not afraid to be seen with the people who are framing this poor, defenseless Indian," Thurman said with mock indignation.

Wilkerson smiled, but in his heart there was still the rage, the rage that had been there for two years. That rage cropped up when anyone mentioned, even in jest, that he or his people would be parties to a frame.

"Thurman," Wilkerson said with pride in his voice, "I'll do my damnedest to get down there tonight and buy every one of you railroading bastards a drink."

A voice from behind Thurman yelled, "Tell that damn civilian to get his ass down here." Wilkerson recognized Ron Shaffer's voice.

"Cary, tell Shaffer that I can't make it because I am going to a Gene Hart chicken dinner." Wilkerson listened as Thurman repeated his remark, which was met with a crescendo of boos and jeers from the crowd in the District Attorney's office.

"I've got to run, Cary, or I will be late for class. Do me a favor, after I hang up tell everybody thanks and that I appreciate them."

"You get your ass down here tonight and tell them yourself," Thurman replied.

"I'll do my damnedest," Wilkerson said as he hung up the phone.

Wilkerson grabbed his books, locked the door to his office, and ran to his car. After fighting rush-hour traffic, he arrived at the law school a couple of minutes before his class began. His best friend, Don Guy, was putting out his cigarette in an ashtray just outside the classroom door as he walked up.

"I thought you would be over at Pryor," Guy said as he opened the door for Wilkerson.

Wilkerson stopped, looked at his friend. "I am."

Guy grinned and yelled, "Be careful!" as Wilkerson ran out of the building and sprinted toward his car.

Bowles and Limke sat eating dinner at a motel restaurant a few miles south of Pryor. As they exchanged talk about the trial, *Daily Oklahoman* reporter Judy Fossett walked up to the table and exchanged greetings with Limke.

Limke began sarcastically chiding Fossett. "How are you, Judy? Still as flakey as ever?"

"I'm not flakey or a kook," she flushed. "You and Dick Wilkerson are wrong about me."

"Aw, Judy, that's okay. Some of my best friends are kooks." Limke smiled. "Of course I wouldn't want my brother to marry one."

Bowles did not like Fossett. She had been transferred to the state desk the year before from her Oklahoma County Courthouse assignment. The transfer came after she had stormed into District Attorney Andrew Coats's office and had begun kicking an assistant district attorney in the leg. A few minutes before, the assistant had jokingly mentioned that the driver of the car that had struck and killed her dog Rags might sue for damages.

The next morning Coats, still appalled, appeared personally at the *Daily Oklahoman* offices and complained to the managing editor. She was finally transferred to general assignment to avoid further problems.

She had befriended both the defense attorneys and Hart's family and had attended numerous rallies in support of Hart. Many officers saw her as a supporter rather than as a reporter.

Bowles bluntly asked, "Are you the reporter who wrote that Bill Stevens confessed to me in the Kansas State Penitentiary?"

Fossett flushed and a nervous tic developed in her facial muscles as she fumbled for words. Before she could find her tongue, Bowles continued, his eyes narrowing.

"Well, I have information that you were the reporter who wrote the story."

Fossett again fumbled for an explanation as Bowles continued mercilessly.

"In fact, another reporter told me it was you. Since it is obvious that you are not going to own up to writing the story, will you answer me one question straight? Did you make a phone call to the Kansas State Penitentiary?"

Fossett, her face ticking badly, admitted that she had telephoned the prison.

"Did Isaacs ask you to write the story?" Bowles demanded.

Fossett did not answer.

"You know," continued Bowles, "I would think that you people would owe it to your profession and the public to check out a story before you write it, but I guess you're only interested in a story."

Fossett whirled about and marched away.

After dinner Bowles was standing at the door of the District Attorney's office when Fossett approached him for the second time that evening.

"You know," Fossett began, "the problem with you people is that you think Gene Hart's whole family is bad."

Bowles stared at her in silence.

"Well, they're not," Fossett continued. "I swam and ate with them last summer and there are some wonderful people among his family."

"I am sure that there are," Bowles replied curtly. "Now, do you really believe that you can be an objective reporter after spending so much time with Hart's family and being such a close friend with Mrs. Isaacs? You are a close friend of Mrs. Isaacs, aren't you?"

"Well, not exactly close friends," Fossett answered.

"You did have lunch with Mrs. Isaacs today, didn't you?" Bowles examined.

"Well, yes," Fossett stammered, and the facial tic returned.

"Another thing, what the hell do you base this great belief in Gene Hart's innocence on?" Bowles demanded.

"Well, I don't see how one man could put all that sperm into those little girls," she reasoned.

Bowles did not comment but instead asked, "Do you really in your heart believe Hart is innocent?"

"Yes," she replied quietly.

"Well, let me ask you this. If you didn't have a way back to Oklahoma City tonight except to ride there with Gene Leroy Hart, would you go?"

The word jumped from the reporter's mouth, "No."

Bowles shook his head, smiled, and turned to walk away. "I rest my case."

In the small motel south of Pryor, most of those involved in the case waited. Shaffer's room was the meeting place for OSBI agents, reporters, and members of the victims' families. Small groups of people could be seen huddling all around the motel. Buddy Fallis had retired early in the evening after having dinner with the Guse and Farmer families. If and when a verdict came, Fallis would not go to the courthouse to hear it. It had been long understood that Ron Shaffer would hear the verdict and report to Fallis. Fallis would be in seclusion the rest of the evening.

Every time Shaffer's phone rang in the room there was suddenly an eerie silence. When Shaffer would say, "No verdict yet," the conversations would again resume, with only an occasional deep sigh revealing the tension.

In one group, Limke assured Dr. Farmer that the worst that would happen would be that the jury would be unable to reach a verdict. Limke, Bowles, Thurman, Shaffer, and Chrisco all expressed the opinion that Hart would be found guilty.

Earlier in the evening the jury had requested to hear again the testimony of Roger Chrisco as he described finding the mirror and corncob pipe, and the testimony of Karen Mitchell as she described her loss and subsequent recovery of the items. Limke told Dr. Farmer, "They are looking at the evidence, Doctor. That means that they will find him guilty. No one looking at the evidence could decide any other way." Everyone nodded in agreement.

Bowles said, "I'll bet there are one or two holding out and the other jurors are just convincing them how strong the evidence is." Again everyone nodded in agreement.

The conversation again halted as Shaffer's telephone rang its alarm. Shaffer lifted the receiver. "Yes?" After a short pause he said, "Okay." He hung up the phone and turned to the expectant crowd. "The jury has retired until 9:00 A.M. in the morning and then they will go back into deliberation."

The news was met with mixed emotion. Most thought it was a good sign. "They probably got one of them holding out and he'll want to sleep on it till morning," one of the agents reasoned.

"Yes, that's probably it," another agent agreed.

"I hope so," sighed Shaffer. "I hope so."

"I'm going to bed," said Bowles.

"Yeah, me too," said another agent.

The small groups began to break up and by 11:00 P.M. most of the motel was quiet.

The night was hot and muggy as usual. It was approximately 11:00 P.M. when Crying Wolf met his coconspirator in the front courtyard of the old courthouse. The old man took a small rawhide bag from his pocket and handed it to his friend, telling him that the bag contained the Old One. He instructed his friend to deposit four equal portions of the tobacco at four different locations within the courthouse. As the man turned and walked toward the courthouse, Crying Wolf's old fingers packed a portion of the Old One into his pipe. With a kitchen match he lit the bowl and the white billowy smoke rose into the cloudless sky. As he puffed he prayed, "Let the smoke and tobacco determine the truth. . . ."

Larry Bowles, Joe Collins, and Trooper Tommy Caldwell stood talking in the hall of the Mayes County Courthouse when they heard someone shout, "They have reached a verdict!"

People began running through the halls shouting the news as Bowles looked at his watch. It was 9:11 A.M.

"What do you think the verdict will be?" Bowles asked.

"They've convicted him," Caldwell answered.

"No way," Collins disagreed. "I say they have acquitted him."

"I agree with you, Joe. They reached the verdict last night. They haven't even deliberated this morning. They're going to turn the sucker loose," Bowles said, hoping he was wrong.

Within fifteen minutes the courtroom was filled to capacity with spectators standing in the doorways and filling the halls. Dick Guse was at the bank across the street cashing a check. Limke managed to squeeze his way into a doorway that led to the District Attorney's office. There was no doubt in Limke's mind that Hart would be found guilty as he watched the solemn jurors file into the jury box and take their seats. Hart sat pale with the look of a terrified animal. Limke took satisfaction in the convict's worry. He felt no pity for the man, only hatred and loathing. He watched the faces of the jurors as they took their seats. An elderly woman juror smiled at Hart as she settled herself in her chair. Limke thought to himself, Oh, God, no. They are going to turn the bastard loose. Then a positive thought pushed the negative thought away. Maybe the smile meant "We've got you, you son-of-a-bitch."

The court was called to order. Judge Whistler addressed the foreman. "Have you reached a verdict?"

"We have, your Honor," the foreman replied.

"Please hand the verdict to the Court Clerk."

It seemed like an eternity as the clerk took the small slip of paper and handed it to the judge. Judge Whistler unfolded the paper, looked at it without expression, and handed it back to the Court Clerk.

"We the jury, duly impaneled, and sworn to try the above entitled cause, upon our oath find the defendant, Gene Leroy Hart, not guilty." The court erupted into pandemonium.

Cary Thurman ran from the courtroom, trying to hide the tears that were filling his eyes. Ron Shaffer lowered his head until it was almost touching the counsel table and fought the tears.

Limke was stunned. They made a mistake, he thought. But there was no mistake. The Court Clerk's words had been burned into his ears like a hot brand. The courtroom was in chaos, and security became a problem as a weeping Gene Hart embraced his attorneys. Hart's family and supporters embraced each other, cheered, and shouted insults to the police officers. Judy Fossett screamed and hugged members of the Hart family. Pete Weaver was pale, shaken, and angry as he shouted to the deputies and highway patrolmen, "Get 'em out of here. Get 'em all out of here." The officers escorted the cheering throng from the courtroom.

The Farmers, Mrs. Guse, and Mrs. Milner were weeping as they walked from the courtroom to the District Attorney's office.

Hart was shackled by highway patrol troopers and led toward the courtroom door. The grin left Hart's face for a moment as his eyes met Crying Wolf's. The old man's eyes belied the faint smile upon his face. Hart nodded uncomfortably as he was led through the door.

Mr. Guse walked back into the courthouse and was confronted by a reporter who asked, "What do you think of the verdict?"

"What verdict?" Mr. Guse asked, puzzled.

"They found him not guilty," replied the reporter. Guse pushed the young man aside and sprinted up the stairs to the courtroom.

Bowles walked up to Judy Fossett, who was standing jubilant in the hall. "I hope you're happy," Bowles said bitterly. "Maybe now you can go back to Oklahoma City and make a hero out of Roger Dale Stafford." Bowles was referring to a recently arrested mass murder suspect. Not waiting for a response, Bowles walked toward the District Attorney's office.

Thurman sat with his head in his hands on the couch in the main prosecutor's office. He didn't want to talk to anyone and he didn't want anyone to talk to him. He arose only when the parents of the victims entered the room. He walked over to Mrs. Milner and embraced her, saying, "I'm so sorry." Mrs. Milner looked at the defeated young man, smiled, and returned his embrace.

"I thank you so much," Mrs. Guse told Bowles as she hugged him. Bowles was unable to say anything.

"Oh, what do we do now?" Sherri Farmer asked a crying Ron Shaffer, but received no answer.

Mr. Guse walked into the room, embraced his wife, and tearfully asked Limke, "Ted, is there any way I can get someone to kill him in the penitentiary?"

Ted shook his head and said, "Don't talk like that, Dick."

"I mean it, Ted," Mr. Guse said.

Mrs. Guse shook her head. "We'll have to live with this thing the rest of our lives," she sobbed.

Roger Chrisco was crying tears of anger and frustration. "Larry, they thought I planted that stuff. That's what they had to think."

Bowles shook his head; he still could not speak.

Joe Collins put his arm around his friend. "They would have turned him loose, Roger, even if he had confessed."

Down the street in the walk-up office the defense attorneys had used as their headquarters, Hart's relatives, supporters, and reporters celebrated. Some drank champagne.

After a while the families of the victims left, still crying, and the agents walked down the stairs of the old courthouse to their cars. Limke walked over to Thurman and shook his hand.

"Ted, I'm sorry. I did all I could. I was the case agent and I . . ." Thurman stopped, looked down at the ground, and took a deep breath, trying to control his emotions.

Limke looked at Thurman. "Cary, it's not your fault. You did all you could. You did your best. The whole damn bunch did all they could. Somewhere during this thing they forgot about what happened that night in June three years ago. They had a folk hero, a Native American accused of the most damnable crime by the establishment. The establishment even looked corrupt with Wise and Grimsley's book. They lost themselves in the accusations, the newspaper articles, the chicken dinners, football, and the circus atmosphere. Somewhere along the line they forgot about the children. Hell, you are going to lose cases and you are going to win cases, but don't forget why you're here. You are young, you have a helluva future ahead of you, and you care for people. Don't let this thing eat you up or sour you. If you are going to cry, don't cry about losing the case, cry for those babies that were killed out there." Limke's voice broke and he slapped Thurman on the shoulder. "Now get your butt home."

As Limke and Thurman got into their cars, Bowles was leaving the Pryor city limits. Four miles out of Pryor Bowles's two-way radio barked, "Vinita OHP—Bureau 33."

Bowles did not answer his call number.

"Vinita OHP—Bureau 33."

Again, Bowles ignored the radio.

"Bureau 33. If you can copy this headquarters, there is a homicide in Tahlequah and your assistance is requested."

Bowles looked at the small white radio on the floorboard as Vinita Highway Patrol Headquarters repeated the message. He reached down, turned the radio off, and continued to drive toward home, occasionally glancing at the radio.

After a minute or so he reached down, turned on the radio, and took the microphone in his hand.

"Bureau 33—Vinita OHP. Please contact Tahlequah PD and advise them my ETA is 45 minutes."

AFTERWORD

Four hours after Gene Leroy Hart was found not guilty, OSBI agents established conclusively that Bill Stevens was working in Seminole, Oklahoma, at the time he was supposed to have been in the Okmulgee and Locust Grove area.

On March 25 the Kansas Bureau of Investigation polygraphed Duane Peters at the request of Joyce Payne's attorney. Peters admitted that he and Payne had fabricated her testimony. They hoped that Peters would be transferred to an Oklahoma penal institution, and then pardoned in exchange for their testimony. Through an administrative error at the KBI, the OSBI had not been informed.

On April 17 Joyce Payne and her son, Larry Short, were arrested and charged with Perjury.*

On April 23 Garvin Isaacs was cited for Contempt of Court for his conduct during the trial.

On May 21 Gene Leroy Hart pleaded guilty to charges of Escape, Burglary, Injury to Public Property, and Possession of a Sawed-off Shotgun. He was sentenced to three years on each charge, to be served concurrently.

On June 4, 1979, Gene Leroy Hart collapsed and died while jogging in the exercise yard at McAlester State Penitentiary. The next day

---

* On May 1, 1980, a mistrial was declared in the case, the jury hopelessly deadlocked seven-to-five in favor of conviction despite Duane Peters's testimony that he and Joyce Payne had made up the story about Bill Stevens killing the children.

an autopsy revealed that Hart, known for his great physical condition, had died from a massive heart attack. The autopsy also revealed that Hart's vasectomy had not been successful; his left seminal vesicle had not been severed.

A few days before his death, Hart had written a letter to a Tulsa newspaper reporter denying a request for an interview. In the letter he also made what many must have seen as a particularly ironic statement. "Most of the media," he wrote, "and I include all forms, did their best to see that I was convicted unjustly of a crime that I had absolutely nothing to do with." Despite this declaration, Hart did grant an interview to *The Cherokee Advocate,* a tribal newspaper. He told the interviewer about OSBI agents taking pictures of him after the capture. When Director Tom Kennedy read the interview he ordered all copies of any pictures sent to his office.

The funeral for Gene Leroy Hart was the largest in Mayes County history. Nearly thirteen hundred people filled the Locust Grove High School gymnasium; another three hundred waited outside in the heat. The middle section of the gym was reserved for three hundred of Hart's relatives. In the crowd were defense attorneys Garvin Isaacs and Gary Pitchlynn. The Chief of the Cherokee Nation, Ross Swimmer, also attended. Hart was eulogized by a local minister: "Just three weeks ago Gene Hart was saved and we see that just four days ago, with the possible one hundred forty-five to three hundred and five years he was facing, God spoke and said, 'Son, you trusted in me and you've been through enough. Come live with me.' And God stepped in with his works and powers and called Gene home." Another minister spoke to the crowd in Cherokee. The casket was then opened and carried outside. For over an hour people lined up to file by Hart's remains. The casket was then brought back inside the gymnasium where a private service was held with Hart's relatives. Pallbearers carried the casket to a hearse which would lead a three-and-a-half-mile procession to Ballou cemetery located near Camp Scott.

Despite the official autopsy report, charges and rumors about the cause of Hart's death began immediately. Some speculated that Hart had been murdered by inmates who believed he was guilty. The rumors appeared to gain credibility when it was learned that a large quantity of cyanide was confiscated from prisoners at McAlester

State Penitentiary the day before Hart died. Enough cyanide to kill eight hundred inmates was uncovered.

The jurors received criticism after the verdict and became very defensive. One juror remarked to a reporter that they had reached a decision five minutes after beginning their deliberation. Another juror said that he believed that Hart had committed the murders, but he just "had a reasonable doubt." Another obstinately said the "evidence wasn't there" and "the investigation was a screwed-up mess." Another juror said that he had disregarded Dr. MacLeod's testimony because the doctor did not define "osmosis" well enough.

Maintaining that the people of Locust Grove no longer want it, Dick Guse has begun to lobby for the permanent closing of Camp Scott. A sign hangs on the padlocked aluminum gate now, announcing that the 410-acre camp is patrolled by armed security guards. Large water-filled chuckholes have eroded the asphalt surface of Cookie Trail leading into the camp. To the left and right, signs identifying the units are tattered but still visible. Camp Ranger Ben Woodward still fights to keep the forest from overrunning the camp area completely. It's a losing battle that he wages while living behind the six-foot-high chain-link fence that surrounds his home. Attack-dogs roam inside the fence. Stacks of brush are everywhere as Woodward has tried to clear out the camping areas. A broken mower lies on the south side of his home.

Down the hill, Kiowa Unit has been reclaimed almost entirely by the trees and brush. The mound of dirt that had been kicked up near the bodies is now a permanent contour of the land. Ravenous ticks continue to infest the woods. White butterflies and bumblebees still lick at the flowers and shrubbery, and songbirds fill the trees. The squirrels, the rabbits, the snakes and toads, and the night crawlers can still be found. But everything human is disappearing. Their gray paint peeling, the tent platforms stand as the only reminders of what Camp Scott used to be.

Locust Grove itself shows little sign of the tragedy that occurred more than three years ago. The small village has seemed to prosper since the murders that brought it such unusual attention in the summer of 1977. At the junction of State Highways 82 and 33, a new convenience store with signs advertising cold beer has replaced the hamburger drive-in. The town also has a new supermarket and a pizza place. But these changes are small. In the summer some of the residents still sit in front of local businesses and watch their town fill with tourists and their expensive fishing boats. Real estate prices have dropped around Camp Scott, but they seem to have held firm elsewhere in the community. It has become fashionable for high school kids to show their bravery by sneaking into the abandoned camp at night. And you can still get involved in either a fistfight or a drunken fest depending on the position you take about Hart's innocence.

Former District Attorney Sid Wise has entered private law practice in Mayes County. He has said that he is seriously thinking about moving to Colorado, but his friends say rather that he is considering a run for the District Attorney's post he vacated.

The Farmers and the Milners are still pursuing their three-and-a-half-million-dollar lawsuit against the Girl Scouts. The Guses still live in Broken Arrow. They confess to being overprotective of their son. Mr. Guse belongs to several committees and organizations in support of scouting and others for families who have lost children. Dr. and Mrs. Farmer have moved into the house they were building when their daughter was murdered: a small upstairs room contains all of Lori's belongings. Mrs. Milner has graduated from college and is working as a medical technician.

The state of Oklahoma never prosecuted the charges against William Smith and Sam Pigeon for Harboring a Fugitive.

Jack Shroff's suit against the Tulsa *Tribune* was dismissed; it had been filed too late to fall within the one-year statute of limitations. The case has been appealed to the Oklahoma Supreme Court.

Dick Wilkerson left the Oklahoma State Bureau of Investigation shortly after Hart's acquittal. He has entered private business with his brother Mike. Larry Bowles stepped down as Inspector-in-charge of the Northeastern Oklahoma Regional Office. He said that he wanted to spend more time with his son and young daughter Kali, whom he named for Lori Farmer's little sister. Mike Wilkerson is now a lawyer in Tulsa. OSBI Agent Sid Cookerly resigned. Agent Dennis Davis resigned. Agent Miles Zimmerman resigned. Agent Jack Lay resigned. Agent Gary Dill resigned. Agent John Gosser resigned. Agent Patty Vaught resigned. Agent Carl Bowhay resigned. Chemist Janice Davis resigned. Agent Tom Lockhart resigned.

Agent Arthur Linville remained with the OSBI to head the investigation that ultimately led to the arrest and conviction of Oklahoma's most prolific mass murderer, Roger Dale Stafford. During a recess in the Stafford trial, reporter Judy Fossett approached Linville to tell him she now thought Hart had been guilty.

Pete Weaver had not planned to run for reelection as Sheriff of Mayes County, convinced that he had little chance of winning. After being encouraged to seek another term by a county commissioner, he has begun active campaigning. Weaver has contacted a prominent Tulsa attorney about filing suit against Garvin Isaacs and Gary Pitchlynn for alleged defamatory statements they made on an Oklahoma City radio talk show.

S.M. "Buddy" Fallis, Jr., remains District Attorney for Tulsa County.

Garvin Isaacs became something of a celebrity after the trial and could be found speaking at various meetings and functions. Since joining an Oklahoma City law firm, however, he has kept a low profile.

Shortly after Gene Hart's acquittal, Inspector Ted Limke had commented to the news media that there was no need to keep the case open because the jury had "turned loose the man who committed the murders." His fellow agents were in complete agreement, but many politicians were not. The OSBI was hit with a rash of criticism because of Limke's statement. Before local television cameras, a Tulsa state senator criticized Limke's comments and chastised the entire OSBI. An OSBI commissioner told Director Tom Kennedy that Limke's comments looked like nothing more than sour grapes. The Governor's office sent unofficial word to "cool it."

While the Oklahoma State Bureau of Investigation inquiry into the murders of the three young Girl Scouts remains officially open, unofficially it is closed.